CAMBRIDGE TEXTS IN THE
HISTORY OF PHILOSOPHY

—

FRIEDRICH SCHLEIERMACHER
On Religion

CAMBRIDGE TEXTS IN THE HISTORY OF PHILOSOPHY

Series editors

KARL AMERIKS
Professor of Philosophy at the University of Notre Dame

DESMOND M. CLARKE
Professor of Philosophy at University College Cork

The main objective of Cambridge Texts in the History of Philosophy is to expand the range, variety and quality of texts in the history of philosophy which are available in English. The series includes texts by familiar names (such as Descartes and Kant) and also by less well-known authors. Wherever possible, texts are published in complete and unabridged form, and translations are specially commissioned for the series. Each volume contains a critical introduction together with a guide to further reading and any necessary glossaries and textual apparatus. The volumes are designed for student use at undergraduate and postgraduate level and will be of interest not only to students of philosophy, but also to a wider audience of readers in the history of science, the history of theology and the history of ideas.

For a list of titles published in the series, please see end of book.

FRIEDRICH SCHLEIERMACHER

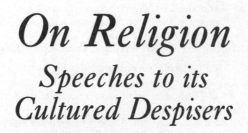

On Religion
Speeches to its
Cultured Despisers

TRANSLATED AND EDITED BY
RICHARD CROUTER

Carleton College,
Northfield, Minnesota

CAMBRIDGE
UNIVERSITY PRESS

PUBLISHED BY THE PRESS SYNDICATE OF THE UNIVERSITY OF CAMBRIDGE
The Pitt Building, Trumpington Street, Cambridge, United Kingdom

CAMBRIDGE UNIVERSITY PRESS
The Edinburgh Building, Cambridge CB2 2RU, UK
40 West 20th Street, New York, NY 10011–4211, USA
477 Williamstown Road, Port Melbourne, VIC 3207, Australia
Ruiz de Alarcón 13, 28014 Madrid, Spain
Dock House, The Waterfront, Cape Town 8001, South Africa

http://www.cambridge.org

First published 1988
Second edition 1996
Reprinted 1997, 1998, 2000, 2002

Printed in the United Kingdom at the University Press, Cambridge

A catalogue record for this book is available from the British Library

Library of Congress Cataloguing in Publication data
Schleiermacher, Friedrich, 1768–1834.
[Über die Religion. English]
On religion: speeches to its cultured despisers / Friedrich Schleiermacher;
edited by Richard Crouter.
p. cm. – (Cambridge texts in the history of philosophy)
Includes index
1. Religion – Early works to 1800. I. Title. II. Series.
BL48.S3313 1966
200–dc20 95–22987 CIP

ISBN 0 521 47448 5 hardback
ISBN 0 521 47975 4 paperback

To
BJC

For without doubt it must hold for art as it does for science that form and content serve mutually to confirm one another.

Schleiermacher, *Kritik der Sittenlehre*

Authors in whose works one finds everything one expects and nothing more are absolutely logical and impersonal. But they are very poor writers. The productive spirit always brings forth something that could not have been expected.

Schleiermacher, *Hermeneutics*

Schleiermacher is the Protestant theologian of the Romantic movement. One will have difficulty imagining Schleiermacher without this, but will also not grasp the significance of the Romantic school for the development of theory in the nineteenth century without knowing and recalling that in him a theologian wholly dedicated to the Romantic school exercised the determining influence on theology. His *Speeches* show this relationship not only in their substance, but also in their form.

Martin Kähler, *Geschichte der protestantischen Dogmatik im 19. Jahrhundert*

Contents

Acknowledgments

Numerous persons assisted me in shaping the original edition of this work published by Cambridge University Press in 1988. For their contributions I am grateful to the library staffs at Carleton College and Luther Northwestern Seminary; former Carleton Deans Roy O. Elveton and Peter W. Stanley; colleagues within the Nineteenth Century Theology Group of the American Academy of Religion, especially Walter W. Wyman, Jr. and John Clayton; my colleague in Carleton's German Department, Julie Klassen; my former student assistant, Barbara Pitkin, Carleton '81; students in my courses on modern religious thought; and readers for Cambridge University Press. Since then I have continued to benefit from stimulating and congenial relations with colleagues at Carleton in Political Science, Philosophy, German Studies, Classics, and Religion. Friedrich Wilhelm Graf and Günter Meckenstock, coeditors of the *Zeitschrift für Neuere Theologiegeschichte / Journal for the History of Modern Theology* (Walter de Gruyter), likewise sustain my intellectual interests. President Stephen R. Lewis, Jr. and Dean Elizabeth McKinsey of Carleton College have been most supportive as has Mrs. Marian Adams Bryn-Jones of Carmel, California. I am also indebted to the Fulbright Commission and the Theology Faculty, Philipps-Universität Marburg, where my colleague Heinrich Leipold and I taught this text to German students of the current generation in 1992. That experience confirmed in my mind the ongoing spiritual and intellectual vitality of encounters with Schleiermacher's thought.

This edition, published in the Cambridge Texts in the History of Philosophy series, keeps the relevant scholarly annotations of the 1988 version intact, while making a few changes to the translation. The Introduction has been somewhat recast, and a Chronology, Further Reading, and a Note on Editions added, in order to produce a leaner, more accessible volume.

Abbreviations

Ath.   *Athenaeum: Eine Zeitschrift.* I–II. Edited by August Wilhelm Schlegel
            and Friedrich Schlegel. 3 vols., Berlin, 1798, 1799, 1800

Br.   *Aus Schleiermacher's Leben. In Briefen.* I–IV. Edited by Ludwig Jonas
            and Wilhelm Dilthey. 4 vols., Berlin, 1860–63

Dierkes   Hans Dierkes, "Die Problematische Poesie: Schleiermachers Beitrag
            zur Frühromantik," *Schleiermacher-Archiv.* Edited by Hermann
            Fischer et al. *Internationaler Schleiermacher-Kongreß Berlin 1984.* Vol.
            I, edited by Kurt-Victor Selge. Berlin, 1985, pp. 61–98

KGA I.1   *Friedrich Schleiermacher Kritische Gesamtausgabe* I *Schriften und Ent-
            würfe. Band 1 Jugendschriften 1787–1796.* Edited by Günter Mecken-
            stock. Berlin, 1984

KGA I.2   *Friedrich Schleiermacher Kritische Gesamtausgabe* I *Schriften und Ent-
            würfe. Band 2 Schriften aus der Berliner Zeit 1796–1799.* Edited by
            Günter Meckenstock. Berlin, 1984

KGA I.3   *Friedrich Schleiermacher Kritische Gesamtausgabe* I *Schriften und Ent-
            würfe. Band 3 Schriften aus der Berliner Zeit 1800–1802.* Edited by
            Günter Meckenstock. Berlin, 1988

KGA V.1   *Friedrich Schleiermacher Kritische Gesamtausgabe* V *Briefwechsel 1774–
            1796 Band 1.* Edited by Andreas Arndt and Wolfgang Virmond.
            Berlin, 1985

Oman   Friedrich Schleiermacher, *On Religion: Speeches to its Cultured Des-
            pisers.* Trans. by John Oman. Louisville, 1994

Introduction

On Religion in its cultural milieu

The work of Friedrich Daniel Ernst Schleiermacher (1768–1834), inaugurated by this book, brilliantly reflects the tensions between the religious thought of the Enlightenment and Romanticism. When *On Religion: Speeches to its Cultured Despisers* was published in 1799, its author was an all but unknown cleric and member of the German Romantic circle. At the time of his death Schleiermacher was the most distinguished theologian of Protestant Germany, the author of a modern post-Enlightenment system of theology that ranks with Calvin and Aquinas in the history of Christian thought. *On Religion* is the premier expression of an understanding of religion as rooted in immediate pre-reflexive feeling and intuition, and only secondarily at the level of intellectual cognition or in moral systems and deeds. This classic theory of religion arose from the Romantics' intense critique of Kant's moral and religious philosophy in the repressive political atmosphere of a Prussia that feared the social upheavals of the French revolution. A many-faceted work, *On Religion* belongs to modern intellectual history, to German studies, to philosophy, religious studies, and theology.

Ultimately Schleiermacher's fame derives from his systematic interpretation of Christian theology, *The Christian Faith* (*Glaubenslehre* [1821–2, 1830–1]), whose relationship to *On Religion* is often disputed. Yet Schleiermacher never renounced his early book and considered his revisions (1806, 1821) to be more stylistic than substantive. Both works share a strategy of moving from abstract to more concrete structures of experience; for both religion arises from immediate self-consciousness and expresses itself individually and socially within a historical community of faith.

For nearly two hundred years *On Religion* has been deeply appreciated and severely criticized. Seekers of a religious perspective that challenges traditional belief find in it a host of stimulating ideas. Students of theology assess the author's heterodox Christian belief alongside its twentieth-century nemesis Karl Barth, whose critique of Schleiermacher's religious liberalism and Romanticism rests on a revealed theology of biblical faith. Yet today Schleiermacher's realism as a thinker and his interdisciplinary cast of mind have been rediscovered by an age that seems unsure of its ability to embrace religious faith even as it remains suspicious of prevailing philosophies, moral creeds, or political ideologies.

Schleiermacher's career was marked by unusual versatility. His work covers fields of Christian theology that range from systematics and ethics, to sermons, historical essays, and exegetical studies. His *Life of Jesus* inaugurated the nineteenth-century quest for the historical Jesus. Lifelong devotion to classical Greek philosophy is reflected in papers presented to the Berlin Royal Academy of Sciences, and his Plato translation became a standard work in modern German philosophy. A pathfinder in interpretation theory and hermeneutics, Schleiermacher moves beyond the specialized concerns of biblical and philological criticism to raise questions about the general conditions and principles that hold sway when we interpret texts. His theory of interpretation constitutes a turning point in the history of the field and still delineates the major problems. Shaped by the Platonic dialogue form, his theory views interpretation on the analogy of speaking and listening, a stance that is emulated in *On Religion*.

Born in Breslau in Lower Silesia, Schleiermacher grew up among the pietistic traditions of the Moravian Brethren (*Herrnhuter*) of southeastern Saxony. Founded by Count Nicholas L. von Zinzendorf in 1722, the Herrnhuter community sought to revive the reformist aims of P. J. Spener's *Pia Desideria* (1675). His schooling included an enlightened humanistic curriculum of languages (Greek, Latin, Hebrew, French, English) and mathematics along with the experiential, biblical, and Jesus-centered piety of the Brethren. At the seminary at Barby, he encountered a narrow, theological pedagogy and took part in a secret club where Kant and Goethe were read and debated. Here he became skeptical about whether the one who called himself "Son of Man was the true, eternal God," and whether "his death was a vicarious atonement, because he never expressly said so himself," and maintained that he cannot believe Christ's death to have been necessary "because God, who evidently did not create men for perfection, but for the pursuit of it, cannot possibly intend to punish them eternally, because they have not attained it."[1] His inability to obtain clear answers to these religious doubts led to disillusionment, a painful exchange of letters with his father ("written with trembling hand and tears"), and his transfer to the (pietistic but more worldly) University of Halle.[2] Yet his early training at boarding school was never renounced. Looking back in 1802 he wrote:

---

[1] Letter to his father (21 January 1787) in *The Life of Schleiermacher as Unfolded in His Autobiography and Letters*, trans. Frederica Rowan (London, 1860), I, pp. 46–7.

[2] See B. A. Gerrish, *A Prince of the Church: Schleiermacher and the Beginnings of Modern Theology* (Philadelphia, 1984), pp. 24f.; *Schleiermacher-Auswahl*, ed. Heinz Bolli (Munich, 1968), pp. 262–8; *KGA* I.I has over fifty letters between father and son, occasionally mother and son, between 1781 (Schleiermacher's thirteenth birthday) and 1794 (shortly before the father's death); see pp. lxvi–lxvii.

Here it was that for the first time I awoke to the consciousness of the relations of man to a higher world . . . Here it was that that mystic tendency developed itself, which has been of so much importance to me, and has supported and carried me through all the storms of skepticism. Then it was only germinating; now it has attained its full development, and I may say, that after all that I have passed through, I have become a Herrnhuter again, only of a higher order.[3]

At Halle, which was dominated by the philosophical rationalism of Leibniz and Christian Wolff (d. 1745), Schleiermacher continued to pursue theology, philosophy, and classical studies.

Schleiermacher passed his theological examinations in 1790 in Berlin under the prominent Berlin churchman and family friend, F. S. G. Sack, who encouraged him to translate Joseph Fawcett's *London Sermons*.[4] Unable to secure immediate church appointment, Schleiermacher became a house tutor (*Hofmeister*) at Schlobitten in East Prussia. The apprenticeship among an upper-class royalist family served, as it were, as a window on the world. During his first year at Halle the storming of the Bastille (14 July 1789) occurred, a foundational experience for his generation. His Schlobitten years coincided with the growing radicalism of the Jacobins in France, the dissolution of the Legislative Assembly, the declaration of a French Republic, and the execution of King Louis XVI (January 1793). Schleiermacher shared his peers' enthusiasm for the movement's aspirations, even if he found the execution of the king repugnant and came to see that peace could only be restored by the overthrow of the Jacobins.[5] Life among the upper classes in Schlobitten provided a taste of the literary and cultural milieu that soon became his own in Berlin.

The tutoring appointment enabled Schleiermacher to continue a process of philosophical and theological self-education. When his duties took him to Königsberg he had a half-hour meeting with Kant, but no obvious intellectual significance was attached to the visit. At the time, the German Enlightenment typified by Kant had not yet undercut efforts to shore up orthodox forms of Protestant Christian belief by appealing to reason. To be sure, naturalistic (today we would say behavioristic) tendencies in human development theory were pursued by Karl Friedrich Bahrdt (1741–92) and Johann Bernhard Basedow (1724–90). The Old Testament scholar Hermann Samuel Reimarus's radically skeptical fragments remained unknown until published by Lessing, while the works of conservative, popular religious poets and writers, like Christian Fürchtegott Gellert (1715–69) and Friedrich Nicolai (1733–1811), enjoyed great popularity. In Germany the new wave of pietistic self-examination and the dominant rationalism of Christian Wolff

---

[3] Letter to Georg Reimer (30 April 1802), *Br.* I, pp. 294–5; Rowan, *Life of Schleiermacher*, I, pp. 283–4.
[4] Joseph Fawcett, *Predigten*, trans. F. Schleiermacher with a preface by F. S. G. Sack (Berlin, 1798).
[5] See Kurt Nowak, *Schleiermacher und die Frühromantik: Eine literaturgeschichtliche Studie zum romantischen Religionsverständnis und Menschenbild am Ende des 18. Jahrhunderts in Deutschland* (Göttingen, 1986), pp. 92–5, and Richard Crouter, "Schleiermacher and the Theology of Bourgeois Society: A Critique of the Critics," *Journal of Religion*, 66 (July 1986), 301–17.

often went hand-in-hand in trying to show that reason and divine revelation were mutually compatible and the existence of God capable of demonstration.

Such defenders of Protestant orthodoxy were, however, being challenged by a newer, more liberal perspective called "neologism," which maintained biblical authority but restricted the content of revelation to what can be known by natural reason. Where the Bible teaches miracles, Jesus and his followers were merely accommodating their views to popular belief. By acknowledging the role of the human will and feeling in shaping biblical faith "neologism" gave fresh impetus to the historical criticism of scripture. Such writers had not yet discovered that a historical understanding of religion confronts them with the radical otherness of the biblical world. Lessing's and Herder's understanding of history as progressive revelation had not penetrated into the world of official theology. Alongside the philosophical challenge to religious belief of a Diderot, Voltaire, Hume, or Kant, both orthodox rationalists and "neologists" seemed like traditional voices. In Berlin circles, the popular preacher Johann Joachim Spalding (1714–1804) represented "neologist" theology. His *On the Usefulness of the Preaching Office and Its Continuity* (1772; 3rd ed., 1791), which demanded that religious doctrines be left out of sermons so the church could attend to society's moral needs, drew ironic commentary from Herder.[6]

The contrast between the "liberalism" of these Enlightenment contemporaries and Schleiermacher's perspective is illustrated by his ecclesiastical superior's comments about *On Religion*. Sack objected to the work as pantheistic and Spinozistic: "No art of sophistry and rhetoric will ever be able to convince any reasonable person that Spinozism and Christian religion can coexist" and strongly disapproved of Schleiermacher's association with Friedrich Schlegel and the Jewish salons.[7] Defending himself, Schleiermacher wrote, "Have I indeed spoken with contempt of religion, in the sense in which you take the word, or of belief in a personal God? Never, certainly. I have only said that religion does not depend upon whether or not in abstract thought a person attributes to the infinite, supersensual Cause of the world the predicate of personality."[8] Spinoza was an example of profound piety, not a model of Christian belief, and his choice of friends was also vigorously defended.

A clash between religious parties and the Prussian state in the last decade and a half of the eighteenth century coincided with German fears regarding the revolution in France. Having entered into coalition with Austria against France (1792), Prussia declared peace in 1795 and preserved its neutrality for the next eleven years. The ethos among Prussian burghers was thoroughly conservative. "Gen-

---

[6] J. G. Herder (1744–1803), *To Preachers, Fifteen Provincial Letters*, in *Sämtliche Werke*, VII, (1774; Hildesheim, 1967), pp. 225–312, was aimed at Spalding; see Robert T. Clark, Jr., *Herder: His Life and Thought* (Berkeley, 1955), pp. 196–201.

[7] Albert L. Blackwell, "The Antagonistic Correspondence of 1801 between Chaplain Sack and His Protégé Schleiermacher," *Harvard Theological Review*, 74 (1981), 113.

[8] Blackwell, "The Antagonistic Correspondence," p. 118.

erally sympathetic to the revolution in France, they attributed it to specifically French causes, without application to themselves."[9] But the issue of badly needed reform raised hopes for greater freedom and constitutionalism.

In this repressive setting fresh interpretations of religion challenged the assumptions of the churches' revealed theology. Rousseau's natural religion in "the confessions of the Savoy vicar" (*Emile*, 1762) and Lessing's understanding of revelation as historical development (*The Education of the Human Race*, 1780) pointed to a more naturalistic and historical understanding of religion. The controversy about Spinoza that broke out after Lessing's death embodied the same tensions. J. G. Hamann's (1730–88) dialectical defense of personal conversion and revelation attacked the spiritual barrenness of the Enlightenment, while Herder's aesthetic appreciation of Hebrew poetry (*The Spirit of Hebrew Poetry*, 1782) provided an alternative deeply aesthetic and literary understanding of the Bible. Hamann's review of Kant's first critique was not published out of deference to Kant, and Herder's *Understanding and Reason: A Metacritique of the Critique of Pure Reason* appeared the same year as *On Religion*.[10] Among contemporary critiques of Kant, only *David Hume on Belief; or, Idealism and Realism* (1787) by F. H. Jacobi (1743–1819) was of direct use to Schleiermacher.

The religious conflicts came to a head as Friedrich Wilhelm II (1786–97) sought to end nearly fifty years of Prussia as a bastion of French thought. In 1788 Johann Christoph Wöllner (1732–1800), a former pastor, landowner, freemason, and Rosicrucianist promulgated his infamous "Edict concerning the constitution of religion in the Prussian states." The edict aimed at suppressing "rampant freedom" and combatting unbelief, superstition, and moral decay by requiring all acts of worship and religious instruction to conform to established church confessions. Such measures were opposed by the "neologists" and by public sentiment. Upon coming to power in 1797, Friedrich Wilhelm III invalidated the edict and dismissed Wöllner. But the decade of state-supported repression of critical thought regarding religion governed the world of the young Schleiermacher.

In this repressive period Kant published *Religion Within the Limits of Reason Alone* (1793).[11] Kant was thus faced with a direct conflict between his duty to uphold the state ("A subject of the Prussian state is declared free to hold what religious views he likes, so long as he quietly performs his duties as a good citizen of the state," in the words of the edict) and his freedom as a scholar. Exercising a right of the German universities to conduct reviews, Kant obtained an imprimatur from the philosophical faculty of Jena for the remaining parts of the book. But Prussia forbade Kant from publishing additional work on religion ("If you continue to resist, you may certainly expect unpleasant consequences to yourself"). In this perilous atmosphere Kant made a "mental reservation" in submitting to the king.

9 R. R. Palmer, *The World of the French Revolution* (New York, 1971), p. 237.
10 Henry E. Allison, *The Kant–Eberhard Controversy* (Baltimore, 1973), p. 5.
11 T. M. Greene (ed.), *Religion Within the Limits of Reason Alone* (New York, 1960), pp. xxxii–xxxvii.

He kept his vow to "refrain from all public statements on religion," but took it as binding only until the king's death in 1797, after which he published a second, larger edition of the book. Like *On Religion*, published two years after the first edition, the book challenged the right of biblical theologians and traditionalists to be the sole interpreters of religion.

Kant's situation typified current relationships between intellectuals and the state. To teach at a university was to be bound to the state as a civil servant. But Germany, which, in the words of R. R. Palmer, had "philosophized the French revolution," could scarcely repress the tide of criticism.[12] It is little wonder that a new generation, nurtured as much by Rousseau and Herder as by rationalism, could no longer espouse the options of religious orthodoxy and dogmatism. Friedrich Wilhelm III's accession was marked by hope for a new beginning. Responding to his troubles with the censor, Kant in *The Conflict of the Faculties* (1798) argued for academic freedom in the life of the university.

Hopes for a greater measure of academic and religious liberty were also present in the mind of the young Schleiermacher. After a brief pastorate in Landsberg, Schleiermacher returned to Berlin in 1796 as the Reformed hospital chaplain at the Charité, an institution that served some three thousand persons a year. His social and intellectual life reached beyond the Charité to include his old schoolmate, Karl Gustav von Brinckmann (1764–1847), who shared his passion for Plato and Kant. Through friendship with his Schlobitten employer's son, Count Alexander von Dohna (1771–1831), Schleiermacher was introduced to the literary salon of Markus Herz (1747–1803), a wealthy Jewish physician and pupil of Immanuel Kant, and his talented wife, Henriette (1764–1847). The circle included the linguist Wilhelm von Humboldt (1767–1835), whom he would later serve in the founding commission of the University of Berlin. In another literary group, the "Wednesday Society," Schleiermacher came to know Friedrich Schlegel (August 1797), who quickly emerged as his most significant friend.[13] Although the venture only lasted three years, Friedrich and his brother August W. Schlegel's literary journal, the *Athenaeum*, remains the best introduction to the intellectual world of the young Schleiermacher.

Collaboration with Friedrich Schlegel was enhanced when he moved into Schleiermacher's house near the Oranienburg Gate on 21 December 1797. Among his many projects, Schlegel was at work on *Lucinde*, a novel that was notorious for its bold literary form as well as for its lightly disguised portrayal of his sexual relationship with Dorothea Veit. Spurred on by these friends, Schleiermacher's work appeared as aphorisms in the *Athenaeum* along with book reviews, poetry, and criticism by the Schlegels and Novalis (Friedrich von Hardenberg; 1772–1801). In quest of a moral philosophy that would challenge rationalism, Schleiermacher

[12] *World of the French Revolution*, pp. 233-50.
[13] F. Schlegel's letter to A. W. Schlegel attests to Schleiermacher's many talents and proposes a role for him in contributing to the *Ath.*; *KGA* I.2, pp. xii–xiii and n. 10.

worked on a study of the principles and conditions of society that enabled free sociability (*Geselligkeit*) to develop. But the project was interrupted by the writing of *On Religion*, where the fruits of these reflections influenced the arguments of the fourth address.[14]

On Religion: Speeches to its Cultured Despisers was conceived amid this literary and philosophical ferment that surrounded Friedrich Schlegel, Henriette Herz, and their friends. As a Christian clergyman – and thus a "natural enemy" of the literary avant-garde – Schleiermacher was an enigma. At a surprise twenty-ninth birthday party on 21 November 1797, Schlegel, Herz, and Dohna urged him to write a book, presumably to explain his view of religion. To some extent his own circle constitutes the "cultured despisers" addressed by the book. The idea of doing the book actually dates from late summer 1798, but the writing only took shape in 1799 when Schleiermacher accepted an interim position as court preacher at Potsdam. There, in the more relaxed atmosphere outside Berlin, *On Religion* was written between mid-February and mid-April. Letters from Henriette Herz and Schlegel helped keep him focused. Schlegel wrote that, "I hope that the boredom, which you seem to enjoy there, will serve it well and chain you to the desk"[15] and, like Herz, commented on style as well as substance. The book arose from the qualities of sociability (*Geselligkeit*) and shared philosophizing (*symphilosophieren*) that the group admired. Schlegel kept Schleiermacher informed about work on his *Lucinde* and affairs in Berlin.[16] While completing the last part of the second speech on God and immortality, Schleiermacher expressed a fear that the work might be suppressed as "atheistic" or possibly turned over to Sack as censor. Pressure to finish was exerted by the publisher, who hoped to have the book in time for the Easter book fair. Its completion brought him exhilaration ("the joy of fatherhood") as well as a curious fear of death.[17]

In addition to the book *On Religion* and his aphorisms in the Schlegels' literary journal, Schleiermacher had begun work on a German translation of David Collins's *An Account of the English Colony in New South Wales* (1798).[18] Upon hearing that his first published sermon would appear in a collection of sermons by the outgoing court preacher, Johann Peter Bamberger, he expressed delight: "I should like someday to write a book about everything; but I shall have to postpone this a good many years. I should require a long time to gather my materials and should also be somewhat at a loss about the form."[19] He ends by remarking that the

[14] *KGA* I.2, pp. l–lii, 163–84.
[15] Jack Forstman, *A Romantic Triangle: Schleiermacher and Early German Romanticism* (Missoula, MT, 1977), pp. 65–6; *KGA* I.2, p. liii; *Br.*, III, p. 103 (2 March 1799).
[16] *KGA* I.2, pp. lvif.; *Br.* III, p. 105.
[17] *KGA* I.2, p. lv, *Br.* I, pp. 197, 201; in *Br.* III, p. 103, Schlegel informs him that the censor was Upper Consistory President von Scheve. *KGA* I.2, p. liv. The book was, however, only completed on 15 April with copies first in circulation in June; see *KGA* I.2, p. lx and also *Br.* I, pp. 217f.
[18] *KGA* I.2, pp. xivf., and n. 27; such travel accounts were immensely popular among Germans in the period; Herz had collaborated on two others, on Africa and on North America.
[19] Rowan, *Life of Schleiermacher*, I, p. 209; *Br.* I, pp. 219–20, letter to Herz.

sermons, aphorisms, book on religion, and Australian travel book "make together a wonderful entry into the literary world. What may I not still become in this sublunary sphere!"

Heightened literary activity continued, undeterred by the author's anticipation of early publishing success. As a friend of the Herz family who was acquainted with the social conditions and aspirations of Berlin's Jews, Schleiermacher entered the debate regarding Jewish emancipation. The issue had attracted a flurry of pamphlets by conservative Jews and Christians as well as by radicals and reformists. His small book, still untranslated, *Letters on the Occasion of the Political-Theological Task and the Open Letter of Jewish Householders* (July 1799), recommends the establishment of a reform sect within Judaism.[20] Concealing his identity behind the dual fictions of an anonymous political editor, who has received six letters on the topic of Jewish emancipation from an anonymous correspondent, Schleiermacher argues against the view of David Friedländer that Christian baptism could be used to "naturalize" Jews into Prussian society. Friedländer's proposal appealed to the common humanity and rational morality of Christian culture, while paying lip service to Christian teaching. Schleiermacher took the stance of advocating full civil rights for Prussia's 30,000 Jews, while denying the appropriateness of "quasi-conversion" as the means of attaining social and political standing. To Schleiermacher, Friedländer's proposal, which was not uncommon in Enlightenment Jewish circles, would water down all religious traditions.

Amid this literary activity Schleiermacher, like Schlegel, fell desperately in love with a married woman. Unlike Schlegel, who eventually married Dorothea Veit (1804), Schleiermacher's hopes for a relationship with Eleanore Grunow, then unhappily married to a fellow clergyman, were never fulfilled. His next publication, the *Soliloquies*, was begun in late fall, 1799, as "a New Year's Gift" to Eleanore. Although never attaining the popularity of *On Religion*, the *Soliloquies* exemplify the Romantics' ideal of bringing philosophy into the world of letters, novels, poetry, and personal reflection. Schleiermacher's assault on the popular Kantian moralism of J. G. Fichte is seen in the *Soliloquies* where we read "I no longer know the thing which men call conscience."[21] Schleiermacher's ethical insight – sometimes missed by readers of *On Religion* – is based more on recognition of the complex determinations of moral choice in lived existence than on the hope that rational action deserving of merit can ever be attained.

All of this literary activity that surrounds *On Religion* shares the early Romantic tendency to experiment with literary form. A case can be made that Schleiermacher's Plato scholarship, love of Socrates, and practice of Romantic literary theory contributed directly in 1835 to Søren Kierkegaard's discovery of the power

---

[20] *KGA* I.2, pp. lxxviii–lxxxv, 327–61 and the facsimile edition with a "Nachwort" by Kurt Nowak (Berlin, Evangelische Verlagsanstalt, 1984).

[21] *Soliloquies*, trans. Horace Friess (Chicago, 1957); *KGA* I.3, pp. 1–61. *Soliloquies*, p. 29; *KGA* I.3, p. 17.

and suggestiveness of indirect communication.[22] A writer can often communicate subtle and controversial thought to an audience more effectively by writing indirectly and anonymously, while freely using irony and allusion. The rhetorical ploy of the fictive letters regarding Jewish emancipation is taken in the controversial defense of Schlegel's *Lucinde*, the *Confidential Letters Concerning Friedrich Schlegel's Lucinde* (1800), which consists of an exchange of letters among friends, and in the *The Celebration of Christmas: A Conversation* (1806), which seeks to discover the meaning of Christian love by focusing on the Christmas Eve celebration of a German family.[23] Later, in the 1820s, when he was involved in controversy about the proper form of Christian liturgy, Schleiermacher wrote under the pseudonym "Pacificus Sincerus."[24] Schleiermacher was himself modest in regard to his literary attainments. Like Friedrich Schlegel, he belongs more to the theoretical than to the practicing artistic side of the movement. The task of finding the rhetorical form that best connects with a particular audience preoccupied him much of his life.

From Kant to Romanticism

Profound criticism appropriately mingles with deep respect in marking the young Schleiermacher's relationship to Kant. Wilhelm Dilthey's view that Schleiermacher was profoundly affected by his struggle with Kant's philosophy continues to have merit. His encounter with Kant began in boarding school with a reading of the *Prolegomena to Any Future Metaphysic*, continued at Halle with J. A. Eberhard, and in a private study of *The Critique of Pure Reason* (1781) and the *Foundations of the Metaphysics of Morals* (1785). In 1790 Schleiermacher observed that his "belief in this [Kant's] philosophy increases day by day, and this all the more, the more I compare it with that of Leibniz."[25] He appears not to have known the *Critique of Judgment*, the work of Kant that comes closest to Romanticism's concern to relate ethics and aesthetics.[26]

---

[22] Richard Crouter, "Kierkegaard's Not so Hidden Debt to Schleiermacher," *Zeitschrift für Neuere Theologiegeschichte/Journal for the History of Modern Theology*, 1 (1994), 205–25.

[23] The *Confidential Letters* (*KGA* I.3, pp. xlviii–lxviii, 139–216) remains untranslated, while *The Celebration of Christmas* appeared in English as *Christmas Eve: Dialogue on the Incarnation*, trans. Terrence Tice (Richmond, VA, 1967).

[24] See "Über das liturgische Recht evangelischer Landesfürsten: Ein theologisches Bedenken" (by "Pacificus Sincerus," 1824) and "Gespräch zweier selbstüberlegender evangelischer Christen über die Schrift: Luther in Beziehung auf die neue preussiche Agende: Ein letztes Wort oder ein erstes" (anonymously, 1827), *Sämtliche Werke* (Reimer, 1846), I.5, pp. 477–625.

[25] *KGA* V.1, no. 134 (2 February 1790), p. 191. The twenty-six letters, which Brinckmann dubs a "philosophical correspondence," are given in *KGA* V.1.

[26] Although the book was in the personal catalogue of books from Schleiermacher's library (Günter Meckenstock (ed.), *Schleiermachers Bibliothek* [Berlin, 1993], p. 210), a remark from 1803 that "Kant only incidentally touches lightly on art" (cited from the *Kritik der Sittenlehre*, p. 290) suggests that the young Schleiermacher had not read the book; see Eilert Herms, *Herkunft, Entfaltung und erste Gestalt des Systems der Wissenschaften bei Schleiermacher* (Gütersloh, 1974), p. 121 n. 5; Günter Scholtz, "Schleiermacher und die Platonische Ideenlehre," *Internationaler Schleiermacher-Kongreß Berlin 1984*, ed. Kurt-Victor Selge (Berlin, 1985), I.1, p. 870 n. 22.

If the *Critique of Pure Reason* restricts metaphysical truth to the realm of appearance, Kant's practical moral philosophy provides access to the supersensible world of noumenal experience. Morality rests on duty in the form of a moral law that is unconditioned, universal, and autonomous. Ethical behavior that is motivated by anything less than rationality conflicts with our freedom as responsible causal agents. Moral law thus constitutes an exception to theoretical reason's restriction of human insight to finite categories. Indeed, for Kant religion answers the first *Critique*'s third question: What can I know? What ought I to do? And what can I hope? "Only if religion is added to it [morals] can the hope arise of someday participating in happiness in proportion as we endeavored not to be unworthy of it."[27]

By what steps, though, does Kant move from morality to postulate religion? Stripped to its essentials, his argument claims that reason everywhere seeks the fullest principles which are absolute and unconditioned. Practical reason also seeks the highest ends of morality. These ends can never be identified with natural desires or with happiness, which all persons desire. To be complete, a moral philosophy must envisage a highest good that combines happiness and virtue, where happiness is proportionate to moral worth. Only virtue that is able to attain its end meets this requirement. But such a level of virtue is impossible to attain by finite beings. In addition, happiness cannot be measured by pleasure and pain, to which we respond so differently. As a complex idea, happiness must be linked to virtue and attainable in principle. "But what man is obligated to achieve he must be able to achieve. It is therefore necessary that the conditions exist by virtue of which he can fulfil his obligation. These conditions are man's immortality and the existence of God."[28] It is beyond doubt that Kant's arguments for a rational faith were seriously intended. His answer to the question "What can I hope for?" is: I can hope that in eternity my efforts will be judged as worthy by the God of spirit and nature, thus (indirectly and after considerable delay) arriving at happiness, which is conceived as the totality of moral ends or as the highest good.

Schleiermacher's youthful works *On the Highest Good* (1789), *On Freedom* (between 1790 and 1792), and *On the Worth of Life* (1792–3) argue against Kant's notion of happiness as part of the highest good ("The land of happiness can only lie in the miraculous region, where the imagination rules unencumbered"[29]) and suggest that Kant's view embodies a concealed premise about perfection that is traceable to Christian sources. Kant infers immortality and the existence of God as necessary and real to ensure the attainability of this highest good. But since Kant acknowledges that the moral law and its obligations exist independently of the question of whether it is possible to attain the highest good, we could drop these

---

[27] *Critique of Practical Reason* (Indianapolis, 1956), p. 134.
[28] Emil L. Fackenheim, "Immanuel Kant" in *Nineteenth Century Religious Thought in the West* I, ed. Ninian Smart et al. (Cambridge, 1985), p. 20.
[29] *KGA* I.1, p. 87.

inferences without giving up our main proposition. Immortality and the existence of God are only posited in place of an infinite regress and an approximation in the quest to attain happiness. They are not, as Kant suggests, discrete inferences; God is already postulated in the idea of immortality, which as the highest condition of happiness must be beyond time, apart from limitations of rational finitude, and supremely rational. Yet why not think of the highest good as infinitely approximated? How much the faculty of desire can realize the highest good cannot be determined by reason apart from circumstances and subjective incentives. Kant errs in taking the highest good as constitutive, whereas for Schleiermacher it stands as a useful regulative principle that does not make perfection the highest possible end.[30] The way Kant connects virtue with happiness is impracticable. Even if a primitive association exists between merit and reward, it is another thing to argue for their necessary connection.

Moreover, if we look closely we see that it is impossible to conceive of happiness as a concept of pure reason. To be conceivable happiness must be construed as a totality that consists of successive parts, for example, a dance, from which the parts are not obliterated, even when temporally past. But as a temporal concept happiness cannot be defined apart from the inclinations. When an inclination is satisfied it grows strong again, while some other inclination grows weaker; thus one never arrives at a coherent concept of happiness as a whole.[31]

Schleiermacher staunchly refuses to accept the "duality" of the human moral agent upon which Kant's system rests. The phenomenal and noumenal selves must be conceived together if we are to consider a person as a moral agent. His answer to the question about how far it is possible to subordinate human actions to rational rules and laws is unambiguous: it is not possible at all, except in the most limited senses, because the law of reason can never determine our will directly. Unless the will is simply another term for reason's self-sufficiency, it must have some relationship to the faculty of desire. And the contents of this faculty are always present, multiple, changing; likewise, the objects of the will are as apt to be mental as physical. Reason and choice (*Willkür*) can only focus on our specific concerns, where actual decisions are made. Human character develops by a long process of training and self-scrutiny, which leads to gradual improvement and only an approximation of happiness.

Schleiermacher's *On the Worth of Life* gives a distinctly un-Kantian restatement of an ideal human nature: "Knowing and desiring [*Erkennen und Begehren*] should not be two in me, but one. Perfect continuous agreement of both, in the fullest measure, in which both are possible in me and the unity of both in purpose and

---

[30] *KGA* I.I, pp. 98–9; *KGA* I.I, pp. 100–1 with apparent reference to *Critique of Practical Reason*, p. 140, where these transcendent objects (freedom, immortality, and God) "become immanent and constitutive, since they are the grounds of the possibility of realizing the necessary object of pure practical reason (the highest good)."

[31] *KGA* I.I, pp. 105–6.

object, that is humanity, that is the beautiful goal, which is attached to the human being." Indeed, even the lovely feeling of pleasure "puts my cognitive powers into play." Schleiermacher makes clear that he is not speaking of a materialist's pleasure in sense experience. "Pleasure in truth is pleasure in rules, joy in agreement of individual things with the rule."[32] Far from being excluded, the material of the faculty of desire continually provides a thousand objects for our reflection.

In addressing the issue of determinism *On Freedom* maintains that rational choice is greatly circumscribed by our situation in life, including our previous thoughts, experiences, and natural capabilities. Schleiermacher's defense of determinism resembles Henry Sidgwick's in *The Methods of Ethics*: "We must therefore accept the conclusion that each such resolve has only a limited effect: and that we cannot know when making it how far this effect will exhibit itself in the performance of the act resolved upon."[33] On the compatibility of free choice with determinism Schleiermacher holds that the attribution of virtue and responsibility requires "nothing more immediate than that the action really is something that occurs in the soul" which acts on the basis of a larger "composite of forces." Confidence that moral accountability is not in danger of ceasing to exist protects the only sense of freedom that is needed. A moral agent is as free in doing a deed as is the painter or artist in completing a work;[34] both pursuits work toward a particular end out of previously given combinations of sensual and spiritual creativity. Like artists, moral agents generally get credit for their deeds.

Although Schleiermacher owned and refers to *Religion Within the Limits of Reason Alone*, he makes no explicit reference to its argument in *On Religion*.[35] Yet it is difficult to maintain that he did not know Kant's arguments for rational religion. The intrinsic importance of Kant's religion book and its proximity in time warrant comparison. Even where their arguments and positions appear similar, resemblances are overshadowed by subtle differences.

First, both works have an eschatological framework. The idea that ultimate religious fulfillment can only occur in an indefinite future is shared by both thinkers. Kant's later thought on politics, peace, morality, and religion is especially couched in an unfolding historical perspective. Yet for Kant the struggle for fulfillment in the form of duty that acts against inclination and desire is dominant, while for Schleiermacher a serene moment of eternity is disclosed in the immediate relationship of an individual to the universe.

Second, both philosophies of religion envisage the human in a broken world. Kant's account of human nature goes far beyond any simple "dualism." In addition to an inherent "propensity for good" the human "inclination to evil" is inextir-

---

[32] *KGA* I.I, p. 410; *KGA* I.I, p. 412.
[33] Sidgwick, *The Methods of Ethics* (London, 1893), p. 75.
[34] *KGA* I.I, p. 260; *KGA* I.I, p. 258.
[35] Meckenstock, *Schleiermachers Bibliothek*, p. 210; *KGA* v.I, no. 259, p. 346, reports to his father that he had not yet read Kant's *Religion Within the Limits of Reason Alone*; no further references to it occur in the correspondence between 1794 and 1799.

pable, even if able to be overcome by a good will. Kant's acknowledgment of "radical evil" in human nature complicates Schleiermacher's perception of a shallow optimism and artificiality in Kant's anthropology. The analogue in *On Religion* lies in the analysis of the interplay of finitude with the infinite, the loss of wholeness that occurs in the quest for higher unity.

Third, external authority cannot be a compelling guide on questions of morality or religion. The moral and rational truth of religion symbolized in biblical and church teachings needs the philosopher for its explication. For Kant, Jesus is the archetype and exemplar of the categorical imperative in the sayings of the Sermon on the Mount. For Schleiermacher, Jesus is the mediator, par excellence, who knows that the finite can only imperfectly become a bearer of the infinite and must undergo death in this cosmic process.

Fourth, the moral community envisaged by Kant genuinely exists in history. But unlike Schleiermacher, especially in the Fourth and Fifth speeches, true religion is less able to find expression in institutions. Both figures seek to ward off the corruption of true religion by the false intrusion of politics and the state. Kant's natural or moral religion contrasts with ecclesiastical faith that is rooted in Scripture, myth, miracles, and ritual. Schleiermacher argues that natural religion is shallow and artificial and sees actual lived religion ("positive religions") as the locus of true faith.

Fifth, it is ironic that *Religion Within the Limits of Reason Alone* rationalizes the claims of dogmatic theology, while *On Religion* stands aloof from the intellectual problems of specific Christian dogmas. Of course, Schleiermacher's mature theological work, *The Christian Faith*, makes good on the omission in ways never attempted by Kant. The two works illustrate the transformation of traditional religion in modern Western thought in ways that confound modernizing "neologists" as much as orthodox Lutherans. The Romantic view seems more radical in reaching towards a religious naturalism that offers a distinctive alternative to traditional theism; yet that reorientation provides a new foundation for theology in the post-Kantian period. If we bear in mind Schleiermacher's radicality on just those issues that Kant defends (God and immortality), his argument stands in stark contrast.

In addition to the impact of Kant, "a Greek ethos" has also been perceived in *On Religion*. Plato the artist, who combines systematic inquiry with concern for the communication of truth, exercises a profound influence – in the form of a dialectical metaphysic and rich explication of human nature – on the present book. Other philosophical influences include F. H. Jacobi (1743–1819), whose *On the Teaching of Spinoza: Letters to Mr. Moses Mendelssohn* (1785), played a key role in the Romantics' Spinozist revival.[36] Schleiermacher took issue with Jacobi's belief that

[36] *KGA* I.1, pp. lxxv–lxxxiii, 511–97, includes his early manuscripts, "Spinozismus," "Kurze Darstellung des Spinozistischen Systems," and "Ueber dasjenige in Jacobis Briefen und Realismus, was den Spinoza nicht betrifft, und besonders über seine eigene Philosophie" (all conjecturally 1793/4);

Spinoza's determinism would lead to atheism, but he admired Jacobi's critique of Kant's teaching on the thing-in-itself in *David Hume on Belief; or, Idealism and Realism*,[37] as well as Jacobi's appeal to an immediate, self-justifying level of insight as the starting point of philosophic thought. Jacobi's "certitude of faith" was not accepted by Schleiermacher as a substitute for knowledge, even though the element of feeling in Jacobi's thought was commensurate with his literary friends' aesthetic theorizing.

There is no evidence that the "German idealists" (Fichte, Schelling, or Hegel) play a foundational role in shaping Schleiermacher's thought, however much he is aware of the two former thinkers and responds to Hegel after 1818 as a colleague at the University of Berlin.[38] Schleiermacher was especially impressed by the early Schelling, a friend of the Schlegels from Jena, whose understanding of nature as physical–spiritual process is incorporated in the present book.[39] By contrast, Fichte's *The Science of Knowledge* (1797) is under sharp attack. If *On Religion* polemicizes against Kant's teaching that an autonomous moral law is the locus of the supersensible world within human experience, the target in the foreground is Fichte's system of transcendental idealism. The suggestion that our moral experience of the categorical imperative is tantamount to being in relationship to God conflicts with Schleiermacher's theological insight into the finite nature of a humanity, which knows its limitations and vulnerability.

Schleiermacher objects not so much to his theological radicality – Fichte was dismissed from his Jena professorship of philosophy in 1799 in the "atheism controversy" – as to the extremes to which Fichte takes the claims of transcendental idealism. As a philosophical realist Schleiermacher sees that the realms of human selfhood (spirit, freedom) and the world (nature) cry out for reconciliation not just intellectually but at the level of human existence. Fundamental self-awareness ("intuition of the universe") is prior to all knowledge claims and rational insight into the matrix of human life. The idea that an immediate sense of the universe impresses itself on human existence anticipates the nineteenth-century movement towards a philosophy of life (*Lebensphilosophie*) championed by Dilthey.

writing to Brinckmann (19 July 1800), *Br.* IV, pp. 72–5, Schleiermacher expresses admiration for Jacobi, even while not in complete agreement. See Jacobi, *Über die Lehre des Spinozas, in Briefen an Herrn Moses Mendelssohn* (Breslau, 1785).

[37] This may be stated, in Henry Allison's words, as "the contradiction between the necessity of appealing to the thing in itself in order to explain experience and the impossibility of justifying such an appeal within the framework of the *Critique*" (*Kant–Eberhard Controversy*, p. 5).

[38] See Richard Crouter, "Hegel and Schleiermacher at Berlin: A Many-sided Debate," *Journal of the American Academy of Religion*, 48 (1980), 25–6.

[39] See *Br.* III, pp. 151, 154, in which Friedrich Schlegel seeks to enlist Schleiermacher to review Schelling's "world soul" for the *Ath.*, while reserving the "philosophy of nature" for himself; Schleiermacher declined, pleading insufficient natural scientific knowledge; Hermann Süskind, *Der Einfluss Schellings auf die Entwicklung von Schleiermachers System* (Tübingen, 1909), pp. 58f., 111–21; see *Ath.*, III, pp. 234–5, for F. Schlegel's sonnets on Schleiermacher's *On Religion* and Schelling's *On the World Soul*; though he initially rejected the book, in 1801 Schelling described himself as an "avid reader and admirer"; Nowak, *Schleiermacher und die Frühromantik*, p. 162 n. 118.

That Schleiermacher is sometimes viewed as a subjective idealist is odd in view of his well-documented critique of this position. In contrast with Fichte, Schleiermacher's notion of selfhood rests on definite individuality rather than the abstract Ego, and his individual person stands in a real spatio-temporal relationship where integration of spirit and nature occur. Fichte's teaching was out of touch with the need for rapprochement between science and art and the need to appreciate religion on its own terms. To deduce human thought and culture from the self-positing Ego put at risk the reality of the objective world. The severity of his quarrel with Fichte did not, however, obscure the formative nature of his debt to Kant. That debt was so great in his age that it shaped the agenda not only of philosophers, but also of literary scholars and poets.

We have seen that Schleiermacher's path towards Romanticism began amid a strand of thought that includes Rousseau, Lessing, and Herder. The malaise of modern culture, the Romantics held, derives in no small part from its lack of common symbols. Schlegel and his associates idealized the socially uniform and harmonious culture of ancient Greece as a contemporary model. Early German Romanticism launched its critique of Kant's transcendental philosophy, of the older rationalism of Leibniz and Wolff, and of the literary genres of French classicism, while subsuming this criticism under the new order of "poesie." In *Athenaeum*, fragment 116, Schlegel maintains that society is to be transformed by this new order: "Romantic poetry is a progressive, universal poetry. Its aim isn't merely to reunite all the separate species of poetry and put poetry in touch with philosophy and rhetoric. It tries to and should mix and fuse poetry and prose, inspiration and criticism, the poetry of art and the poetry of nature; and make poetry lively and sociable, and life and society poetical." Far from viewing philosophy as the universal arbiter of truth, that role is taken over by critical insight, which for Schlegel is characterized by "wit" and "irony": "Society is a chaos that only wit can organize and bring into harmony."[40]

Hans Eichner offers the apt reminder that "romanticism is an unpleasantly vague term, whose meaning depends only too often on the preoccupations of the person who happens to use it."[41] But Schleiermacher's involvement in Romanticism can be approached on the basis of something more than whim. As Friedrich Schlegel's intellectual confidant, Schleiermacher shared his friend's sensibility and intellectual belief. If little scholarly consensus exists regarding Schleiermacher's relationship to Romanticism, this is partly due to efforts to explain away the relationship. Since Paul Kluckhorn, German literary scholars readily acknowledge that Schleiermacher fully shares the Romantic world view. Some writers in theology and literary studies (Dilthey, Haym, Redeker) resist this view and present Romanticism as a passing phase of his thought, while still others (Forstman, Dierkes, Nowak) recognize the

---

[40]   Peter Firchow (ed.), *Friedrich Schlegel's Lucinde and the Fragments* (Minneapolis, MN, 1971), p. 175; ibid., p. 76.

[41]   Eichner, "The Genesis of German Romanticism," *Queen's Quarterly*, 72 (1965), 213.

commonalities but stress Schleiermacher's distinctive contribution to a movement that was always heterogenous.[42] A proper estimate of Schleiermacher's relationship to the Romantics must see this relationship in the context of the criticism of Kant by Friedrich Schlegel. As a young literary and philosophical rebel, Schlegel sought to get beyond Kant's restrictive understanding of transcendental freedom as the postulate of practical reason. For Schlegel the full round of life, including aesthetic sensibility and the ambiguity of politics, seemed distorted in Kant's teaching. "For want of a political and aesthetic sense, Kant has confused the ethical maxim (holy will and kingdom of God in his sense) with the practical."[43] Thus "freedom," the rallying cry of the French revolution, remained the theme of the Romantics' revolt against rationalism.

Schleiermacher's rebellion against Kant's division of reality into the realms of necessity and freedom, the unknowable world of things-in-themselves and the intelligible world of categories, the determinism of natural science and the realm of freedom in moral law, art, philosophy, and religion occasions no surprise. The category of the understanding "held sway only in the field of empirical reality, which was inexorably ruled by the law of cause and effect." The Romantics understood radical freedom as *Willkür*, a German term with connotations of "capricious" or "arbitrary." By contrast Kant was suspicious of the power of *Willkür* to turn away from the moral law and took pains in *Religion Within the Limits of Reason Alone* to minimize its link with the faculty of desire and to identify it with the higher intellectual faculty. The view of Kantianism held by these young writers is vividly captured by Eichner: "Kant's idea of freedom was that you were unfree when you did what you wanted to do, because then you were subject to psychological causation; and you were free when you did what you didn't want to do, when you obeyed the moral law imposed by your own reason. To make matters worse, reason was the same in everybody; and consequently you were free only when you were least original."[44] Eichner further observes that "this was an impossible position for a group of young writers, who . . . were desperately trying to vindicate their individuality." Against the normative and legalistic character of Kantianism, self-development of the individual person stands at the center of Romanticist thought. A universal dimension still holds sway. But the vehicle of expression is literature in the form of a "universal poetry."

For Schlegel God's "creation from nothing" points to an utterly creative

---

[42] Cf. Dierkes, pp. 66, 87 on Dilthey's "total opposition"; Martin Redeker, *Life and Thought* (Philadelphia, 1973), p. 33, under the heading "Was Schleiermacher a Romantic?" asserts: "Some have claimed that the basic original ideas of his creative Berlin period, for instance, the concepts of individuality and the universe, were derived from romanticism. Such a claim is untrue, for he had the idea of individuality earlier"; Forstman, *A Romantic Triangle*, pp. 65–94, recognizes similarities but stresses the distinctive features of Schleiermacher's thought; Nowak, *Schleiermacher und die Frühromantik*, pp. 11–16.

[43] *Schriften und Fragmente*, ed. Ernst Behler (Stuttgart, 1956), p. 156.

[44] Eichner, "The Genesis of German Romanticism," p. 221.

freedom and suggests "the artistic view of God as a poet and of the world as a work of art."[45] Deity is the ground of rationality and the center of all productive possibilities. For Schlegel religious and literary ways of appreciating the world are innate, whereas philosophy, which insists on fathoming the mysteries of nature, does violence to reality and is a secondary and artificial endeavor.[46] The Romantics' discovery of freedom as divine possibility (the artistic counterpart of the *creatio ex nihilo*) is related to the categories of action, possibility, becoming, infinitude, and individuality. While freedom in Kant is restricted to the realm of the mind and cognitive insight, and freedom in the French Revolution is politically ambiguous, the Romantics posit absolute freedom only in a love and art that are intuitively connected to an existing, real world. As Hans Dierkes puts it: "Ethics must – in a word – dissolve into aesthetics."[47] A universally valid ethic is no longer needed since a sequence of contingent events that require a uniform response is not present. Schleiermacher and Schlegel happened upon the same insight into the new divine role of art in 1797.

Love and art converge to form a "religion of love" in Schlegel's *Lucinde*, where his love for Dorothea is set forth through the combination of letters, diaries, dialogue, and essays with Julius and Lucinde playing the parts of "priest and priestess in the religion of love." The common Romantic view of love shared by Schleiermacher and Schlegel contrasts sharply with the understanding of love as platonic virtue, which puts one's moral fiber to the test, or as pure libertine behavior, which reduces the distinctively human to animality. Yet Schleiermacher's reservations about Schlegel's notion of a "universal poeticization" cause his version of Romanticism to be more reformist than revolutionary.[48] Schleiermacher's fictive *Confidential Letters* on the *Lucinde* stops short of endorsing Schlegel's unity of "spiritual voluptuousness and sensual beatitude."[49] At the end of his third letter (from Ernestine) Schleiermacher incorporates material from an earlier paper "On the sense of shame." This tacit response to Schlegel, which insists upon respect for the spiritual condition of another person, places constraints on one's own freedom: "Here I stand at the boundary where my will is limited by another freedom, and, by the course of life, a mystery of nature" (*Soliloquies*).[50] Compared with Schlegel's

---

[45] Dierkes, pp. 61–2.

[46] *Kritische Ausgabe* XI, ed. Ernst Behler (Munich, 1958), p. 116.

[47] Dierkes, p. 65.

[48] Firchow, *Friedrich Schlegel's Lucinde*, pp. 23, 44: "We embraced with as much wantonness as religion." In the section, "A dithyrambic fantasy on the loveliest situation in the world": "So is it that the religion of love weaves our love ever more closely together," and "The religion I have returned to is the oldest, the most childlike and simple. I worship fire as the best symbol of the Godhead" (pp. 49, 61); Dierkes, pp. 65–6.

[49] Firchow, *Friedrich Schlegel's Lucinde*, p. 44; M. E. Philipp (ed.), *Lucinde* (Leipzig, n.d.), p. 5: "die geistige Wollust und die sinnliche Seligkeit."

[50] *KGA* I.3, pp. 168–78. *Soliloquies*, p. 79; Dierkes, pp. 72–4; *KGA* I.3, p. 172, where the discussion of shame (*Schaamhaftigkeit*) recognizes that modesty insists on "respect for the spiritual condition of another person," and asks "Are there not also similar indispensable intrusions into freedom in other fields?"

virtual poetizing of nature, Schleiermacher acknowledges a degree of separateness between spirit and nature. In addition, moral conflict has a legitimate place in human relationships; Schleiermacher passes over in silence the chapter of *Lucinde* in praise of idleness ("The Idyll of Idleness"), and by defending the legitimate rights of civil society he issues a caveat with respect to Schlegel's interpretation of art as the divine resolution of chaos.[51]

What, then, are we able to conclude regarding Schleiermacher's relationship to the Romantics? As noted, Romanticism fed on the unresolved problems of Kantian thought in ways that reveal a surprising degree of continuity between the Enlightenment and Romanticism. Kant's own admiration of Rousseau is well known. When the matter is put in perspective, Schleiermacher's distinctive embodiment of Romanticism warrants greater recognition. Such a view differs from the efforts of Christian apologists to minimize Schleiermacher's Romanticism in order to protect the theological orthodoxy of his mature teaching. The early Romantics were a loosely knit group of aesthetic theorists, artists, and poets. If the subtle differences between Schleiermacher and Schlegel soon became more pronounced – as seen in Schlegel's nuanced review of *On Religion* in the *Athenaeum*[52] – this does not warrant the conclusion that Schleiermacher is un-Romantic or anti-Romantic, so much as it points to the distinctiveness of his contribution to the movement.

An awareness of certain "doctrinal differences" or heterodox opinions ought not to obscure the large number of common images and symbols that unite Schleiermacher's work with these contemporaries. Dominant Romantic symbols, the quest for a center, the image of an open circle, the ellipse, and eccentric path are all present in *On Religion*.[53] At the level of the imagination, Schleiermacher is of one mind with the Romantics. For all their talk about darkness, night, and chaos – *On Religion* accepts "infinite chaos" as an appropriate symbol for the universe – neither his Romanticism, nor that of his friends, approaches the utter despair of a metaphysical nihilism. While stopping short of a "religion of art," the literary form of the young Schleiermacher's work attests to the impact of Schlegel's belief (*Lyceum*, fragment 117) that "Poetry can only be criticized by way of poetry."[54]

Far from being a theological interloper among the writers and poets of the Romantic movement, Schleiermacher fully contributes to the movement as a "thinker of finitude." His involvement is not limited to Schlegel, but includes a profound, though brief, relationship with the poet Novalis. The young poet responded appreciatively to *On Religion* in *Christendom or Europe*; his famous

[51] Dierkes, p. 84.

[52] Dierkes, p. 88; *Ath.* ii, pp. 289–300.

[53] Marshall Brown, *The Shape of German Romanticism* (Ithaca, NY, 1979); Philippe Lacoue-Labarthe and Jean-Luc Nancy, *The Literary Absolute: The Theory of Literature in German Romanticism*, trans. Philippe Barnard and Cheryl Lester (New York, 1988).

[54] Dierkes, p. 90; Firchow, *Friedrich Schlegel's Lucinde*, p. 157: "Poetry can only be criticized by way of poetry. A critical judgment of an artistic production has no civil rights in the realm of art if it isn't itself a work of art."

poems, *Hymns to the Night*, were written when Schleiermacher was completing his *Soliloquies*. The German Romantics' sense of "unfulfilled longing" is perhaps nowhere better expressed than in Novalis's words (from *Blütenstaub*): "We *seek* the unconditioned everywhere, and always *find* only things."[55] Especially in his Fifth Speech, Schleiermacher presents the incompletion of the finite that struggles against the infinite as the most sublime expression of the Christian faith, which is embodied in "holy sadness." This Romantic belief in the final inexpressibility of reality was paralleled, for Schleiermacher, by the teaching of Plato. These ways of viewing the world posit a higher unity amid multiplicity, even when the knower is unable to comprehend the mystery of the whole. Unlike Kant's and Fichte's way of defending these claims in a philosophical system, the young Schleiermacher seeks an open-ended, literary-rhetorical way of defending a philosophical interpretation of religion that will give religion its due. If the Kantian dichotomy between spirit and nature, represented by the realms of noumena and phenomena, is too great for Schleiermacher, the Romantics' insistence on collapsing these distinctions into a single mode of poetic awareness ends with too vacuous a line being drawn between spirit and nature. Although Schleiermacher finds the notion of the thing-in-itself obscure, his realism keeps him in touch with the objective world and serves as a restraint on the efforts of the young Schlegel to poetize reality. In view of these exacting discriminations, it is little wonder that Schleiermacher's relationship to Kantian thought as well as to Romanticism is so frequently misrepresented. The chief poles of his formative youthful thought were complementary. The present book was conceived by a writer who stood at the confluence of the most vivid intellectual options of his day and whose thought is incomprehensible apart from these alternatives.

Rhetoric and argument in the work

Readers of the 1799 text cannot fail to be struck by the book's rhetorical power and design. With audacious confidence the young author assaults his audience's certitude that religion deserves contempt. By casting doubt on interpretations of religion as right knowledge (metaphysics) or right action (morals), Schleiermacher relentlessly exposes their ignorance of religion. A reader who approaches the work looking for didactic guidance ("What shall I believe?", "Is Christ God's Son?", or "Is the Bible true?") is sure to miss its central argument. Schleiermacher is less concerned to tell us "what to believe" than he is with showing "what it is to believe" by showing how religious life arises from the self's relationship to the universe. The text evokes an awareness of the way our partial, fragmented experience relates to larger, systemic wholes. The hardened lines of academic (literary,

---

[55] *Ath.* I, p. 70.

philosophical, or theological) discourse that we bring to such texts are of our own making.

Starting with an ironic title, a process of intellectual seduction anticipates, plays upon, and seeks to subvert reader reactions. In the end, the "cultured despisers of religion" are viewed as more authentically religious than many orthodox church-goers or professional clergy. The poet-writer not only speaks about religion but is directly under its sway, though his clerical status remains concealed. Given the degeneracy of modern religious life, his audience's contempt is understandable, even though it rests on the ill-founded assumption that religion is necessarily restrictive, dogmatic, and exclusivistic. He ridicules his audience's notions of religion, while appealing to prejudices of his fellow Germans, especially their contempt for clergy, suspicion of the French and English, dislike of official creeds, and revulsion with the materialism and utilitarianism that shape modern politics.

Readers may be surprised at the vehemence with which Schleiermacher attacks the Enlightenment view of religion as rational or moral teaching. His biting irony often shifts to a form of endorsement and flattery, for the author believes that his audience's aesthetic sense predisposes them to doubt the received opinion about religion's demise. He appeals to the divine muse, to human individuality and genius, and to hope for an emancipation of the human spirit from the dull conformism of modern life. To fulfill this strategy the author must persuade his audience that the views they already hold about life, far from being inimical to religion, are the basis for its authentic expression and rebirth. Literary devices and figures of speech abound in the work. When politics is chastized for bestowing a "fatal kindness" on religion, the oxymoron conveys the author's sense of irony. "Not only . . . but also" constructions build to a climax and contribute to reader suspense. The technique of "false denial" weaves material into the argument which might be objectionable if it were directly asserted. When Schleiermacher writes, "About all that I do not inquire" (Fifth Speech), we can be sure that he has just asked a whole series of penetrating questions on the matter. Ironic inversions (e.g., "natural religion" as decidedly unnatural) seek to undermine his opponents' arguments, while creating space for a new concept of religion. No side issue is too peripheral when readers are asked to examine their experience in regard to a matter as complex, and as widely misunderstood, as religion.

A preference for organic metaphors exemplifies the Romantics' "nostalgia for the natural object."[56] Countless metaphors and similes from biology and physical science bring home the ways that finite processes relate to the oneness of reality. Organic images suggest the dynamic tension between birth and death, while physical images better convey the endless cycle of permanence amid change. Together they set a mood and awaken a reader's sense of the universe. Like other philosophical-religious writers (one thinks of Kierkegaard or Buber), Schleier-

---

[56] Paul de Man, "Intentional Structure of the Romantic Image" in *Romanticism and Consciousness: Essays in Criticism*, ed. Harold Bloom (New York, 1970), pp. 70, 76.

Table 1   *Rhetorical structure and dynamics of the work*

Problem	Oppositions	Resolutions
1. Foundational assumption	Two–opposing forces	Demand for mediation (not a midpoint or equilibrium)
2. Intellectual definition	Manifest activity (thinking, doing) *versus* secret inactivity (feeling, intuition)	Intuition of the universe as mediatory
3. Personal formation	Outer forms (language, creeds, political constraints) *versus* personal, inward appropriation of truth	Indirect communication (Socratism)
4. Institutional and social embodiment	Institutional with standard leadership (coerciveness) *versus* community (mutuality)	Reconceptualized ideal of religious community
5. Religious tradition	Natural religion (limited) *versus* historical religion (expansive/universal)	Christianity as universal religion; holy sadness as symbol of lack of finality

Note: The chart shows the problem addressed by each speech, the oppositional terms or polarities in which a dialogue with the reader occurs, and a new mediating idea or reality that is introduced as a means of living with these tensions and oppositions. Also shown is the argument's movement from abstract foundational insight to the concrete particularity of Christian religiousness.

macher speaks at deeply personal levels of human self-awareness. By playing off personal address (the German *Ihr*) against third person perspectives, Schleiermacher aligns himself with his audience against a rising tide of social conformity, materialism, and confidence in science. For some readers the book's intensely personal nature presents a problem. How shall we respond to someone who claims to speak "of necessity from his own soul"? Such a stance places a person, not just an argument, on the line. This highly personal cast of mind is, of course, also a reason for the book's popularity. Students of religion and philosophy are often struck by its author's ability to speak across the standard barriers of academic discourse. Novice readers occasionally have the feeling that a timeless sage has crept into modern Berlin. Yet analysis must sometimes appear as the betrayal of a friend, if only to get inside the arguments in an objective manner.

The work's structure and arrangement moves from abstract to concrete levels of experience. It begins with the premise that reality consists of "two opposing forces" (First Speech). (Who among us wishes to deny that we relate to the world in modes that are passive as well as active? Which of us ever truly knows how to keep these impulses in proper balance?) Subsequent speeches delineate more particular horizons of reality and move from the essence of religion (Second Speech), to its role in human self-formation (Third Speech), to its manifestation in communities (Fourth Speech), and finally to its concrete reality within a historical tradition (Fifth Speech). Thematic repetitions and recapitulations provoke a reader into fresh insight. Richly textured allusions (to politics, technology, contemporary letters, schools of psychology, historical events) connect the book with its immediate setting. A rhetoric of persuasion needs time and conceptual space to produce the insight that invites reader confidence and conviction.

In addition to the text's rhetorical structure, literary and ironic stratagems, its actual polemical arguments also deserve our attention. To what extent are his arguments of interest only to history? Which of his perspectives is still influential today? Which issues remain unresolved and are the subject of ongoing debate?

We may single out five issues in *On Religion* for brief analysis, each of which has momentous implications for modern culture and each of which is, arguably, as unresolved today as it was in Schleiermacher's lifetime. The aim is not to contend against Schleiermacher's choices on these matters – which, after all, now belong to history – but to suggest that this text, though it plays a significant role in a continuing dialogue, does not automatically provide answers to these issues.

(1) *The cognitive status of religion.* The most abiding philosophical question raised by the work concerns the relationship of religion, understood as feeling and intuition, to our knowledge claims about the universe. The text rests its case on the primacy of prereflective experience and in so doing confronts a host of issues that cry out for resolution. Schleiermacher's approach to religious truth is experiential, based on a personal encounter with truth in the form of immediate intuition and feeling. In his own time the appeal to immediacy was countered by Hegel's claim that there is nothing in heaven or earth, nature or spirit that is not mediated as well as immediate. If correct, then claims that rest on immediate experience lose their privileged status. To Schleiermacher's neoorthodox Christian critics in the twentieth century, Emil Brunner and Karl Barth, who base religious truth on scriptural revelation, such an experiential stance was deeply suspect. Even an opponent of neoorthodox theology like Paul Tillich, whose thought is much indebted to Schleiermacher, never overcame a suspicion that Schleiermacher's appeal to feeling is based on an emotivist account of religion.[57] Yet the experiential path to religious insight has a continual appeal. Its early twentieth-century champion, Rudolf Otto, acknowledged a considerable debt to the present book.[58] Through Otto the legacy of Schleiermacher is also linked to Mircea Eliade and the study of the history of

---

57 Tillich, *Systematic Theology* (Chicago, 1951), I, pp. 15, 42, 45, 215; *What Is Religion?*, trans. James Luther Adams (New York, 1973), p. 160; *Perspectives on 19th and 20th Century Protestant Theology*, ed. Carl E. Braaten (New York, 1967), pp. 95–102.

58 Otto, *The Idea of the Holy*, trans. John W. Harvey (London, 1923); cf. Otto's introduction to *Friedrich Schleiermacher. On Religion: Speeches to its Cultured Despisers*, trans. John Oman (New York, 1958), pp. vii–xx, and "How Schleiermacher Re-discovered the Sensus Numinis" in *Religious Essays: A Supplement to the "Idea of the Holy"* (Oxford, 1931), pp. 68–77.

religions. Recent work by philosophers and theologians has defended the experiential and relational aspects of his thought against charges of subjectivism and emotivism.[59] Indeed, it is difficult to see how a religious argument which seeks to demonstrate its cogency can escape the need to join issue with the nature of experience in pressing its claims.

Recently, the weight of opinion among philosophers of religion and theologians has seemed to favor the critics of unmediated insight. These views claim that experience is necessarily "constructivist," i.e., assumes linguistic form, takes on implicit categories and assumptions, and that we never attain coherent awareness of some substratum of raw experience.[60] Thus one might ask whether Schleiermacher comes any closer to talking about the objective nature of reality than did Kant, whom he criticizes, in positing the unknowable realm of the thing-in-itself. John E. Smith's view that experiences of God can be direct but not immediate, since the purely immediate is a category that lies beyond interpretation, might lead to a counterargument to Schleiermacher's critics which would distinguish the talk about immediacy in *On Religion* from the reality itself. In such a case, the unspeakable depths of experience are logically distinguished from the book's argument, which seeks to make these depths evident.[61] Newer work on mystical and religious perception strongly defends nonconceptual claims and suggests that the debate about this religious epistemology will continue.[62] For his part Schleiermacher knew full well that there was a crucial sense in which he could not speak about the object of his discourse.

However one may judge the problem of cognitivity in *On Religion*, one can inquire further about the larger function of thought in the book. If it is a systematic inquiry into the topic of religion, which seems not implausible, how does the work escape the numerous strictures of the 1799 text against systems? Wherein does the

[59] As related to H. Richard Niebuhr see Hans W. Frei, "Niebuhr's theological background" in *Faith and Ethics: The Theology of H. Richard Niebuhr*, ed. Paul Ramsey (New York, 1957), especially, pp. 32–40; Van A. Harvey, "A Word in Defense of Schleiermacher's Theological Method," *Journal of Religion*, 42 (July 1962), 151–70; Louis Dupré, "Toward a Revaluation of Schleiermacher's Philosophy of Religion," *Journal of Religion*, 44 (April 1964), 97–112; Charles E. Scott, "Schleiermacher and the Problem of Divine Immediacy," *Religious Studies*, 3 (April 1968), 499–512 and "Preconceptuality and Religious Experience," *Southern Journal of Philosophy*, 7 (Fall 1969), 239–47; Robert R. Williams, *Schleiermacher the Theologian: The Construction of the Doctrine of God* (Philadelphia, 1978); Peter L. Berger's *The Heretical Imperative* argues for Schleiermacher's experiential approach under the heading, "The Inductive Possibility" (New York, 1979), pp. 125–56.

[60] N. R. Hanson, *Perception and Discovery: An Introduction to Scientific Inquiry*, ed. Willard C. Humphries (San Francisco, 1969), pp. 298–313; Steven T. Katz (ed.), *Mysticism and Philosophical Analysis* (New York, 1978), pp. 1–9, 22–74, and Katz (ed.), *Mysticism and Religious Traditions* (Oxford, 1983); George A. Lindbeck, *The Nature of Doctrine: Religion and Theology in a Postliberal Age* (Philadelphia, 1984); Wayne Proudfoot, *Religious Experience* (Berkeley, 1985).

[61] Smith, "The Experiential Foundations of Religion," *Reason and God* (New Haven, CT, 1961), pp. 181f.

[62] See the essays in Robert K. C. Forman (ed.), *The Problem of Pure Consciousness: Mysticism and Philosophy* (New York, 1990) as well as William P. Alston, *Perceiving God: The Epistemology of Religious Experience* (New York, 1991).

ground of unity that Schleiermacher associates with religion (and denies to metaphysics and ethics) actually exist? Can this ground, if it exists on his terms, be argued about at all? If not, what purposes are served by an allusive, poeticizing account? If intuitions, in Schleiermacher's sense of the term, involve active as well as passive dimensions, how are they related to our intellectual activity, our choices, and our efforts to justify these choices? Such questions as these, which quickly lead to complex levels of debate, arise from a reading of this work. If pursued, they will drive a reader either to develop a defense of immediate experience as providing grounds for religious belief, or to move on to yet other views. They may even lead to a prolonged engagement with Schleiermacher.

(2) *The relationship between religion and art.* Schleiermacher seeks to avoid equating religion with aesthetics and enters a caveat against Schlegel's effort to merge literature and religion into a new "religion of art." The view that art and religion have an affinity has long been recognized, even amid disagreements. Like religious practitioners and theorists, creative artists know that it is impossible to exclude feeling and emotion from their work. The special affinity between religion and art is especially noteworthy in Paul Tillich.[63] Other twentieth-century philosophers as well as historians of religion have observed the similarity between aesthetic and religious insight, while literary critics in North America who specialize in "religion and literature" turn theorizing about this affinity into a career.[64]

Schleiermacher recognizes that there is a special affinity between an artistic sensibility and the conditions that make the human soul receptive to religion. But when the question is posed "What precisely differentiates religion and aesthetics?," answers are far less clear. If art and religion both serve as the basis for an intuition of the infinite universe – a view that undeniably follows from Schleiermacher's argument – what makes religion distinctive and worthy of pursuit for its own sake? The answer cannot be made, at least by Schleiermacher, with reference to the external trappings of religion. Of course, it is a mark of Schleiermacher's candor when he tells us that he cannot explain but only acknowledge that a "passing over"

---

[63] Tillich, "Art and Ultimate Reality," an address at the Museum of Modern Art, 17 February 1959 in *Cross Currents*, 10 (1959), 1–14; Robert P. Scharlemann, "Tillich and the Religious Interpretation of Art" in *The Thought of Paul Tillich*, ed. James Luther Adams, Wilhelm Pauck, Roger Shinn (San Francisco, 1985), pp. 156–74.

[64] Cook Wilson, "The Existence of God" in *Historical Selections in the Philosophy of Religion*, ed. Ninian Smart (New York, 1962), pp. 440–63; Suzanne L. Langer, *Philosophy in a New Key* (New York, 1942); Gerardus van der Leeuw, *Sacred and Profane Beauty: The Holy in Art* (New York, 1963); H. G. Hubbeling, "Das Heilige und das Schöne: Gerardus van der Leeuws Anschauungen über das Verhältnis von Religion und Kunst," *Neue Zeitschrift für Systematische Theologie und Religionsphilosophie*, 25 (1983), 1–19; Nathan A. Scott, Jr., "Criticism and Theology – the Terms of the Engagement" in *Negative Capability: Studies in the New Literature and the Religious Situation* (New Haven, CT, 1969), pp. 112–44; Giles Gunn, "Threading the Eye of the Needle: The Place of the Literary Critic in Religious Studies," *Journal of the American Academy of Religion*, 43 (June 1975), 164–84; Robert Detweiler (ed.), "Art–Literature–Religion: Life on the Borders," *Journal of the American Academy of Religion: Thematic Studies*, 49 (1983), 1–201.

often occurs between art and religion. On this entire question there is room for further discussion. Although at one with his Romantic peers' view of the world, Schleiermacher expresses a wariness about art even while acknowledging that it has successfully adorned religion. If one thinks of the rich artistic traditions of Asia, the ancient Hindu and Buddhist traditions with their elaborate temple cultures and ritualized forms of religious celebration, not to mention the interweaving of creative art forms with the Christian West, Schleiermacher's reserve on this matter may seem unduly cautious, and the grounds for this caution are not fully given in the present text.

(3) *The problem of religious pluralism.* Today the quest for a comparative philosophy of religion or a theology of world religions stands near the center of present-day interest.[65] In his day Schleiermacher identified the problem of developing a historical and theological understanding of world religions, even if his attention is focused only on Greek, Judaic, and Christian religions. His contribution to this matter is both theoretical and personal. *On Religion* insists that we must get the categories straight if we are to study religions effectively; for him, that meant a rejection of efforts to posit either total uniformity of belief ("Everyone believes the same, after all") or exclusivity ("Only one religion is correct"). Having set aside these extremes, it remained for him to give a reasoned defense of his position.

Schleiermacher's appeal to Protestant Christian tradition, especially in the Fifth Speech, assumes a stance in the comparative study of religion, which is made as much on "confessional" as on purely scholarly or philosophical grounds. To say this is not to say that his answer lacks merit. The issue of how best to relate the insight of one historical, positively manifest religious tradition to other religious traditions, or to the secular world, remains vexing. In breaking with natural religion and the Enlightenment's moral-rational interpretations of religion Schleiermacher sides with particularity as the starting point for analysis of religion.[66] Since religion arises within human culture, a denial of historically manifest religion in effect constitutes a denial of humanity. It is shortsighted to pretend that the depth of personal emotion, the joy and despair, the creeds, ritual behavior, and strange or exotic beliefs and practices of religious life can be ignored in an account of the human. Schleiermacher contends that the risks of particularity outweigh the gains of a more abstract comparative analysis. To engage in the latter, he argues, is to invoke extraneous categories, like nature or universal morality, as standards of judgment.

But whether he has fully resolved the dilemma may be doubted. To claim that he has done so is to affirm that the singular "great idea" embodied by Jesus of Nazareth that the finite is always striving with the infinite while seeking higher

---

[65] John Clayton's Stanton lectures to be published by Cambridge University Press.

[66] Gerardus van der Leeuw, *Religion in Essence and Manifestation* (1933; New York, 1963), II, the fifth section on "Religions," pp. 591–649, starts with a direct allusion to Schleiermacher's Fifth Speech; see especially pp. 645–46.

mediation is at once so particular and yet universal that it evades the charge of prejudice and can become an adequate standard of judgment through which other religious intuitions are analyzed. In strict terms, Schleiermacher adopts a version of relativism and in no way seeks to legislate anyone's relationship to the universe. But his own choice, when presented as "religion raised to a higher power," builds a heavy Christian bias into his account of religions. Although less blatant than Karl Rahner's formulation of "anonymous Christianity," Schleiermacher's model has the appearance of universality but is Christian in derivation.[67] In saying this, one can also acknowledge that the theme of struggle between the finite and infinite has had an impressive appeal in modern Protestant Christian thought and that this position continues to have advocates. But if, as the argument suggests, Christianity is "religion raised to a higher power," then this idea appears to take on a privileged capacity to stand in judgment of all others, simply because, as a polemical and self-critical religious principle, it is willing to stand in judgment of itself.

A reader might well ask what prevents that insight, which is grounded in confessionalism, from distorting one's vision of the very thing one is searching for, namely, the essential nature of religion as it is humanly embodied. If it is not grounded in confessionalism, but is admitted as an abstract philosophical principle, Schleiermacher's argument has failed to sustain its overall point about the need for concrete historical religion. If all religions have "basic intuitions" and "essences," then one should be able to compare and to assess the relative merits of these features. To accomplish this, however, requires one either to follow a path similar to Schleiermacher's or to posit some other nonreligious philosophical principle as the basis of judgment. If humanity is universal and each individual constitutes a compendium of the whole of humanity, why cannot an appeal to one's common humanity provide a more appropriate basis of judgment? In Schleiermacher's discussion of Judaism, the problem with his approach to religious pluralism comes to a head. While his view that Judaism is dead may be explained in its historical setting (the belief was held by some Enlightenment Jews as well as by their opponents), what looks like patent anti-Judaism is scarcely in accord with his argument for an open, nonprivileged perspective on religion. At such points, the experiential ground of his argument again comes to the fore; if we argue primarily out of *our own* experience, then the experience of *others* may inadvertently undergo significant distortion.

(4) *The classic problem of liberalism: the free individual person in human communities. On Religion* presents arguments that stem directly from Enlightenment thought on individual personhood and liberty, even if Schleiermacher's fundamental affinity is with the Romantic critics of the Enlightenment. On the Lockean view, inherited by Schleiermacher, religion consists of the voluntary association of freely choosing persons. Only such a model can do justice to individual liberty.

---

[67] Karl Rahner, *Foundations of Christian Faith*, trans. William V. Dych (New York, 1978), pp. 311–21.

Among the Romantics the cult of individual creativity was carried to even greater lengths. Schleiermacher's early thought guards against the view that individual creativity can ever be experienced autonomously. Like human nature, religion is necessarily social.[68] All too frequently readers miss the communal dimension of Schleiermacher's teaching. But even full acknowledgment of the rootedness of Schleiermacher's anthropology in a sense of community leaves open the question of the proper relationship between religion and politics. How far can or should a defense of individual liberty extend toward delineating the proper role and function of the state? The Fourth Speech's trenchant cultural and political critique of the forces of dehumanization, the rampant utilitarian and materialistic tendencies of the modern period, places Schleiermacher as a forerunner of critics of modernity like José Ortega y Gasset, Martin Buber, Gabriel Marcel, Martin Heidegger, Hannah Arendt, and Jacques Ellul.[69] The critique of the state's undue exercise of power in relation to religion of the Fourth Speech has a pertinence that is rediscovered in each age.

But *On Religion* does not directly address the question of the nature of political life beyond the family and religious community. In view of the history of church-state relations in the West the theoretical and practical problems loom large. The unresolved nature of these questions has in our day provoked interest in "civil religion," Rousseau's answer in *The Social Contract* (1762) to the age-old rivalry of religious and secular authority. One might well wonder what conception of the state Schleiermacher actually holds and how this relates to his idea of religious community. If the terms of a proper relationship between religion and politics are not spelled out, then the religious community in practice might function as surrogate for the larger social engagements of the political order. A reader may ask what keeps Schleiermacher's "voluntaristic" understanding of the church from drifting into a religious enclave and approximating the groups that he identifies as "sects." To think that all persons must seek their own spiritual community for it to reflect their interests and adequately minister to them places a heavy burden of choice on the individual and is very possibly not sustainable over time.

(5) *The estimate of human nature as positive and progressive.* Schleiermacher's reformist political impulses are rooted in a positive and progressivist understanding of human nature and the march of history.[70] The present book exemplifies the relative optimism about the human condition from which those reformist impulses

---

[68]   Peter L. Berger describes the Fourth Speech as "essentially a sort of precocious treatise in the sociology of religion," *The Heretical Imperative: Contemporary Possibilities of Religious Affirmation* (Garden City, NY, 1979), p. 131.

[69]   See Ortega y Gasset, *The Revolt of the Masses* (1930; New York, 1977); Buber, *I and Thou*, especially Part Two, pp. 87–122, on the world of I-It; Marcel, *Man Against Mass Society* (1952; Chicago, 1967); Heidegger, *The Question of Technology and Other Essays* (New York, 1977); Arendt, *The Human Condition* (Chicago, 1958) and *Eichmann in Jerusalem: A Report on the Banality of Evil* (New York, 1963); Ellul, *The Technological Society* (New York, 1964).

[70]   Crouter, "Schleiermacher and the Theology of Bourgeois Society," pp. 302–23.

derive. Rousseau's "natural human goodness" is reflected in Schleiermacher's understanding of human nature. As a time of sanctity, childhood is idealized for its fantasy and imaginative games, and the human heart remains pure as long as it is uncorrupted by political society. The human predicament is described more in terms of a rift with the universe than by a rift within oneself, which in classical Christian teaching is analyzed as sin that needs redemption through Christ as its necessary remedy. There is little of an Augustinian or Calvinist perspective on the sinful human condition in the 1799 work or its revisions, even if this element is strongly evident in Schleiermacher's mature dogmatics and, among other teachings, marks his continuity with the historic Protestant reformation.[71]

It is difficult to imagine the young Schleiermacher acknowledging that "radical evil" is present in human experience. Ironically, the moral rationalism of Kant's *Religion Within the Limits of Reason Alone* with its analysis of our propensity toward good *and* our inclination to evil resonates more fully with the wider Christian tradition. Whether on tactical grounds or as a substantive choice *On Religion* does not dwell at length on the point, even though the relative optimism about the human potential appears to be in tension with his attack on perfectionism in moral philosophy. If so much potential creativity exists within each individual, what is to keep this from being realized in a state of happiness in this life? In passing, a reader may note that there is limited awareness of the corporate and institutional dimension of evil in the present work of the sort that has been familiar to the western world since Marx. Post-Marxian, twentieth-century European religious writers with a leaning towards socialism, like Buber, Tillich, or Gollwitzer, posit an understanding of religious community that seeks to approximate the utopian goals of the religious life. Although less obvious in the present text, Schleiermacher also sees the need for greater approximations of social justice; his arguments for community in the Fourth Speech constitute an indirect call to rescue human life from enslavement to the oppressive systems of modernity.

Yet the dominant teaching of this text appeals to the direction of history and the progressive unfolding of a new future. Allusions to the future help readers to see that a resolution of our problems will occur in some other time and place. When this dimension is acknowledged, one is not far removed from Kant's moral arguments for deity, except that the arguments and hopes of *On Religion* are transposed into the stream of history and away from a traditional theology of eternal life. It is, of course, unfair to criticize a writer for matters that could not possibly have been anticipated in his lifetime. But one can at least understand, even if not always agree with, persons who wonder what Schleiermacher's response might have been to the horrors of Nazism and the Holocaust. The Christian heart that Schleiermacher writes about is a redeemed heart that is already, as it were, "on the way." *On Religion* does not dwell much on the more radical forms of human

---

[71] *The Christian Faith*, ed. H. R. Macintosh and J. S. Stewart (Edinburgh, 1928), see especially, pp. 269–354, on the consciousness of sin.

self-estrangement, a theme that the reformed and Calvinist theological tradition in which he stands has richly analyzed. In this last area, as with the four preceding issues, readers must weigh in their minds how far Schleiermacher's suggestions can or should apply to our own time and place. An expectation that his answers will readily resolve the major dilemmas in our contemporary understanding of religion is unrealistic and anachronistic. Yet past texts, when they are classics, continue to inform and challenge our thinking.

Chronology

1798	Schelling publishes *On the World Soul*
1799	Schleiermacher publishes first edition of *On Religion: Speeches to its Cultured Despisers*
1800	Friedrich Schlegel publishes *Lucinde*; Novalis (Friedrich von Hardenberg) publishes *Hymns to the Night*; Schleiermacher publishes *Soliloquies* and *Confidential Letters Concerning Friedrich Schlegel's Lucinde*
1803–6	Schleiermacher assumes post as university preacher at Halle
1804–28	Schleiermacher publishes German translation of Plato
1806	University of Halle overrun by Napoleon's troops; Schleiermacher publishes 2nd edition of *On Religion* and *The Celebration of Christmas: A Conversation*; Hegel publishes *The Phenomenology of Spirit*
1809	Founding of the University of Berlin by Wilhelm von Humboldt with Schleiermacher as secretary to the founding commission
1809–34	Schleiermacher at the University of Berlin as professor of theology, member of philosophical and historical sections of the Berlin Academy of Sciences
1810–34	Schleiermacher is preacher at the Holy Trinity Church in Berlin
1813	Birth of Kierkegaard in Copenhagen
1814	Death of Fichte at University of Berlin
1815	Congress of Vienna settles the Napoleonic wars
1818–32	Hegel at the University of Berlin
1821	Schleiermacher publishes 3rd edition of *On Religion* with "Explanations" attached to each speech
1821–2	Schleiermacher publishes first edition of his systematic theology, *The Christian Faith* [*Glaubenslehre*]
1830–1	Schleiermacher publishes 2nd edition of *The Christian Faith*
1832	Deaths of Goethe and Hegel
1834	Death of Schleiermacher, 6 February

Further reading

For an estimate of the legacy of Schleiermacher and his work see B. A. Gerrish, "Friedrich Schleiermacher" in *Nineteenth Century Religious Thought in the West* I, ed. Ninian Smart et al. (Cambridge, 1985), pp. 123–56 and *Tradition and the Modern World: Reformed Theology in the Nineteenth Century* (Chicago, 1978), pp. 13–48, *The Old Protestantism and the New: Essays on the Reformation Heritage* (Chicago, 1982), pp. 179–207, and *Continuing the Reformation: Essays on Modern Religious Thought* (Chicago, 1993), pp. 147–216, 249–73. A survey of recent German and English-language Schleiermacher literature is given in Richard Crouter, "Friedrich Schleiermacher: A Critical Edition, New Work, and Perspectives" in *Religious Studies Review*, 18 (January 1992), 20–7.

No full-scale intellectual biography exists. Cf. Martin Redeker *Schleiermacher: Life and Thought* (Philadelphia, 1973); Stephen Sykes, *Friedrich Schleiermacher* (Richmond, VA, 1971); B. A. Gerrish, *A Prince of the Church: Schleiermacher and the Beginnings of Modern Theology* (Philadelphia, 1984) gives an illuminating portrait. The classic work, Wilhelm Dilthey's *Life of Schleiermacher* (Berlin, 1870) only covers the years through 1802, though a recent edition includes papers on Schleiermacher's hermeneutics, philosophy, and theology; *Leben Schleiermachers* I–II ed. Martin Redeker (Berlin, 1970). On the work in its setting, see Albert L. Blackwell, *Schleiermacher's Early Philosophy of Life: Determinism, Freedom, and Phantasy* (Chico, CA, 1982), which draws from the years 1789–1804 and contains an attractive series of plates. Rudolf Otto's introduction to *Friedrich Schleiermacher, On Religion: Speeches to its Cultured Despisers*, trans. John Oman (New York, 1958) pp. vii–xx, and "How Schleiermacher Re-discovered the Sensus Numinis" in *Religious Essays: A Supplement to the "Idea of the Holy"* (Oxford, 1931), pp. 68–77 remain pertinent, while Jack Forstman, *A Romantic Triangle: Schleiermacher and Early German Romanticism* (Missoula, MT, 1977) provides a vivid account of the origin of the work.

Two of Schleiermacher's philosophical concerns, Plato and hermeneutics, bear on this text. Schleiermacher's attempt to locate each Platonic dialogue within the unfolding dialectic of Plato's thought led to the modern historical understanding of Platonic philosophy. Werner Jaeger credits Schleiermacher with being the "founder of modern Platonic scholarship": see *Paideia: The Ideals of Greek Culture*, II (Oxford, 1933–44), pp. 78f., 383. On his contributions to hermeneutical theory, see Heinz Kimmerle (ed.), *Hermeneutics: The Handwritten Manuscripts*, trans. James Duke and Jack Forstman (Missoula, MT, 1977), p. 1; Kurt Mueller-Vollmer (ed.), *The Hermeneutic Reader: Texts of the German Tradition from the Enlightenment to the Present* (New York, 1985), pp. 8–12; cf. Paul Ricouer, "The Task of Hermeneutics," *Philosophy Today*, 17 (1973), 112–28; Schleiermacher, "*The Hermeneutics*: Outline of the 1819 Lectures," *New Literary History: A Journal of Theory and Interpretation*, 10 (Autumn 1978), 1–16; for readers with German, Manfred Frank (ed.), *Friedrich Schleiermacher Hermeneutik und Kritik* (Frankfurt am Main, 1977) with his Introduction (pp. 7–67) is indispensable.

Extant literature on German Romanticism, especially the ways in which newer recognition is given to its bold literary and philosophical theories, can overwhelm a novice reader. These ideas are boldly set forth in Philippe Lacoue-Labarthe and Jean-Luc Nancy, *The Literary Absolute: The Theory of Literature in German Romanticism*, trans. Philippe Barnard and Cheryl Lester (New York, 1988), while a readable account of the emergence of the movement compared with English Romanticism may be found in Nicholas V. Riasanovsky, *The Emergence of Romanticism* (New York, 1992); for readers with German, the philosophical side of Romantic theory, often with direct reference to Schleiermacher, may be explored in relevant titles by Manfred Frank.

A note on editions

Ever since Rudolf Otto published his jubilee edition of *On Religion* in 1899 and dramatized the work's "re-discovery of the numinous," the original 1799 version has dominated German study of the young Schleiermacher's thought. Widely available in Germany, the text has been reprinted thirty-one times in the twentieth century. This original edition, here presented in translation, was substantially revised by Schleiermacher in 1806 and 1821 and reissued with slight alterations in 1831.[1] Since Schleiermacher's lifetime, questions have been raised about the extent and nature of the changes he made to the 1799 text. In sheer textual intricacy the study of these revisions rivals "the synoptic problem" of the New Testament gospels, except that here we have an exercise in self-redaction. Nonetheless, some basic features of the revisions can be reliably sketched.

(1) Schleiermacher never renounced the youthful work. Rather he continually sought to relate his evolving ideas to his original understanding of religion. His mind on these matters is seen in the 1806 and 1821 dedications to his friend, Karl Gustav von Brinckmann, and in his Preface and "Explanations" from 1821.

(2) As a reflection of fervent debates about religion among the early German Romantics, the 1799 version is without doubt a rhetorically and substantively radical work. Readers invariably conclude that the earliest version is more immediate, vivid, and, for all its complex design, succinctly argued. Along with certain other early works by Schleiermacher (e.g., *The Celebration of Christmas: A Conversation*), the present text does not conform to an established genre of academic theology; its revisions only make significant gestures in this direction.

(3) Several different levels of motivation lie behind the revisions. First, Schleiermacher makes an obvious effort to play down his apparent Christian

---

[1] Prior to 1988 readers had access to the text in English only in its third edition, translated by John Oman in 1893, a work long carried by Harper and Row and re-issued by Westminster/John Knox in 1994 (this omits Rudolf Otto's introduction found in the 1958 printing). The forthcoming critical edition of the revised versions in the German *KGA* (Walter de Gruyter) will put study of the text's revisions on a new footing. For a fuller account, see the editor's Introduction, *On Religion* (Cambridge, 1988), pp. 55–73.

heterodoxy ("[W]hether we have a God as a part of our intuition depends on the direction of our imagination").[2] Second, he seeks to strengthen his basic convictions regarding the nature of religion, and its relation to philosophic thought and to social-political life, by giving the text's rhetoric a more "scientific" form. In 1806 a didactic tendency masks the original work's passion, while revisions in 1821 relate the argument directly to his concurrently published magnum opus, *The Christian Faith*. Third, he uses the publics' interest in the book as an occasion to address changing circumstances affecting Protestantism in Berlin, which had lived through the Napoleonic wars and a failed Prussian reform movement to find itself in a new era of conservatism where strident forms of biblically-based pietism replaced the exultant voices of Romantics. Constant editing and revision was the mental habit of a philosopher-theologian who, as Plato translator and preacher, sought to connect with his audience.

[2]   See p. 53.

On Religion
Speeches to its Cultured Despisers

First Speech
Apology

It may be an unexpected undertaking, and you might rightly be surprised that someone can demand from just those persons who have raised themselves above the herd, and are saturated by the wisdom of the century,[1] a hearing for a subject so completely neglected by them. I confess that I do not know how to indicate anything that presages a fortunate outcome for me, not even the one of winning your approval of my efforts, much less the one of communicating my meaning and enthusiasm to you. From time immemorial faith has not been everyone's affair,[2] for at all times only a few have understood something of religion while millions have variously played with its trappings with which it has willingly let itself be draped out of condescension.

Especially now, the life of cultivated persons is removed from everything that would in the least way resemble religion. I know that you worship the deity in holy silence just as little as you visit the forsaken temples, that in your tasteful dwellings there are no other household gods than the maxims of the sages and the songs of the poets, and that humanity and fatherland, art and science (for you imagine yourselves capable of all of this) have taken possession of your minds so completely that no room is left over for the eternal and holy being that for you lies beyond the world, and that you have no feelings for and with it. You have succeeded in making your earthly lives so rich and many-sided that you no longer need the eternal, and after having created a universe for yourselves, you are spared from thinking of that

---

[1] On the heightened sense of the Enlightenment in eighteenth-century Prussia, see Immanuel Kant, "What is Enlightenment" in *Foundations of the Metaphysics of Morals* (New York, 1959), pp. 90–1, which attests to "the age of Enlightenment, or the century of Frederick" (Friedrich II, 1740–86, patron of artists and philosophers), while adding that even in that era, "much is lacking which prevents men from being, or easily becoming, capable of correctly using their own reason in religious matters with assurance and free from outside direction."

[2] Thessalonians 3:2: "For not all have faith" (unless otherwise noted, English Bible references are to the Revised Standard Version); cf. Luther's, *Der Glaube ist nicht jedermanns Ding*.

which created you. You are agreed, I know, that nothing new and nothing convincing can be said anymore about this matter, which has been sufficiently belabored in all directions by philosophers and prophets and, if only I might not add, by scoffers and priests. Least of all – something that can escape no one – are you inclined to listen to something on this subject from the last mentioned, who have long since made themselves unworthy of your trust, as the kind of people who best like to dwell only in the dilapidated ruins of the sanctuary and who cannot live even there without disfiguring and damaging it still more. All this I know and am nevertheless convinced to speak by an inner and irresistible necessity that divinely rules me, and cannot retract my invitation that you especially should listen to me.

With regard to this last point I could probably ask you, How does it happen that on every subject, be it important or insignificant, you most desire to be instructed by persons who have dedicated their lives and their intellectual powers to it, and your thirst for knowledge does not shun even the huts of peasants and the workshops of humble artisans,[3] and yet in matters of religion you consider everything more suspicious that comes from those who claim to be experts on the subject and are considered to be such by the state and the people? You will surely not be able to show that they are not that and that they rather hold and preach everything else but religion. Thus reasonably disdaining such an unfounded judgment, I confess before you that I also am a member of this order and I do so at the risk, if you do not listen to me attentively, of being thrown into the same category with the same bunch.

It is at least a voluntary confession, for my speech would not have betrayed me, and the eulogies of my fellow guildmembers would not either. What I intend lies almost completely outside their sphere and would hardly resemble what they want to see and hear. I do not chime in with the cry for help of most of them concerning the demise of religion, for I would not know what other age may have accommodated it better than the present; and I have nothing to do with the old-fashioned and barbaric lamentation with which they would like to clamor for the caved-in walls of their Jewish Zion and its Gothic pillars.[4] I am aware that I fully deny my profession in all that I have to say to you; why should I not, therefore, acknowledge it like any other contingency? The prejudices desirable for it shall not hinder us, and the boundaries of all questioning and communicating it holds sacred shall have no validity among us. I speak to you as a human being about the holy mysteries of humanity according to my view; about that which was in me when, still with youthful enthusiasm, I sought the unknown; about that which has been the innermost mainspring of my existence ever since I have thought and been alive and

---

[3] Schleiermacher alludes to the scientific investigation of artisans' procedures that characterizes the scientific revolution from Frances Bacon (1561–1626) through the *Encyclopédie raisonné des sciences, des arts, et des métiers (1751–1772)* of Diderot and d'Alembert.

[4] The text plays upon the dominant Enlightenment view of Judaic and Roman Catholic traditions as closed, legalistic systems that are out of keeping with the age.

which shall eternally remain for me the highest, whichever way the fluctuations of time and humanity might move me. That I speak does not originate from a rational decision or from hope or fear, nor does it happen in accord with some final purpose or for some arbitrary or accidental reason. It is the inner, irresistible necessity of my nature; it is a divine calling; it is that which determines my place in the universe and makes me the being I am. Even if it were neither suitable nor prudent to speak of religion, the thing that thus drives me crushes these petty notions with its heavenly power.

You know that the deity, by an immutable law, has compelled itself to divide its great work endlessly, to fuse together each definite being only out of two opposing forces, and to realize each of its eternal thoughts in twin forms that are hostile to each other and yet exist inseparably only through each other. This whole corporeal world, penetration into whose interior is the highest goal of your investigations, appears to the best informed and most thoughtful among you only as an eternally prolonged play of opposing forces.[5] Every life is only the result of a continuous appropriation and repulsion; everything has its determinate being only by virtue of the way in which it uniquely combines and retains the two primal forces of nature: the thirsty attraction and the expansion of the active and living self. It seems to me as if even the spirits, as soon as they are transplanted into this world, would have to follow such a law.

Each human soul – its transitory actions as well as the inner peculiarities of its nature that lead us to this conclusion – is merely a product of two opposing drives. The one strives to draw into itself everything that surrounds it, ensnaring it in its own life and, wherever possible, wholly absorbing it into its innermost being. The other longs to extend its own inner self ever further, thereby permeating and imparting to everything from within, while never being exhausted itself. The former desire is oriented toward enjoyment; it strives after individual things that bend toward it; it is quieted so long as it has grasped one of them, and always works only mechanically on whatever is at hand. The latter drive despises enjoyment and only goes on to ever-increasing and heightened activity; it overlooks individual things and manifestations just because it penetrates them and finds everywhere only the forces and entities on which its own force breaks; it wants to penetrate and to fill everything with reason and freedom, and thus it proceeds directly to the infinite and at all times seeks and produces freedom and coherence, power and law, right and suitability. But just as among corporeal things no individual exists alone through one of the two forces of material nature, so each soul participates in the two original functions of spiritual nature. The perfection of the intellectual world consists in the fact that not only are all possible combinations of these two forces between the two opposed ends really present in humanity, with now one and now the other nearly excluding everything and leaving only an infinitely small part to its

[5] Schleiermacher's "two opposing drives" reflect a fundamental polarity that is widely shared in eighteenth-century aesthetics, literary theory, natural philosophy, and physics.

opposite, but also a common bond of consciousness embraces them all so that each person, even though he can be nothing other than what he must be, nevertheless recognizes all others as clearly as himself and perfectly comprehends all individual manifestations of humanity.[6]

Those who lie at the extreme ends of this great series are fervent natures, who are completely turned in upon themselves and self-isolating. The insatiable sensuality commands the ones at this extreme to gather around them an ever greater amount of earthly things that it would gladly tear from the context of the whole in order to absorb them solely for itself. In the eternal alternation between desire and pleasure, they never get beyond perceptions of the individual phenomenon; always occupied with egoistic concerns, the nature of the rest of humanity remains unknown to them. An uncultivated enthusiasm that flies beyond its goal restlessly drives the others about in the universe; without forming and fashioning something really better, they hover around empty ideals and, uselessly diluting and expending their energy, return to their starting point, inactive and exhausted. How shall these remote extremes be brought together in order to shape the long series into that closed ring that is the symbol of eternity and perfection?

There is indeed a certain point where an almost perfect equilibrium unites the two. This you are accustomed to overestimate far more often than to underestimate, in that it is generally only the magic of nature playing with the ideals of humanity, and only seldom the result of strenuous and accomplished self-formation. But if all those who no longer dwell at the extremes were to stand at that point, no uniting of those ends with this middle would be possible, and the final purpose of nature would be wholly thwarted. Only the thoughtful expert penetrates into the secrets of such a combination brought to rest; the individual elements in it are completely hidden for every common eye, and it would never recognize either its own element or that opposed to it.

Therefore at all times the deity sends people here and there in whom both tendencies are combined in a more fruitful manner, equips them with wondrous gifts, prepares their way with an all-powerful word,[7] and employs them as translators of its will and its works and as mediators of what would otherwise remain eternally separated. Look to those whose nature demonstrated a high level of that force of attraction that actively seizes surrounding things, but who also possess so much of the spiritual penetration drive, which strives for the infinite and impregnates all spirit and life, that they express it in the actions to which the former impels them. It is not sufficient for these, as it were, destructively to devour

[6] An initial version of the translation rendered Schleiermacher's highly personal prose without using generic male language. In the end, however, I realized that consistent translation of singular male pronouns as plurals interferes with the movement of the text from individual to plural examples. Since I wished to let Schleiermacher speak as nearly as possible within the idiom of his own world, a decision was made to emulate his usage in this respect, as well as in others. The work's argument makes it clear that human beings as such, and not just males, are being addressed.

[7] Wisdom of Solomon 18:15.

earthly things in a raw state, but they have to place something in front of themselves, order and shape it into a small world that bears the impress of their spirit, and thus rule it more rationally while enjoying it more constantly and humanely. Thus they become heroes, lawgivers, inventors, conquerors of nature, and benevolent genies who quietly create and disseminate a nobler happiness. By their mere existence such people prove themselves to be ambassadors of God and mediators between limited man and infinite humanity. They show the inactive, merely speculative idealist,[8] who splits his nature into individual empty thoughts, that this thing is active, which he merely imagined, and that what he hitherto despised is the material he should actually treat; they explain to him the misunderstood voice of God, and reconcile him with the earth and with his place in it. Merely earthly and sensual people, however, require such mediators even more, who teach them to comprehend that higher elemental force of humanity, since they embrace everything in a contemplative and illuminating manner without the drive and activity of mediators and wish to know no other limits than the universe they have found. If God also adds that mystical and creative sensuality, which seeks to give external reality to everything inward, to the striving toward extension and penetration of those who move in this course, then after every flight of their spirit to the infinite they must set down in pictures or words the impression it made on them as an object so as to enjoy it themselves afresh, transformed into another form on a finite scale. They must also instinctively and, as it were, enrapturedly – for they would do it even if no one were there – represent for others what they have encountered as poets and seers, as orators or as artists.[9] Such people are true priests of the Most High,[10] for they bring deity closer to those who normally grasp only the finite and the trivial; they place the heavenly and the eternal before them as an object of enjoyment and unification, as the sole inexhaustible source of that toward which their creative endeavors are directed. Thus they strive to awaken the slumbering seed of a better humanity, to ignite love to the Most High, to transform the common life into something higher, to reconcile the children of earth with the heaven that belongs to them, and to counter the ponderous attachment of the age to baser things. This is the higher priesthood that proclaims the inner meaning of all spiritual secrets and speaks down from the kingdom of God; this is the source of all visions and prophecies, of all holy works of art and inspired speeches that are

[8] An explicit allusion to the philosophy of Johann Gottlieb Fichte (1762–1814), whose major work, *The Science of Knowledge* (Cambridge, 1982) had appeared in 1794. Schleiermacher's early encounter with Fichte, mediated through Friedrich Schlegel after Fichte's dismissal from his Jena professorship, is reflected in his notebooks ("Gedanken I," p. 10), letters (*Br.* I, pp. 222, 229, 230); cf. the review of Fichte's *The Vocation of Man* in *Ath.* III, pp. 283–97.

[9] "Gedanken I" (no. 154), *KGA* I.2, p. 36: "To what extent can the priest be compared with the writer?" This and subsequent translations of cross-references from the new critical edition to Schleiermacher's early notebooks (1796–9) are my own.

[10] Genesis 14:18; cf. Hebrews 7:1.

scattered abroad on the chance that a receptive mind might find them and let them bring forth fruit in itself.

May it yet happen that this office of mediator should cease and the priesthood of humanity receive lovelier definition! May the time come that an ancient prophecy describes when no one will need a teacher because all will be taught by God![11] If the holy fire burned everywhere, fiery prayers would not be needed to beseech it from heaven, but only the gentle quiet of holy virgins to tend it; thus it probably would not break out in dreaded flames, but its sole striving would be to put the inner and hidden glow into balance among everyone.

Individuals would then silently light the way for themselves and for others, and the communication of holy thoughts and feelings would consist only in the easy game of now unifying the different beams of this light and then again breaking them up, now scattering it and then again concentrating here and there on individual objects. The softest word would be understood, whereas now the clearest expressions do not escape misinterpretation. One could jointly penetrate into the interior of the sanctuary, whereas now one must be occupied only with the rudiments in the forecourts. How much more delightful it is to exchange completed ideas with friends and participants than to have to burst into an empty space with barely sketched outlines. But how far removed from one another are those people now between whom such communication could take place. They are distributed among humanity with such wise economy as are the hidden points in space from which supple primal matter expands in all directions;[12] namely, only just the outermost limits of their spheres of influence are contiguous – so that nothing is, after all, completely empty – but one point probably never meets the other. A wise arrangement indeed: For the whole longing for communication and sociability is all the more directed only toward those who need it most; it works all the more unceasingly toward obtaining the companions it lacks.

To this very power I submit. This very nature is my calling. Permit me to speak of myself: You know that what bids religion to speak can never be proud, for it is always full of humility. Religion was the maternal womb in whose holy darkness my young life was nourished and prepared for the world still closed to it. In it my spirit breathed before it had discovered the world of external objects, experience, and scholarship. Religion helped me when I began to examine the ancestral faith and to purify my heart of the rubble of primitive times. It remained with me when God and immortality disappeared before my doubting eyes. It guided me into the active life. It taught me, with my virtues and defects, to keep myself holy in my undivided

[11] Jeremiah 31:34: "I will put my law within them, and write it upon their hearts"; cf. Hebrews 8:11, John 6:45, and 1 Corinthians 13:12.

[12] Like his contemporaries, Fichte, Schelling, Novalis, and Friedrich Schlegel, Schleiermacher's early work reflects a preoccupation with natural philosophy and physical speculation in the wake of the teaching of Leibniz (1646–1716) and Kant (1724–1804). See the early notebooks in this regard, "Gedanken I" (1796–9) and "Leibniz I, II", in *KGA* I.2, pp. 1–49, 75–103. By 1799 Schleiermacher had read the earliest nonsystematic, natural philosophical works of Schelling (1775–1854).

existence, and only through it have I learned friendship and love. As regards the other advantages and attributes of humanity, I well know that it proves little before your judgment seat, you wise and prudent ones of the people, if a person can say how he possesses those qualities; for he can know them from the descriptions and observations of others, or as all virtues are known, from the common ancient tradition of their existence. But the matter of religion is so arranged and so rare that a person who expresses something about it must necessarily have had it, for he has not heard about it anywhere. Of all that I praise and feel as its work there stands precious little in holy books, and to whom would it not seem scandal or folly[13] who did not experience it himself?

If I am so permeated by religion that I must finally speak and bear witness to it, to whom shall I turn with this matter other than to you? Where else would there be listeners for my speech? It is not blind partiality for my native soil or for my companions in disposition and language that makes me speak thus, but the deep conviction that you are the only ones capable, and thus also worthy, of having the sense for holy and divine things aroused in you.[14] Those proud islanders, whom many among you venerate so unduly, know no other watchword than to profit and enjoy. Their zeal for the sciences, for the wisdom of life, and for holy freedom, is merely an empty sham battle. Just as the most inspired champions of freedom among them do nothing but defend the national orthodoxy with rage and delude the people with miracles so that superstitious devotion to old customs might not vanish, so they are no more serious with all the rest that goes beyond the sensual and nearest immediate use. Thus they seek knowledge; their wisdom is only directed toward a lamentable empiricism, and thus religion can be nothing else for them than a dead letter,[15] a holy article in the constitution in which nothing is real.

For other reasons I turn away from the French, whose sight a lover of religion can hardly bear, for in every act, in every word, they all but trample on its most holy laws. The frivolous indifference with which millions of the people, the witty levity with which brilliant individual spirits look upon the most sublime act of the universe, which not only occurs before their eyes but takes hold of them all and determines every movement of their lives, sufficiently demonstrates how little they

---

[13] 1 Corinthians 1:23: "We preach Christ crucified, a scandal to the Jews and folly to the Greeks."

[14] The passage appeals to the resurgence of Prussian patriotism in the Napoleonic era and hopes for the new monarchy of Friedrich Wilhelm III (1797–1840). A sense of the special mission of Germany to save Europe is seen in Novalis's hope for a new golden age, in Hölderlin's, "Song of the Germans" (1801), and after the rout of Prussia at the battles of Jena and Auerstadt in 1806, in Fichte's *Addresses to the German Nation* (1808; New York, 1968). By contrast Schleiermacher perceived movements in England (mercantilism and industrialism, empirical philosophy, and the union of throne and altar) and in France (the *philosophes'* ridicule of religion and the violent secularizing of the French revolution) as inimical to his view of religion.

[15] 2 Corinthians 3:6: "For the letter kills, but the spirit gives life" (RSV, modified), the most often cited biblical allusion in the speeches, expresses Schleiermacher's view of hermeneutics as consisting of the continuous interplay between the assumptions and conditions of a text and those of its interpreter.

are capable of holy awe and true adoration.[16] And what does religion abhor more than the unbridled arrogance with which the rulers of people defy the eternal laws of the world? What does religion inculcate more than the circumspect and humble moderation of which not even the slightest feeling seems to reach them? What is more holy to it than the lofty Nemesis whose most dreadful acts they, in the intoxication of blindness, do not even understand? Where successive decrees of judgment, which formerly were allowed to strike only individual families in order to fill whole peoples with awe before the heavenly being and to dedicate the works of poets for centuries to eternal fate – where these repeat themselves a thousandfold in vain, how one solitary voice would fade away there, unheard and unnoticed to the point of ridiculousness! Here in my ancestral land is the fortunate climate that denies no fruit completely; here you find everything scattered that adorns humanity, and everything that prospers fashions itself somewhere, at least individually, in its most beautiful form; here neither wise moderation nor quiet contemplation is lacking. Here, therefore, it must find a refuge from the coarse barbarism and the cold earthly sense of the age.

Only do not relegate me without a hearing to those whom you look down upon as common and uncultivated as if the sense for the holy, like an old folk-costume, had passed over to the lower class of people to whom alone it is still seemly to be gripped by awe and belief in the unseen. You are very well disposed to these our brothers and might like it if they were also addressed on other higher subjects, on morality and law and freedom, and so at least for individual moments their inner striving would be raised to better things and an impression of the dignity of humanity awakened in them. Accordingly, one would speak with them concerning religion; one might occasionally cut through their whole being until that point is struck where this holy instinct lies concealed; one might captivate them through particular flashes one elicits from it, open a way from the innermost center of their narrow confines to a glimpse of the infinite and, for a moment, elevate their animal sensuality to the high consciousness of a human will and existence; a great deal will always be gained. But, I ask you, do you then turn to them when you want to disclose the innermost connection and the highest ground of those holy sanctuaries of humanity? Do you turn to them when concept and feeling, law and deed are to be traced to their mutual source, and the real is to be exhibited as eternal and necessarily grounded in the essence of humanity?

Would it not really suffice if your wise men were only understood by the best among you? But even that is my final goal with religion. I do not wish to arouse particular feelings that perhaps belong in its realm, nor to justify or dispute particular ideas. I wish to lead you to the innermost depths from which religion first addresses the mind. I wish to show you from what capacity of humanity

16 An allusion to the wry, ironic, and detached view of religion of the *philosophes* of which Voltaire's (1694–1778), *Candide* (1759; New York, n.d.) and *Philosophical dictionary* I–II (1764; New York, 1962) serve as representative works.

religion proceeds, and how it belongs to what is for you the highest and dearest. I wish to lead you to the pinnacles of the temple[17] that you might survey the whole sanctuary and discover its innermost secrets. Can you seriously expect me to believe that those who daily torment themselves most tiresomely with earthly things are most preeminently suited to become intimate with heaven? That those who brood anxiously over the next moment and are firmly chained to the nearest objects can raise their eyes the furthest to the universe? And that persons who have not yet found themselves in the uniform succession of a dead industriousness will most clearly discover the living deity? Therefore, I can call only you to me, you who are capable of raising yourselves above the common standpoint of humanity, you who do not shrink from the burdensome way into the depths of human nature in order to find the ground of its action and thought.

Ever since I admitted this to myself I have long found myself in the fearful mood of one who, missing a beloved jewel,[18] does not yet want to search thoroughly the last place where it could be hidden. There were times when you considered it a mark of special courage to free yourselves partially from religion, and happily read and heard about some particular subjects if it resulted in the eradication of a traditional concept; when it pleased you to see a refined religion go about adorned in eloquence, because you wished to preserve a certain feeling for the holy at least in the gracious sex. All that is no more. Religion is not supposed to be spoken of any longer, and even the Graces themselves, with unfeminine severity, are supposed to spoil the most delicate blossoms of human imagination. I can thus relate the interest I demand of you to nothing else than to your contempt itself; I wish only to call upon you to be properly informed and thoroughgoing in that contempt.

Let us, then, I beg you, examine whence your contempt properly originates, from the individual or from the whole? Does it start with differing types and sects of religion as they have been in the world or from the concept itself?[19] Some will without a doubt profess the latter view, and this always includes the unjustly vigorous despisers of religion, who extract their speculation from themselves and have not taken the pains to acquire a precise knowledge of the matter as it actually is. Fear of an eternal being and reliance on another world seem to you to be the hinges of all religion and that is, on principle, contrary to you. Tell me, then, dear friends, whence have you derived these concepts of religion that are the object of your contempt? Every expression, every product of the human spirit can be viewed

---

[17] In contrast to the New Testament allusion to Matthew 4:5, where the devil leads Christ to the pinnacle of the temple to tempt him to evil, Schleiermacher here "tempts" his audience to take an objective view of religion.

[18] Possible allusion to the "pearl of great price" (Matthew 13:45).

[19] Schleiermacher chides his readers for having proceeded abstractly to deduce concepts of religion (fear of a deity, longing for eternal life) without having taken the trouble to justify this understanding inductively through knowledge of particular instances of actual religion. The theme recurs in the Fifth Speech, pp. 96–102.

and apprehended from a dual standpoint. If one considers religion from its center according to its inner essence, it is a product of human nature, rooted in one of its necessary modes of action or drives, or whatever you wish to call it, for I do not now want to pass judgment on your technical language. If one considers it from its extremities, according to the definite bearing and form it has here and there assumed, it is a product of time and of history. From which aspect have you considered this spiritual phenomenon in order to arrive at those concepts that you pass off as the common content of everything that anyone has ever designated by the name religion? You will hardly say that this is a consideration of the first type, for, good friends, you would then have to admit that at least something in these ideas would belong to human nature. And if you also wish to say that religion, as one now encounters it, has sprung only from misinterpretations or false correlations of a necessary striving of humanity, it would become you to unite yourselves with us to seek out what is true and eternal in it and to free human nature from the wrong it always suffers when some part of it is misunderstood or misdirected. By all that is holy to you – and there must be something holy for you according to this confession – I implore you, do not neglect this business so that humanity, which you honor with us, is not angry with you, with good reason, as persons who have forsaken it in an important concern. And if you find that this business is already done, then I can count on your thanks and your approval.

But you will probably say that your concepts of the content of religion are merely the other view of this spiritual manifestation. And for just that reason, you say religion is empty and despised by you because what lies at the center is completely heterogeneous with it; it can in no way be called religion, and thus it cannot have arisen from there at all; and religion everywhere can be nothing other than an empty and false delusion that, as a gloomy and oppressive atmosphere, has enshrouded a part of the truth. Certainly that is your true and actual opinion. But if you consider those two points to be the content of religion in all forms under which it has appeared in history, then am I permitted to ask whether you have correctly observed all its manifestations and rightly comprehended its common content? If your concept has arisen thus, you would have to justify it from the particulars, and if someone tells you that it is wrong and in error and points to something else in religion that is not empty, but that has a center as valid as any other, then you should first hear and judge before you may continue to despise.

Do not let it perturb you to listen to what I now want to say to those who, right at the start, have proceeded more correctly but also more painstakingly from the particular instance. Without doubt, you are familiar with the history of human follies and have perused the different edifices of religion, from the meaningless fables of barbarous nations to the most refined deism, from the crude superstition of our people to the poorly stitched together fragments of metaphysics and morals that are called rational Christianity, and you have found them all without rhyme or reason. I am far from wishing to contradict you in that. On the contrary, if you but honestly mean that the most developed religious systems bear these characteristics no less than the crudest, if you would only realize that the divine cannot lie in a series that terminates on both sides in something common and despicable, than I shall gladly spare you the trouble of evaluating more closely all those that lie between. They all appear as transitions to and approximations of the former; each comes from the hand of its age somewhat more honed until finally art has ascended to that perfected plaything with which our century has until now whiled away the time.[20]

But this consummation is almost anything but an approximation of religion. I cannot speak of it without indignation. For everyone who has a feeling for all that issues from the depths of the heart and who takes it seriously that every side of human nature should be formed and exhibited must bewail how the high and noble has strayed from its vocation and has lost its freedom in order to be held in a despicable slavery by the scholastic and metaphysical spirit of barbaric and cold times. Where it is present and effective it must so reveal itself that it moves the mind in a peculiar manner, mingling or rather removing all functions of the human soul and resolving all activity in an astonishing intuition of the infinite. Do you feel this way about these systems of theology, about these theories of the origin and end of the world, about these analyses of the nature of an incomprehensible being, where everything amounts to cold argumentation and nothing can be treated except in the tone of an ordinary didactic controversy?[21] In all these systems you despise, you have accordingly not found religion and cannot find it because it is not there, and if it were shown to you that it were elsewhere, you would still not be capable of finding and honoring it. But why have you not descended any more to the particular?

I wonder at your voluntary ignorance, you good-natured investigators, and your all too calm persistence with what is simply there and praised by you! What you did not find in these systems you would necessarily have to have seen in the rudiments of these systems, and, to be sure, not in one or the other, but certainly in all. In all of them something of this spiritual material lies latent, for without it they could by no means have arisen. But those who do not know how to release it, no matter how finely they dissect it, no matter how thoroughly they investigate everything, always retain in their hands only the dead cold mass. The injunction to seek the true and the right, which you have not found in the great multitude, in the first apparently unformed rudiments cannot seem strange to any of you, who are more or less concerned about philosophy and are familiar with its fortunes. Recall how few of those who have descended on their own path into the inner side of human nature

---

[20] Reference is made to Friedrich Schiller's term "play impulse" (*Spieltrieb*), which refers to the interplay between our sensible and formal impulses within aesthetic experience in "Fourteenth Letter," *On the Aesthetic Education of Man*, trans. Reginald Snell (1795; New York, 1954), p. 7.

[21] This is the sole reference to "theology" in 1799; changes of the text in 1806 and 1821 modify the impression that, like his Romanticist contemporaries, the author is opposed to the forms of didactic, systematic reflection.

and the world, and who have intuited and portrayed their mutual relationship and inner harmony in a unique light, have formed their own system of philosophy. Have not all communicated their discoveries in a more delicate – be it also more fragile – form? But are there not systems from all the schools? Yes, precisely from the schools, which are nothing but the habitations and nurseries of the dead letter;[22] for the spirit lets itself neither be bound in academies, nor be poured successively into eager skulls; it usually evaporates on the way from the first mouth to the first ear. Would you not call instructively to one who considered the makers of these great bodies of philosophy to be philosophers themselves and wanted to find the spirit of scholarship in them, "Not so, good friend!"? In all things those who have only followed and collected and have stopped with what someone else has provided do not have the spirit of the matter. This is based solely on its discoverers, and to them you must go. But you shall have to confess that this is even more the case with religion, for by its whole nature it is just as far removed from all that is systematic as philosophy is by its nature inclined toward it.

Consider by whom these artificial edifices are raised? Consider whose changeableness you mock, whose disproportion offends you, and whose inadequacy on account of their petty tendencies is so ludicrous to you? By chance one of the heroes of religion? Name me one individual among all those who have brought down to us some new revelation, from whoever first conceived the one universal God – certainly the most systematic thought in the whole field of religion – to the most recent mystic in whom perhaps an original beam of the inner light still gleams. (You will not blame me if I do not include the literalistic theologians who believe the salvation of the world and the light of knowledge is to be found in the new garb of their formulas or in the new arrangements of their calculating proofs.) Name me a single individual among all of these who would have thought it worth the effort to be occupied with this Sisyphean labor. Only single sublime thoughts flash through their soul that ignited from an ethereal fire, and the magic thunder of a charmed speech accompanied the lofty appearance and proclaimed to a worshiping mortal that the deity had spoken.[23] An atom impregnated by a celestial power fell into their mind, assimilated everything there, expanded it mightily, and then burst, as if by divine decree, in a world whose atmosphere offered too little resistance and brought forth in its final moments one of those heavenly meteors, one of those significant signs of the times whose origin no one mistakes and which fill all mortals with awe. You must seek these heavenly sparks that arise when a holy soul is stirred by the universe, and you must overhear them in the incomprehensible moment when they are formed. Otherwise it fares with you as with one who

---

[22] See n. 15 above.

[23] The mystic with the magic thunder of charmed speech very likely refers to the poet Novalis, whose remarkable *Blütenstaub* aphorisms had recently appeared in *Ath.* I, pp. 70–106, and are cited elsewhere in *On Religion*; see n. 21 in the Second Speech. The immediate, revelatory power of these fragments ("We seek everywhere the unconditioned [*das Unbedingte*] and only find things [*Dinge*]") is contrasted with the work of the literalistic, orthodox theologians.

seeks out too late with combustible material the fire that the flint has drawn from the steel and then finds only a particle of crude metal which cannot be ignited.

I ask, therefore, that turning from all that is usually called religion you aim your attention only at these individual intimations and moods that you will find in all expressions and noble deeds of God-inspired persons. If you then discover nothing new and pertinent even in the particular, as I hope may occur despite your learning and your knowledge, if your narrow concept that is produced only by superficial observation does not expand and transform itself, if you could then still despise this bent of the mind toward the eternal – if all that is important to humanity can still seem ludicrous to you even from this point of view, than I shall believe that your disdain of religion is in conformity with your nature and shall have nothing further to say to you. Only do not worry that I still might, in the end, resort after all to those common measures of demonstrating to you how necessary religion is for maintaining right and order in the world and for coming to the aid of the shortsightedness of human perspective and the narrow limits of human power with the reminder of an all-seeing and infinite power.[24] Nor shall I say that religion would be a true friend and a saving support of morality, since its holy feelings and its brilliant prospects make the struggle with the self and the accomplishment of good very much easier for a weak humanity.[25] Thus indeed do those speak who pretend to be the best friends and most zealous defenders of religion. But I shall not decide for whom the most contempt is due in this chain of ideas, whether it be right and morality, which are represented as in need of support, or religion, which is supposed to undergird them, or you, to whom this is addressed.

If even this wise counsel were given to you differently, with what sort of impudence could I expect you to play an empty game with yourselves in your inner selves that you should let yourselves be spurred on by something you would otherwise have no reason to honor and love to something else you already honor without this and about which you concern yourselves? Or if perhaps through these speeches something is supposed to be whispered in your ears concerning what you are to do for the sake of the people, how should you, who are called to educate others and to make them like yourselves, begin by deceiving them and by passing something off to them as holy and effective that is, in the highest degree, indifferent to you and that they are to reject as soon as they have raised themselves to the same level as you? I cannot demand such a course of action. It entails the most destructive hypocrisy toward the world and toward yourselves. Whoever intends to recommend religion in this way cannot help magnifying the contempt under which it already suffers.

[24] "Gedanken I" (no. 88), *KGA* I.2, p. 25: "Whatever is supposed to be defended must be defended completely from within itself, thus also religion [is to be defended], not as a means."
[25] "Gedanken I" (no. 89), *KGA* I.2, p. 89: "One can be fully lawful without religion but perhaps not completely moral, for the renunciation of individuality points, for all that, finally to a highest individual. Ethics is also historical."

I will grant that our civil institutions still sigh under a high degree of imperfection and have as yet demonstrated little power to prevent injustice or to eradicate it. What a culpable abandonment of a weighty matter, what timid disbelief in the approach to something better it would be, if religion had to be called in because of that! Would you have a lawful situation if its existence depended on piety? Would not the whole concept that you, after all, consider so holy disappear for you as soon as you start from that point? Deal with the situation directly if it seems so bad to you; improve the laws, shake up the constitutions with each other, give the state an iron hand, give it a hundred eyes if it does not yet have them. Only do not lull to sleep with a deceitful lyre those eyes that it has. Do not insert a business like this into another one or you have not attended to it at all; and do not, to the insult of humanity, declare its most sublime work of art to be a parasitic plant that can nourish itself only with alien fluids.

Law must not even require ethical life, which is, after all, intimately related to it but is still far from it, in order to secure for itself the most unlimited sovereignty in its realm; it must stand completely alone for itself.[26] Whoever administers justice must be able to engender it everywhere, and anyone who claims that this can only happen when religion is communicated – as if that which only exists by proceeding from the heart can be communicated other than voluntarily – likewise claims that only those should be administrators of justice who are skilled at infusing the spirit of religion into the human soul. To what dark barbarism of unholy times would that return us? But ethical life probably has just as little to share with religion; those who make a distinction between this world and the world beyond delude themselves; at least all who have religion believe in only one world.[27]

If, therefore, the desire for well-being is something foreign to ethical life, then the latter must be worth no more than the former, and awe of the eternal not more than that of a wise human being. If ethical life loses its glory and firmness through every addition to it, how much more through something whose lofty and alien colors can never be denied. You have heard this enough from those who defend the independence and the omnipotence of the moral laws,[28] but I add that it also shows the greatest contempt for religion to wish to transplant it into another realm and expect it to serve and work there. It would not even want to reign in a foreign kingdom, for it is not so desirous of conquest that it wishes to enlarge what is its own.

[26] "Gedanken I" (no. 153), *KGA* I.2, p. 36: "That religion is supposed to be the source of ethics is not true and that ethics is supposed to be the source of religion is also not true. But it is true that religiosity is the source of morality and that morality is the source of religiosity. Therefore, here one of the three nouns must be taken in a different sense. Is it not immaterial which term one chooses for that? From this it follows that the ambiguity emerges from the connecting word (source)."

[27] The attack on the traditional view (ridiculed by the Enlightenment) that religion has chiefly to do with "the other world" and with the hope for rewards in a "hereafter" is maintained throughout subsequent editions of the work.

[28] An allusion to Kant's teaching on the autonomy and unconditioned nature of the moral law.

Second Speech
On the Essence of Religion

You know how the aged Simonides, through repeated and prolonged hesitation, reduced to silence the person who had bothered him with the question, "What are the gods after all?"[1] I should like to begin with a similar hesitation about the far greater and more comprehensive question, "What is religion?"

Naturally, this would not be with the intention of keeping silent and leaving you in embarrassment as he did, but that, kept waiting in impatient expectation, you might for a time steadily direct your gaze to the point we seek, while completely excluding all other thoughts. It is, after all, the first requirement of those who only conjure common spirits that onlookers, who want to see their manifestations and be initiated into their secrets, prepare themselves through abstinence from earthly things and through holy silence; then, without distracting themselves by the sight of other objects, they look with undivided attention at the place where the vision is to show itself. How much more will I be permitted to insist on a similar obedience, since I am to call forth a rare spirit that does not deign to appear in any oft-seen familiar guise, a spirit you wi.! have to observe attentively a long time in order to recognize it and understand its significant features. Only if you stand before the holy circles with the most unprejudiced sobriety of mind that clearly and properly comprehends every contour and, full of desire to understand the presented object on its own terms, is neither seduced by old memories nor corrupted by preconceived suspicions, can I hope that, even if you do not come to like my manifestation, you will at least agree with me concerning its form and recognize it as a heavenly being.

I wish I could present religion to you in some well-known form so that you

---

[1] The story is from Cicero, *De natura deorum*, 1.22. Simonides of Ceos (c. 556–468 BC) was a lyric poet and epigrammist from the Aegean, who served after 476 at the court of Hieron in Syracuse. Schleiermacher frequently appeals, often ironically, to his audience's post-Winckelmann love of Hellenism; see the references in this speech to Prometheus, Greek mythology, Eleusinian mysteries, and Greco-Roman deities and religion; and in the Fourth Speech to Greek poets, sages, and Plato.

The power that is religion's due, which it merits anew in every moment, satisfies it; and for religion, which considers everything holy, what maintains the same rank with it in human nature is even holier. But it is actually supposed to serve as those wish; it is to have a purpose, and is to render itself useful. What denigration! And should its defenders greedily procure this for religion? Yet those who thus proceed from utility, for whom, in the end, even ethical life and law are there for the sake of another advantage, might themselves better founder in this eternal cycle of general utility in which they allow everything good to perish and of which no person who even wishes to be something for himself understands a sound word. Better that than to set themselves up as defenders of religion whose cause they are truly the most inept to lead. A lovely fame for heavenly religion, if it were now able to provide so passably for the earthly affairs of humanity! Much honor to this free and carefree one, if it were only somewhat more vigilant and active than the conscience! Religion does not descend to you from heaven for such purpose. What is loved and esteemed only for an advantage that lies outside may well be needed, but it is not in itself necessary; it can always remain a pious wish that never comes into existence, and a reasonable person places no extraordinary value on it, but merely the value that is appropriate to the other thing. And this would be little enough in the case of religion. I, at least, would bid for it stingily, for I must only confess that I do not believe that the unjust actions it hinders and the ethical deeds it is supposed to have produced are so serious. If that should be the only thing that can command respect for it, I want to have nothing to do with its cause. To recommend it merely as an aside is too insignificant. An imagined praise that disappears when one observes it more closely cannot assist something that deals in higher claims. What I assert and what I should like to establish for religion include the following: It springs necessarily and by itself from the interior of every better soul, it has its own province in the mind in which it reigns sovereign, and it is worthy of moving the noblest and the most excellent by means of its innermost power and by having its innermost essence known by them. Now it is up to you to decide whether it is worth your while to listen to me before you become still more entrenched in your contempt.

I will grant that our civil institutions still sigh under a high degree of imperfection and have as yet demonstrated little power to prevent injustice or to eradicate it. What a culpable abandonment of a weighty matter, what timid disbelief in the approach to something better it would be, if religion had to be called in because of that! Would you have a lawful situation if its existence depended on piety? Would not the whole concept that you, after all, consider so holy disappear for you as soon as you start from that point? Deal with the situation directly if it seems so bad to you; improve the laws, shake up the constitutions with each other, give the state an iron hand, give it a hundred eyes if it does not yet have them. Only do not lull to sleep with a deceitful lyre those eyes that it has. Do not insert a business like this into another one or you have not attended to it at all; and do not, to the insult of humanity, declare its most sublime work of art to be a parasitic plant that can nourish itself only with alien fluids.

Law must not even require ethical life, which is, after all, intimately related to it but is still far from it, in order to secure for itself the most unlimited sovereignty in its realm; it must stand completely alone for itself.[26] Whoever administers justice must be able to engender it everywhere, and anyone who claims that this can only happen when religion is communicated – as if that which only exists by proceeding from the heart can be communicated other than voluntarily – likewise claims that only those should be administrators of justice who are skilled at infusing the spirit of religion into the human soul. To what dark barbarism of unholy times would that return us? But ethical life probably has just as little to share with religion; those who make a distinction between this world and the world beyond delude themselves; at least all who have religion believe in only one world.[27]

If, therefore, the desire for well-being is something foreign to ethical life, then the latter must be worth no more than the former, and awe of the eternal not more than that of a wise human being. If ethical life loses its glory and firmness through every addition to it, how much more through something whose lofty and alien colors can never be denied. You have heard this enough from those who defend the independence and the omnipotence of the moral laws,[28] but I add that it also shows the greatest contempt for religion to wish to transplant it into another realm and expect it to serve and work there. It would not even want to reign in a foreign kingdom, for it is not so desirous of conquest that it wishes to enlarge what is its own.

---

[26] "Gedanken I" (no. 153), *KGA* 1.2, p. 36: "That religion is supposed to be the source of ethics is not true and that ethics is supposed to be the source of religion is also not true. But it is true that religiosity is the source of morality and that morality is the source of religiosity. Therefore, here one of the three nouns must be taken in a different sense. Is it not immaterial which term one chooses for that? From this it follows that the ambiguity emerges from the connecting word (source)."

[27] The attack on the traditional view (ridiculed by the Enlightenment) that religion has chiefly to do with "the other world" and with the hope for rewards in a "hereafter" is maintained throughout subsequent editions of the work.

[28] An allusion to Kant's teaching on the autonomy and unconditioned nature of the moral law.

seeks out too late with combustible material the fire that the flint has drawn from the steel and then finds only a particle of crude metal which cannot be ignited.

I ask, therefore, that turning from all that is usually called religion you aim your attention only at these individual intimations and moods that you will find in all expressions and noble deeds of God-inspired persons. If you then discover nothing new and pertinent even in the particular, as I hope may occur despite your learning and your knowledge, if your narrow concept that is produced only by superficial observation does not expand and transform itself, if you could then still despise this bent of the mind toward the eternal – if all that is important to humanity can still seem ludicrous to you even from this point of view, than I shall believe that your disdain of religion is in conformity with your nature and shall have nothing further to say to you. Only do not worry that I still might, in the end, resort after all to those common measures of demonstrating to you how necessary religion is for maintaining right and order in the world and for coming to the aid of the shortsightedness of human perspective and the narrow limits of human power with the reminder of an all-seeing and infinite power.[24] Nor shall I say that religion would be a true friend and a saving support of morality, since its holy feelings and its brilliant prospects make the struggle with the self and the accomplishment of good very much easier for a weak humanity.[25] Thus indeed do those speak who pretend to be the best friends and most zealous defenders of religion. But I shall not decide for whom the most contempt is due in this chain of ideas, whether it be right and morality, which are represented as in need of support, or religion, which is supposed to undergird them, or you, to whom this is addressed.

If even this wise counsel were given to you differently, with what sort of impudence could I expect you to play an empty game with yourselves in your inner selves that you should let yourselves be spurred on by something you would otherwise have no reason to honor and love to something else you already honor without this and about which you concern yourselves? Or if perhaps through these speeches something is supposed to be whispered in your ears concerning what you are to do for the sake of the people, how should you, who are called to educate others and to make them like yourselves, begin by deceiving them and by passing something off to them as holy and effective that is, in the highest degree, indifferent to you and that they are to reject as soon as they have raised themselves to the same level as you? I cannot demand such a course of action. It entails the most destructive hypocrisy toward the world and toward yourselves. Whoever intends to recommend religion in this way cannot help magnifying the contempt under which it already suffers.

---

[24] "Gedanken I" (no. 88), *KGA* 1.2, p. 25: "Whatever is supposed to be defended must be defended completely from within itself, thus also religion [is to be defended], not as a means."

[25] "Gedanken I" (no. 89), *KGA* 1.2, p. 89: "One can be fully lawful without religion but perhaps not completely moral, for the renunciation of individuality points, for all that, finally to a highest individual. Ethics is also historical."

might immediately remember its features, its movements, and its manners and exclaim that you have here or there seen it just this way in real life. But I would deceive you. For it is not found among human beings as undisguised as it appears to the conjurer, and for some time has not let itself be viewed in the form peculiar to it. The particular disposition of various cultivated peoples no longer shows itself so purely and distinctly in individual actions, since their commerce has become more many-sided and what they have in common has increased through all sorts of connections. Only the imagination can grasp the entire idea behind these qualities, which are encountered only singly as dispersed and mixed with much that 'is foreign. This is also the case with spiritual things, and among them with religion. It is well known to you how everything is now full of harmonious development; and precisely this has caused such a completed and extended sociability and friendliness within the human soul that none of the soul's powers in fact now acts among us distinctly, as much as we like to think of them as distinct. In every accomplishment each is immediately precipitated by polite love and beneficial support of the other and is somewhat deflected from its path. One looks around vainly in this cultured world for an action that could furnish a true expression of some capacity of spirit, be it sensibility or understanding, ethical life or religion.

Do not, therefore, be indignant and explain it as disdain for the present if, for the sake of clarity, I frequently lead you back to those more childlike times where, in a less perfected state, everything was still, distinct and individual. If I begin at once with that theme, and in some way or other meticulously come back to it, this is to warn you emphatically about the confusion of religion with things that sometimes look similar to it and with which you will everywhere find it mixed.

If you put yourselves on the highest standpoint of metaphysics and morals, you will find that both have the same object as religion, namely, the universe and the relationship of humanity to it. This similarity has long since been a basis of manifold aberrations; metaphysics and morals have therefore invaded religion on many occasions, and much that belongs to religion has concealed itself in metaphysics or morals under an unseemly form. But shall you, for this reason, believe that it is identical with one of these? I know that your instinct tells you the contrary, and it also follows from your opinions; for you never admit that religion walks with the firm step of which metaphysics is capable, and you do not forget to observe diligently that there are quite a few ugly immoral blemishes on its history. If religion is thus to be differentiated, then it must be set off from those in some manner, regardless of the common subject matter. Religion must treat this subject matter completely differently, express or work out another relationship of humanity to it, have another mode of procedure or another goal; for only in this way can that which is similar in its subject matter to something else achieve a determinate nature and a unique existence. I ask you, therefore, What does your metaphysics do – or, if you want to have nothing to do with the outmoded name that is too historical for you, your transcendental philosophy?[2] It classifies the universe and divides it into this being and that, seeks out the reasons for what exists, and deduces the necessity of what is real while spinning the reality of the world and its laws out of itself. Into this realm, therefore, religion must not venture too far. It must not have the tendency to posit essences and to determine natures, to lose itself in an infinity of reasons and deductions, to seek out final causes, and to proclaim eternal truths.

And what does your morality do? It develops a system of duties out of human nature and our relationship to the universe; it commands and forbids actions with unlimited authority. Yet religion must not even presume to do that; it must not use the universe in order to derive duties and is not permitted to contain a code of laws. "And yet what one calls religion seems to consist only of fragments of these various fields." This is indeed the common concept. I have just imparted to you doubts about that; now it is time to annihilate it altogether. The theorists in religion, who aim at knowledge of the nature of the universe and a highest being whose work it is, are metaphysicians, but also discreet enough not to disdain some morality. The practical people, to whom the will of God is the primary thing, are moralists, but a little in the style of metaphysics. You take the idea of the good and carry it into metaphysics as the natural law of an unlimited and plenteous being, and you take the idea of a primal being from metaphysics and carry it into morality so that this great work should not remain anonymous, but so that the picture of the lawgiver might be engraved at the front of so splendid a code. But mix and stir as you will, these never go together; you play an empty game with materials that are not suited to each other. You always retain only metaphysics and morals. This mixture of opinions abut the highest being or the world and of precepts for a human life (or even for two) you call religion! And the instinct, which seeks those opinions, together with the dim presentiments that are the actual final sanction of these precepts, you call religiousness! But how then do you come to regard a mere compilation, an anthology for beginners, as an integral work, as an individual with its own origin and power? How do you come to mention it, even if only to refute it? Why have you not long since analyzed it into its parts and discovered the shameful plagiarism?

I would take pleasure in alarming you with some Socratic questions and bringing you to confess that, even in the most common things, you know the principles according to which like must be related to like and the particular subordinated to the universal, and that you only wish not to apply these principles here in order to be able to make fun of a serious subject in a worldly manner. Where, then, is the unity in this whole? Where does the unifying principle lie for this dissimilar material? If it is an attractive force of its own, then you must confess that religion is the highest in philosophy and that metaphysics and morals are only subordinate divisions of it; for that in which two varied but opposed concepts are one can only

---

[2]   A polemic against the newest wave of "transcendental philosophy," which Schleiermacher associates with Fichte's *Science of Knowledge* (1794), is one of the major aims of his work.

be the higher under which the other two belong. If this binding principle lies in metaphysics, you have recognized, for reasons that are related to metaphysics, a highest being as the moral lawgiver. Therefore annihilate practical philosophy, and admit that it, and with it religion, is only a small chapter of the theoretical. If you want to assert the converse, then metaphysics and religion must be swallowed up by morality, for which indeed, nothing may any longer be impossible after it has learned to believe and in its old age has acquiesced in preparing a quiet spot in its innermost sanctuary for the secret embraces of two self-loving worlds.

Or do you want to say that the metaphysical in religion does not depend on the moral, nor the latter on the former? Or that there is a remarkable parallelism between the theoretical and the practical, and that to perceive and represent this is religion? To be sure, the solution to this parallelism can lie neither in practical philosophy, which is not concerned about it, nor in theoretical philosophy, which, as part of its function, strives most zealously to pursue and annihilate the parallelism as far as possible. But I think that you, driven by this need, have already been seeking for some time a highest philosophy in which these two categories unite and are always on the verge of finding it; and religion would lie so close to this! Would philosophy really have to flee to religion as the opponents of philosophy like to maintain? Pay close heed to what you say there. With all this either you receive a religion that stands far above philosophy as it exists at present, or you must be honest enough to restore to both parts of philosophy what belongs to them and admit that you are still ignorant of what concerns religion. I do not wish to hold you to the former, for I want to take no position that I could not maintain, but you will very likely agree to the latter.

Let us deal honestly with one another. You do not like religion; we started from that assumption. But in conducting an honest battle against it, which is not completely without effort, you do not want to have fought against a shadow like the one with which we have struggled. Religion must indeed be something integral that could have arisen in the human heart, something thinkable from which a concept can be formulated about which one can speak and argue. I find it very unjust if you yourselves stitch together something untenable out of such disparate things, call it religion, and then make so much needless ado about it. You will deny that you have begun deceitfully. You will call upon me to roll out all of the ancient sources of religion – since I have, after all, already rejected systems, commentaries, and apologies – from the beautiful compositions of the Greeks to the holy writings of the Christians, and to state whether I would not find the nature of the gods and their will everywhere, and everywhere praise persons as holy and blessed, who acknowledge the former and fulfill the latter.

But that is precisely what I have said to you. Religion never appears in a pure state. All these are only the extraneous parts that cling to it, and it should be our business to free it from them. After all, the corporeal world provides you with no primal element as nature's pure product – you would then, as happens to you in the intellectual world, have to regard very rough things as simple – but rather it is only the ceaseless aim of analytic skill to be able to depict such a primal element. In spiritual things the original cannot be brought forth for you, except when you beget it through an original creation in yourselves, and even then only in the moment when you beget it. I beg you, understand yourselves on this point, for you shall be ceaselessly reminded of it. But as far as the sources and original documents of religion are concerned, this interference of metaphysics and morals with them is not merely an unavoidable fate; it is rather an artificial plan and a lofty intention. What is presented as the first and last is not always the truest and highest. If you only knew how to read between the lines! All holy writings are like the modest books that were in use some time ago in our modest fatherland, which treated important matters under a sketchy title. To be sure, they only give notice of metaphysics and morals, and in the end are happy to return to that which they have announced, but you are encouraged to crack open this shell. Thus even the diamond lies wholly enclosed in a base substance, yet surely not in order to remain hidden but rather to be found all the more certainly. To make proselytes out of unbelievers is deeply engrained in the character of religion; those who impart their own religion can have no other purpose. Thus it is in fact hardly a pious deception but an appropriate method to begin with and appear concerned about a matter for which the sensibility already exists, so that something may occasionally and unnoticeably slip in for which the sensibility must first be aroused.[3] Since all communication of religion cannot be other than rhetorical, it is a clever engagement of an audience to introduce them into such good company. Yet this device has not only reached but overstepped its goal, since even for you religion's essence has remained hidden under this mask. Therefore it is time to take up the subject from the other end and to start with the sharp opposition in which religion is found over against morals and metaphysics. That was what I wanted. You distracted me with our ordinary concept; I hope it is now settled and you will interrupt me no more.

In order to take possession of its own domain, religion renounces herewith all claims to whatever belongs to those others and gives back everything that has been forced upon it. It does not wish to determine and explain the universe according to its nature as does metaphysics; it does not desire to continue the universe's development and perfect it by the power of freedom and the divine free choice of a human being as does morals. Religion's essence is neither thinking nor acting, but intuition and feeling. It wishes to intuit the universe, wishes devoutly to overhear the universe's own manifestations and actions, longs to be grasped and filled by the universe's immediate influences in childlike passivity. Thus, religion is opposed to these two in everything that makes up its essence and in everything that character-

---

[3] Paul Seifert, *Die Theologie des jungen Schleiermacher* (Gütersloh, 1960), p. 118, cites this as the most explicit "methodological" passage in the work; the passage justifies the rhetorical stance and hermeneutic of the work, which seeks out common assumptions with its audience, even if the argument eventually challenges these assumptions.

izes its effects. Metaphysics and morals see in the whole universe only humanity as the center of all relatedness, as the condition of all being and the cause of all becoming; religion wishes to see the infinite, its imprint and its manifestation, in humanity no less than in all other individual and finite forms. Metaphysics proceeds from finite human nature and wants to define consciously, from its simplest concept, the extent of its powers, and its receptivity, what the universe can be for us and how we necessarily must view it.[4] Religion also lives its whole life in nature, but in the infinite nature of totality, the one and all; what holds in nature for everything individual also holds for the human; and wherever everything, including man, may press on or tarry within this eternal ferment of individual forms and beings, religion wishes to intuit and to divine this in detail in quiet submissiveness. Morality proceeds from the consciousness of freedom; it wishes to extend freedom's realm to infinity and to make everything subservient to it.[5] Religion breathes there where freedom itself has once more become nature; it apprehends man beyond the play of his particular powers and his personality, and views him from the vantage point where he must be what he is, whether he likes it or not.

Thus religion maintains its own sphere and its own character only by completely removing itself from the sphere and character of speculation as well as from that of praxis. Only when it places itself next to both of them is the common ground perfectly filled out and human nature completed from this dimension. Religion shows itself to you as the necessary and indispensable third next to those two, as their natural counterpart, not slighter in worth and splendor than what you wish of them.[6] To want to have speculation and praxis without religion is rash arrogance. It is insolent enmity against the gods; it is the unholy sense of Prometheus, who cowardly stole what in calm certainty he would have been able to ask for and to expect. Man has merely stolen the feeling of his infinity and godlikeness, and as an unjust possession it cannot thrive for him if he is not also conscious of his limitedness, the contingency of his whole form, the silent disappearance of his whole existence in the immeasurable. The gods have also punished this crime from the very beginning. Praxis is an art, speculation is a science, religion is the sensibility and taste for the infinite. Without religion, how can praxis rise above the common circle of adventurous and customary forms? How can speculation become anything better than a stiff and barren skeleton? Or why, in all its action directed outwardly and toward the universe, does your praxis actually always forget to cultivate humanity itself? It is because you place humanity in opposition to the universe and do not receive it from the hand of religion as part of the universe and as something holy. How does praxis arrive at an impoverished uniformity that

---

[4] The metaphysical stance sketched here alludes to Kant's reduction of metaphysics to the realm of finite human experience in the *Critique of Pure Reason*.

[5] An allusion to the *Critique of Practical Reason*.

[6] The notion of religion as a necessary counterpart to "speculation" and "praxis" is retained, though embellished and elaborated in the 1806 and 1821 revisions.

knows only a single ideal and lays this as the basis everywhere? It is because you lack the basic feeling for infinite and living nature, whose symbol is multiplicity and individuality. Everything finite exists only through the determination of its limits, which must, as it were, "be cut out of" the infinite. Only thus can a thing be infinite and yet be self-formed within these limits; otherwise you lose everything in the uniformity of a universal concept. Why, for so long, did speculation give you deceptions instead of a system, and words instead of real thoughts? Why was it nothing but an empty game with formulas that always reappeared changed and to which nothing would ever correspond? Because it lacked religion, because the feeling for the infinite did not animate it, and because longing for it and reverence for it did not compel its fine, airy thoughts to assume more rigorous consistency in order to preserve itself against this powerful pressure. Everything must proceed from intuition, and those who lack the desire to intuit the infinite have no touchstone and indeed need none in order to know whether they have given any respectable thought to the matter.

And how will the triumph of speculation, the completed and rounded idealism, fare if religion does not counterbalance it and allow it to glimpse a higher realism than that which it subordinates to itself so boldly and for such good reason?[7] Idealism will destroy the universe by appearing to fashion it; it will degrade it to a mere allegory, to an empty silhouette of our own limitedness. Respectfully offer up with me a lock of hair to the manes of the holy rejected Spinoza![8] The high world spirit permeated him, the infinite was his beginning and end, the universe his only and eternal love; in holy innocence and deep humility he was reflected in the eternal world and saw how he too was its most lovable mirror; he was full of religion and full of holy spirit; for this reason, he also stands there alone and unequaled, master in his art but elevated above the profane guild, without disciples and without rights of citizenship.

I entreat you to become familiar with this concept: intuition of the universe. It is the hinge of my whole speech; it is the highest and most universal formula of religion on the basis of which you should be able to find every place in religion, from which you may determine its essence and its limits. All intuition proceeds from an influence of the intuited on the one who intuits, from an original and independent action of the former, which is then grasped, apprehended, and

---

[7] The designation "higher realism" describes Schleiermacher's philosophical position as compared to Fichte's speculative thought. Like Goethe and Schelling, Schleiermacher felt a deep spiritual kinship with Spinoza and delights in the irony of playing off this pious atheist against Fichte, who had just lost his Jena professorship in the "atheism controversy" and whose *Science of Knowledge* views Spinozism as a form of consistent dogmatism. The chief tenet of this "realism" is that the highest principle of reality, which alone is divine, is inexpressible in thought and that the infinite is knowable only as mediated through the finite.

[8] See F. Schlegel: "Indeed, I barely comprehend how one can be a poet without admiring Spinoza, loving him, and becoming entirely his" ("Dialogue on poetry (1799–1800)" in *Friedrich Schlegel: Dialogue on Poetry and Literary Aphorisms*, ed. Ernst Behler and Roman Struc [University Park, PA, 1968], p. 84).

conceived by the latter according to one's own nature.[9] If the emanations of light –
which happen completely without your efforts – did not affect your sense, if the
smallest parts of the body, the tips of your fingers, were not mechanically or
chemically affected, if the pressure of weight did not reveal to you an opposition
and a limit to your power, you would intuit nothing and perceive nothing, and what
you thus intuit and perceive is not the nature of things, but their action upon you.
What you know or believe about the nature of things lies far beyond the realm of
intuition.

The same is true of religion. The universe exists in uninterrupted activity and
reveals itself to us every moment. Every form that it brings forth, every being to
which it gives separate existence according to the fullness of life, every occurrence
that spills forth from its rich, ever-fruitful womb, is an action of the same upon us.
Thus to accept everything individual as a part of the whole and everything limited
as a representation of the infinite is religion. But whatever would go beyond that
and penetrate deeper into the nature and substance of the whole is no longer
religion, and will, if it still wants to be regarded as such, inevitably sink back into
empty mythology.

Thus it was religion when the ancients, annihilating the limitations of time and
space, regarded every unique type of life throughout the whole world as the work
and reign of an omnipresent being. They had intuited a unique mode of acting of
the universe in its unity, and designated this intuition accordingly. It was religion
when, for every helpful event whereby the eternal laws of the world were
illuminatingly revealed through contingency, they gave the god to whom it
belonged its own name and built its own temple to it; they had comprehended an
act of the universe and thus denoted its individuality and its character. It was
religion when they rose above the brittle iron age of the world, full of fissures and
unevenness, and again sought the golden age on Olympus among the happy life of
the gods; thus they intuited the ever-active, ever-living, and serene activity of the
world and its spirit, beyond all change and all the apparent evil that only stems
from the conflict of finite forms. But when they keep a wondrous chronicle of the
descent of these gods or when a later faith trotted out for us a long series of
emanations and procreations, that is empty mythology. To present all events in the
world as the actions of a god is religion; it expresses its connection to an infinite
totality; but while brooding over the existence of this god before the world and
outside the world may be good and necessary in metaphysics, in religion even that
becomes only empty mythology, a further development of that which is only the

---

9   The universality, necessity, independence, and nonconceptual nature of Schleiermacher's notion of
    intuition are commensurate with Kant's use of intuition, even if Schleiermacher's broad, all-
    encompassing notion of intuition and its intimate association with religion are notably unlike Kant.
    Cf. *Critique of Pure Reason* (1781; London, 1961), p. 65: "In whatever manner and by whatever
    means a mode of knowledge may relate to objects, *intuition* is that through which it is in immediate
    relation to them, and to which all thought as a means is directed. But intuition takes place only in so
    far as the object is given to us."

means of portrayal as if it were the essential itself, a complete departure from its characteristic ground.

Intuition is and always remains something individual, set apart, the immediate perception, nothing more. To bind it and to incorporate it into a whole is once more the business not of sense but of abstract thought. The same is true of religion; it stops with the immediate experiences of the existence and action of the universe, with the individual intuitions and feelings; each of these is a self-contained work without connections with others or dependence upon them; it knows nothing about derivation and connection, for among all things religion can encounter, that is what its nature most opposes. Not only an individual fact or deed that one could call original or first,[10] but everything in religion is immediate and true for itself.

A system of intuitions? Can you imagine anything stranger? Do views, and especially views of the infinite, allow themselves to be brought into a system? Can you say that one must look at a thing a certain way just because one had to look at something else in such a manner? Others may stand right behind you, right alongside you, and everything can appear differently to them. Or do by chance the possible standpoints on which a mind can stand in order to observe the universe progress in measured intervals so that you can exhaust, enumerate, and precisely determine the characteristic of each? Are there not infinitely many of these, and is not every entity only a continual transition between two others? I speak your language in these matters, for it would be an infinite business, and you are not accustomed to connect the concept of something infinite with the term "system," but rather the concept of something that is limited and completed in its limitation. Elevate yourselves at once – after all, it is still an elevation for most of you – to that infinite dimension of sensible intuition,[11] to the wondrous and celebrated starry sky. The astronomical theories, which orient a thousand suns with their world systems around a common point and seek for each common point again a higher world system that could be its center, and so on into infinity, outwardly and inwardly – surely you would not want to call this a system of intuitions as such? The only thing to which you could attribute this name would be the age-old work of those childlike minds that have gathered the infinite mass of these phenomena into definite, but scanty and unseemly, pictures. But you know that there is no semblance of a system in that, that still other stars are discovered between these pictures, that even within their limits everything is undetermined and endless, and that the pictures themselves remain something purely arbitrary and highly change-

---

[10] The German terms *Tatsache, Handlung, erst,* and *ursprünglich,* which are used to express the first principle of consciousness, the principle of identity, or A=A, leave no doubt that the target is Fichte's *Science of Knowledge.* See Fichte, *Sämtliche Werke* (Berlin, 1845), I, pp. 91ff.

[11] The expression *sinnliche Anschauung* is traceable to Kant's *Critique of Pure Reason,* p. 93, and elsewhere. Schleiermacher uses the term for our immediate apprehension of objects in the world in which concepts play no mediating role. Schleiermacher comes closest to his predecessor where Kant plays tribute at the end of the *Critique of Practical Reason* (Indianapolis, 1956), p. 166, to the wondrous effect on the human mind of "the starry heavens above me and the moral law within me."

able. When you have persuaded another person to join you in drawing the image of the Big Dipper onto the blue background of the worlds, does he not nevertheless remain free to conceive the adjacent worlds in contours that are completely different from yours? This infinite chaos, where of course every point represents a world, is as such actually the most suitable and highest symbol of religion. In religion, as in this chaos, only the particular is true and necessary; nothing can or may be proved anything else. Everything universal under which the particular is supposed to be treated, each collection and combination of this sort, either exists in a different territory, if it is to be referred to the inner and essential realm, or is only the work of playful imagination and freest caprice. If thousands of you could have the same religious intuitions, each of you as an individual would certainly draw other outlines in order to portray how you viewed them alongside or in succession to one another; that would depend not on each mind but, rather, on an accidental condition, on a triviality. Individual persons may have their own arrangement and their own rubrics; the particular can thereby neither win nor lose. Those who truly know about their religion and its essence will utterly subordinate to the particular every apparent connection and will not sacrifice the smallest part of the particular to it. The realm of intuition is so infinite precisely because of this independent particularity.

If you place yourself at the most distant point of the material world, you will not only see from there the same objects in another order; and if you wish to cling to your former arbitrary images that you do not find there again, you will be completely in error. Instead you will even discover wholly new objects in new regions. You cannot say that your horizon, even the broadest, comprehends everything and that nothing more is to be intuited beyond it, or that nothing within this horizon escapes your eye, even the best aided. You find limits nowhere and are not able to think of any. This is true of religion in an even far higher sense; from an opposite point you would receive new intuitions not only in new regions; but also in old, well-known places the first elements would unite in different forms and everything would be different. Religion is infinite not only because acting and being acted upon ceaselessly alternate between the same limited matter and the mind – you know that such thinking is the sole infinity of speculation – not only because it is, like morality, internally incapable of completion; it is infinite in all respects, an infinity of matter and form, of being, of vision, and of knowledge about it. This feeling must accompany everyone who really has religion. Each person must be conscious that his religion is only a part of the whole, that regarding the same objects that affect him religiously there are views just as pious and, nevertheless, completely different from his own, and that from other elements of religion intuitions and feelings flow, the sense for which he may be completely lacking.

You see how immediately this lovely modesty, this friendly inviting tolerance springs from the concept of religion and how intimately tolerance nestles up to it. How wrongly, therefore, do you turn on religion with your reproaches that it is bent on persecution[12] and spitefulness, that it wrecks society and makes blood flow like water. Indict those who corrupt religion, who want to inundate it with philosophy and fetter it to a system. What is it in religion over which men have argued, taken sides, and ignited wars? Sometimes over morals and always over metaphysics, and neither of these belongs to it. Philosophy indeed strives to accommodate those who wish to know under one common knowledge, as you can daily see; but religion does not strive to bring those who believe and feel under a single belief and a single feeling. It strives, to be sure, to open the eyes of those who are not yet capable of intuiting the universe, for every one who sees is a new priest, a new mediator, a new mouthpiece; but for just this reason it avoids with aversion the barren uniformity that would again destroy this divine abundance.

The mania for system does indeed reject what is foreign, even if it is quite conceivable and true, because it could spoil one's own well-formed ranks and disturb the beautiful connections by claiming its place. In this mania lies the seat of contradiction; it must quarrel and persecute; for to the extent that the particular is again related to something individual and finite, the one can indeed destroy the other through its existence. But in the infinite everything finite stands undisturbed alongside one another; all is one, and all is true. Moreover, only the systematizers have caused all this. Modern Rome, godless but consistent, hurls anathemas and excommunicates heretics; ancient Rome, truly pious and religious in a lofty style, was hospitable to every god and so it became full of gods. The adherents of the dead letter that religion casts out have filled the world with criers and tumult; the true contemplators of the eternal have ever been quiet souls, either alone with themselves and the infinite or, if they glanced around themselves, happily granting his own way to everyone who only understood the mighty word. But with this broad view and this feeling of the infinite, religion also looks at what lies outside its own realm and contains in itself the capacity for unlimited multiplicity in judgment and in contemplation that, in fact, cannot be found elsewhere. No matter what inspires a person – I exclude neither ethical life nor philosophy but rely instead, as far as they are concerned, on your experience – his thinking and striving, to whatever object they may be directed, draw a narrow circle around him in which his highest lies enclosed and outside of which everything appears to him to be common and unworthy. Whoever only thinks systematically and acts from principle and design and wants to accomplish this or that in the world inevitably circumscribes himself and constantly sets himself in opposition to what as an object of aversion does not further his actions. Only the drive to intuit, if it is oriented to the infinite, places the mind in unlimited freedom; only religion saves it from the most ignominious fetters of opinion and desire. Everything that exists is necessary for religion, and everything that can be is for it a true indispensable image of the infinite; it is just a question of finding the point from which one's relationship to

---

[12] "Gedanken I" (no. 121), *KGA* I.2, p. 31: "Religion has never persecuted."

the infinite can be discovered. However reprehensible something may be in another connection or in itself, in this respect it is always worthy of existence and of being preserved and contemplated. To a pious mind religion makes everything holy and valuable, even unholiness and commonness itself, everything it comprehends and does not comprehend, that does or does not lie within the system of its own thoughts and is or is not in agreement with its peculiar manner of action; religion is the only sworn enemy of all pedantry and all one-sidedness.

Finally, to complete the general picture of religion, recall that every intuition is, by its very nature, connected with a feeling. Your senses mediate the connection between the object and yourselves; the same influence of the object, which reveals its existence to you, must stimulate them in various ways and produce a change in your inner consciousness. This feeling, of which you are frequently scarcely aware, can in other cases grow to such intensity that you forget both the object and yourselves because of it; your whole nervous system can be so permeated by it that for a long time that sensation alone dominates and resounds and resists the effect of other impressions. But that an action is brought forth in you, that the internally generated activity of your spirit is set in motion, surely you will not ascribe this to the influence of external objects? You will, of course, admit that this lies far beyond the power of even the strongest feelings and must have a completely different source in you. The same is true for religion. The same actions of the universe through which it reveals itself to you in the finite also bring it into a new relationship to your mind and your condition; in the act of intuiting it, you must necessarily be seized by various feelings. In religion, however, a different and stronger relationship between intuition and feeling takes place, and intuition never predominates so much that feeling is almost extinguished.

On the contrary, is it really a miracle if the eternal world affects the senses of our spirit as the sun affects our eyes? Is it a miracle when the sun so blinds us that everything else disappears, not only at that moment, but even long afterward all objects we observe are imprinted with its image and bathed in its brilliance? Just as the particular manner in which the universe presents itself to you in your intuitions and determines the uniqueness of your individual religion, so the strength of these feelings determines the degree of religiousness. The sounder the sense, the more sharply and definitely will it apprehend every impression. The more ardent the thirst and the more persistent the drive to grasp the infinite, the more manifoldly will the mind itself be seized by it everywhere and uninterruptedly, the more perfectly will these impressions penetrate it, and the more easily will they awaken again and again and retain the upper hand over everything else. That is how far the realm of religion concerns us in this respect; its feelings are supposed to possess us, and we should express, maintain, and portray them.

But should you wish to go beyond that dimension with these feelings, should they cause actual actions and incite you to deeds, then you find yourselves in an alien realm. If you still hold this to be religion, however rational and praiseworthy your action may appear, you are absorbed in an unholy superstition. All actual action should be moral, and it can be too, but religious feelings should accompany every human deed like a holy music; we should do everything with religion, nothing because of religion. If you do not understand that all action is supposed to be moral, then I add that this also applies to everything else. People should act calmly and whatever they may undertake should be done with presence of mind. Ask the moral, the political, and the artistic person, and all will say that this is their first precept; but calm and thoughtfulness are lost when a person permits himself to be driven to action by the powerful and disturbing feelings of religion. It is also unnatural that this should happen, for by their very nature religious feelings inhibit the strength of our action and invite us to calm and dedicated enjoyment; that is why the most religious people, for whom other impulses to action were lacking and who were nothing but religious, forsook the world and yielded themselves wholly to leisurely contemplation. Man must first master himself and his pious feelings before they press actions out of him; and, if I may refer directly to you, it is a part of your accusation that so many senseless and unnatural things have come to pass in this way. You see, I concede not only this point to you but also the most excellent and most praiseworthy ones. Whether meaningless rites are manipulated or good works performed, whether humans are slaughtered on bloody altars or whether they are made happy by a charitable hand, whether life is spent in dead inactivity or in dull, tasteless order or in frivolous and sumptuous sensual desire, these are certainly things that differ widely from one another if we wish to talk about morality or life and worldly affairs; but if they are supposed to pertain to religion and to have arisen from it, then they are all the same as one another, only slavish superstition, each one like the others.[13]

You reproach the person who lets his behavior toward another person be determined by the impression the other makes upon him. You desire that even the most accurate feeling about the impact of a human being should not lead us to action for which we have no better grounds; thus that person is also to be reproached whose actions, which should always be oriented toward the whole, are solely determined by the feelings that precisely this whole awakens in him. He is singled out as someone who sacrifices his honor, not only from the standpoint of morality, because he gives way to extraneous motives, but also from that of religion, because he ceases to be what, in its eyes, alone gives him unique worth, a free part of the whole, active through his own power. This entire misunderstanding that religion is supposed to act can, at the same time, be nothing other than a dreadful misuse, and to whichever side the activity should turn, it ends in mischief and ruin. But to have the soul full of religion while performing a calm action that must

[13] Negative references to practices of human sacrifice, religions of good works, mystical quietism, and the routine behavior of monastic life vividly illustrate Schleiermacher's affinity with the eighteenth-century Enlightenment's desire to distinguish true religion from superstition. See, e.g., David Hume, *The Natural History of Religion* (1757; Stanford, CA, 1957).

proceed from its own source, that is the goal of the pious. Only evil spirits, not good ones, possess a person and drive him, and the legions of angels with which the heavenly Father had equipped his Son were not in him but around him;[14] they also did not help him in his actions, nor were they supposed to, but they instilled serenity and rest into a soul wearied by deed and thought. Occasionally he lost sight of them in the moments when his whole power was roused to action, but then they hovered around him again in joyous throng and served him.[15]

But before I lead you into the particulars of these intuitions and feelings, which must certainly be my next business with you, permit me first for a moment to mourn the fact that I cannot speak of both other than separately. The finest spirit of religion is thereby lost for my speech, and I can disclose its innermost secret only unsteadily and uncertainly. But reflection necessarily separates both; and who can speak about something that belongs to consciousness without first going through this medium? Not only when we communicate an inner action of the mind, but even when we merely turn it into material for contemplation within ourselves and wish to raise it to lucid consciousness, this unavoidable separation immediately occurs. This state of affairs intermingles with the original consciousness of our dual activity, what predominates and functions outward and what is merely sketching and reproducing, which seems rather to serve things. Immediately upon this contact the simplest matter separates itself into two opposing elements, the one group combining into an image of an object, the other penetrating to the center of our being, there to effervesce with our original drives and to develop a transient feeling. We cannot escape this fate even with the innermost creation of the religious sense; we cannot call up its products to the surface again and communicate them except in this separate form. Only do not think – for this is one of the most dangerous errors – that in the first stirring of the mind religious intuitions and feelings may originally be as divided as we must unfortunately consider them here. Intuition without feeling is nothing and can have neither the proper origin nor the proper force; feeling without intuition is also nothing;[16] both are therefore something only when and because they are originally one and unseparated.

That first mysterious moment that occurs in every sensory perception, before intuition and feeling have separated, where sense and its objects have, as it were, flowed into one another and become one, before both turn back to their original position – I know how indescribable it is and how quickly it passes away.[17] But I

---

[14] Matthew 26:53.

[15] Matthew 4:1–11.

[16] This passage plays on the Kantian dictum: "Thoughts without content are empty, intuitions without concepts are blind" (*Critique of Pure Reason*, p. 93).

[17] The "love scene" passage, which expresses the idea that the highest principle (reality itself or the divine) is inexpressible yet nonetheless of deepest significance in human experience, may be compared to the Socratic "myth of the soul" in Plato's *Phaedrus* 244-57, where sexual imagery expresses the union of passion and intellectual eros. Schleiermacher views *Phaedrus* as the programmatic statement of the Platonic corpus; see his *Introductions to the Dialogues of Plato* (reprint 1836; New York, 973), pp. 48f.

wish that you were able to hold on to it and also to recognize it again in the higher and divine religious activity of the mind. Would that I could and might express it, at least indicate it, without having to desecrate it! It is as fleeting and transparent as the first scent with which the dew gently caresses the waking flowers, as modest and delicate as a maiden's kiss, as holy and fruitful as a nuptial embrace; indeed, not *like* these, but it *is itself* all of these. A manifestation, an event develops quickly and magically into an image of the universe. Even as the beloved and ever-sought-for form[18] fashions itself, my soul flees toward it; I embrace it, not as a shadow, but as the holy essence itself. I lie on the bosom of the infinite world. At this moment I am its soul, for I feel all its powers and its infinite life as my own; at this moment it is my body, for I penetrate its muscles and its limbs as my own, and its innermost nerves move according to my sense and my presentiment as my own. With the slightest trembling the holy embrace is dispersed, and now for the first time the intuition stands before me as a separate form; I survey it, and it mirrors itself in my open soul like the image of the vanishing beloved in the awakened eye of a youth; now for the first time the feeling works its way up from inside and diffuses itself like the blush of shame and desire on his cheek. This moment is the highest flowering of religion. If I could create it in you, I would be a god; may holy fate only forgive me that I have had to disclose more than the Eleusinian mysteries.

This is the natal hour of everything living in religion. But the same thing happens with it as with the first consciousness of human beings that retires into the darkness of an original and eternal creation and leaves behind for us only what it has produced.[19] I can only make present to you the intuitions and feelings that develop out of such moments. But let this be said to you: If you understand these ever so completely, if you believe you have them in clearest consciousness, but you do not know and cannot show that they have arisen in you from such moments and that they have been originally one and unseparated, then prevail upon yourself and me no further, for surely it is not so; your soul has never conceived. They are only illegitimate children, productions of other souls that you have adopted in the secret feeling of your own weakness. I would characterize such people as unholy and far from all divine life who thus parade around with religion and put on airs. The one individual has intuitions of the world and formulas that are supposed to express them, while the other has feelings and inner experiences by which to document them. The first braids formulas over one another, and the second weaves a scheme of salvation out of experiences; and now conflict ensues as to how many concepts and explanations and how many stirrings and sensations one has to lay hold of in order to *assemble* a sound religion from them that would be neither cold nor overenthused. You fools and slow of heart! Do you not know that all those things,

---

18 Like Plato, Schleiermacher holds that one comes to know the essence or nature of a thing (*Wesen*) only in its manifestation in finite form (*Gestalt*).

19 The reference to "eternal creation" appears to have been inspired by the Platonic myth of the transmigration of souls.

which your own reflection would have had to make, are only dissolutions of religious sensibility; and if you are not now conscious of having had something reflection was able to disintegrate, where then did you get these? You have memory and imitation, but no religion. You have not produced the intuitions for which you know the formulas, but have learned them by heart and preserved them, and your feelings are mimetically reproduced like alien physiognomies, and for just that reason are caricatures.

Do you want to put together a religion out of these dead and decayed fragments? One can break down the fluids of an organic body into its constituent parts; but now take these separated elements, mix them in every proportion, treat them in every way. Will you be able to make life's blood out of them again? Will what was once dead be able to move again in a living body and become one with it? Every human art runs aground in trying to restore the products of living nature out of their separated constituent parts, and thus you will not succeed in doing it with religion, even though you have imagined its individual elements ever so completely from outside; they must proceed from within. The divine life is like a tender plant whose blossoms are fertilized while enclosed in the bud, and the holy intuitions and feelings you are able to dehydrate and preserve are the beautiful calyxes and corollas that open soon after that secret action, but which also soon drop away again. Yet new blossoms always spring from the fullness of the inner life – for the divine plant forms a paradisiacal climate about itself that no season of the year can harm – and the old ones bestrew and thankfully adorn the earth that covers the roots from which they were nourished and still give up a fragrance in fond memory of the stem that bore them. From these buds and corollas and calyxes I intend to weave a holy wreath for you.

To external nature, which so many consider the first and foremost temple of divinity, the innermost sanctuary of religion, I lead you only as far as its outermost forecourt.[20] Neither fear of the material forces you see operating on this earth nor joy at the beauty of corporeal nature will or can give you the first intuition of this world and its spirit. Neither in the thunder of the heavens nor in the frightful rolling of the sea are you to recognize the presence of the almighty being; neither in the bloom of the flowers nor in the brilliance of the sunsets are you to recognize the lovely and benevolent. It may be that both fear and joyous pleasure first prepared the unrefined sons of the earth for religion, but these sentiments themselves are not religion. All presentiments of the invisible that have come to us in this way were not religious but philosophical, not intuitions of the world and its spirit – for they are merely glimpses of the incomprehensible and immeasurable particular – but a seeking and a searching for causation and primal power. These crude beginnings in religion are like everything else that belongs to the original simplicity of nature.

[20] Schleiermacher's resistance to a deification of nature is found in the following section, the themes of which recur in the Fifth Speech's critique of "natural religion."

Only so long as this simplicity is still there does this raw state have power to move the mind; thus it will attain the peak of perfection, on which we do not yet stand, perhaps transformed again into a higher form through art and caprice; but on the path of formation it inevitably and fortunately gets lost, for these crude beginnings would only restrict this cultivation's progress. We find ourselves on this path, and no religion can come to us through these motions of the mind. Indeed, it is the great aim of all diligence that is applied to the formation of the earth[21] that the dominance of the forces of nature over us would be annihilated and all fear of them cease. How, therefore, could we intuit the universe in what we endeavor to master and have in part already mastered? Jupiter's lightning no longer frightens us since Vulcan has prepared a shield against it. Vesta protects what she won from Neptune against the angriest blows of his trident, and the sons of Mars unite with those of Aesculapius in order to protect us against the quick and deadly arrows of Apollo. Thus, the one god annihilated the other, insofar as fear had formed them, and since Prometheus has taught us to bribe now this one, now that one, we stand as the victor, smiling about their general war.

To love the world spirit and joyfully observe its work is the goal of our religion, and in love there is no fear.[22] It is no different with those beauties of the terrestrial globe that the childlike person embraces with such heartfelt love. What is the delicate play of colors that delights your eye in all phenomena of the firmament and with so much pleasure attaches your gaze to the most lovely products of vegetative nature? What is it, not in your eyes, but in and for the universe? For thus you would have to ask if this delicate play is to have some significance for your religion. It disappears as an accidental appearance as soon as you think of the all-pervasive material whose developments it attends. Consider that you can rob all of this beauty from a plant in a dark cellar without destroying its nature; consider that the splendid appearance in whose tendrils your whole soul dwells is nothing other than that the same streams of light are only refracted differently in a greater sea of earthly vapors, that the same midday beams whose glare you cannot endure already appear to those in the East as glimmering twilight – and you must consider this, if you want to regard these things as a whole. You will then find that these phenomena, no matter how strongly they move you, are still not suited to be intuitions of the world. Perhaps someday, at a higher stage, we shall find that to which we are to submit here on earth spread abroad and ruling in the whole of space, and that then a holy thrill concerning the unity and universality of even corporeal power will fill us. Perhaps someday, we shall also be amazed to discover in this appearance the same spirit that animates the whole. But that will be something different from and higher than this fear and this love. Right now the heroes of reason among you do not need to ridicule the fact that some people wish

---

[21] Cf. Novalis, "Blütenstaub," *Ath.* I, p. 80, "We are on a mission: to form the earth [*zur Bildung der Erde*] is our calling."

[22] 1 John 4:18: "Perfect love casts out fear."

to guide fear and love to religion through humiliation under inanimate matter and through empty poetry, and the sensitive souls must not believe that religion might be so easily arrived at.

Certainly there is something more essential to be intuited in corporeal nature than this. Its infinity, the prodigious masses scattered in that boundless space that runs through immeasurable paths – are we not overcome with reverence at the thought and sight of the world? I only ask you not to identify as religion what you hereby feel. Space and mass do not make up the world and are not the material of religion; to seek the infinite in them is a childish way of thinking. When not half of those worlds were discovered, indeed, when it was not even known that the illuminated points were celestial bodies, the universe was nevertheless no less splendid to behold than now, and there was then no more excuse for the despisers of religion than now. Is not the most limited body just as infinite in this respect as all those worlds? The incapacity of your senses cannot be the pride of your spirit; and what does the spirit care about numbers and quantities, since it sums up the whole of infinity in little formulas and reckons with it just as with the most insignificant things? What actually appeals to the religious sense in the external world is not its masses but its laws. Raise yourselves to the view of how these laws embrace everything, the largest and the smallest, the world systems and the small mote of dust that flutters about restlessly in the air, and then say whether you do not intuit the divine unity and the eternal immutability of the world. What the common eye first perceives of these laws in this intuition of the universe is precisely the least: the order in which all movements return in heaven and on earth, the definite course of the stars and the uniform coming and going of all organic forces, the perpetual uniformity in the striving of malleable nature.

If you only consider a single fragment of a great work of art and in turn perceive in the individual parts of this fragment, outlines and proportions, quite beautiful in themselves, which are contained in this fragment and whose principle can be completely surveyed from this point, will not this fragment seem to you to be more a work in itself than a part of a work? Will you not conclude that the whole, if it is executed in this style throughout, would have to be lacking in inspiration and boldness and all that portends a great spirit? Wherever you suspect a sublime unity, a relationship that reflects greatness, there must necessarily be circumstances in the particular, in addition to the general tendency toward order and harmony, which cannot be completely understood in terms of the individual. Even the world is a work of which you survey only a part, and if this part were perfectly ordered and complete within itself, you would not be able to formulate any lofty concept of the whole. You see that the feature that is often meant to serve to reject religion actually has a greater value for it in its intuition of the world than the order that first presents itself and can be surveyed from a smaller part. In the religion of the ancients only lower deities and ministering virgins had superintendence over what uniformly recurs, whose order was already discovered. The deviations that were not understood, the revolutions for which there were no laws, were the work of the father of the gods. The perturbations in the course of the stars indicate a higher unity, a bolder combination than that which we have already proved true from the regularity of their paths, and the anomalies, the superfluous touches of malleable nature, compel us to see that it treats its most definite forms with an arbitrariness, with an inventiveness, as it were, whose principle we can discover only from a higher standpoint.[23]

How far distant we still are from that which would be the highest, and how incomplete, therefore, remains our intuition of the world! Consider the law according to which everywhere in the world, so far as you survey it, everything alive behaves toward that which in regard to itself can be considered as dead. See how everything living nourishes itself and forcibly draws dead matter into its life, how on all sides there presses in upon us the stored-up supply for everything living, which does not lie there dead but is itself living and everywhere reproduces itself anew, how with all the multiplicity of forms of life and the prodigious mass of material each form consumes in turn, each nevertheless has enough to run through the cycle of its existence, and each is subordinated only to an inner fate and not an external scarcity. What infinite fullness is revealed there, what superabundant riches! How we are seized by the impression of maternal provision and by childlike confidence to play away sweet life in the full and rich world without any cares. Consider the lilies of the field; they neither sow nor reap, and our heavenly Father still nourishes them; wherefore, do not worry.[24] But this happy sight, this serene and lighthearted mind was also the highest, indeed, the only thing one of the greatest heroes of religion obtained for his own religion from the intuition of nature. How very much nature must have been located only in the forecourt of religion!

Certainly a greater yield is vouchsafed to us who have been permitted by a richer age to penetrate deeper into nature's interior.[25] Its chemical powers, the eternal laws according to which bodies themselves are formed and destroyed, these are the phenomena in which we intuit the universe most clearly and in a most holy manner. See how attraction and repulsion determine everything and are uninterruptedly active everywhere, how all diversity and all opposition are only apparent and relative, and all individuality is merely an empty name. See how all likeness strives to conceal itself and to divide into a thousand diverse forms, and how nowhere do you find something simple, but everything is ornately connected and intertwined. That is the spirit of the world that reveals itself in the smallest things

---

[23] See Marshall Brown, *The Shape of German Romanticism* (Ithaca, NY, 1979), pp. 161–70, on the penchant of the Romantic mind for deviant, anomalous, and eccentric (literally, "outside the circle") phenomena as pointing to the need of a higher unity for their completion.

[24] Matthew 6:28–9; Luke 12:27–8. Although the descriptions of the forecourt of religion may be beautiful, even Jesus of Nazareth only had limited intuitions of external nature.

[25] These references to contemporary natural scientific theories allude to the organic and holistic perspective in the early works of Schelling.

just as perfectly and visibly as in the greatest; that is an intuition of the universe that develops out of everything and seizes the mind. But only the person who in fact sees it everywhere, who, not only in all alterations but in all existence, finds nothing else but a production of this spirit and a representation and execution of these laws, only to him is everything visible really a world, formed and permeated by divinity, and is one. Even with a total lack of all the knowledge that adorns our century, the oldest wise men of the Greeks did not, nevertheless, lack this view of nature, a clear proof of how everything that is religion spurns and easily dispenses with every external aid; and if this view had penetrated from the wise men to the people, who knows what exalted path their religion would have taken!

But what are love and resistance? What are individuality and oneness? Did you get these concepts, by means of which nature first actually becomes for you an intuition of the world, from nature? Do they not derive originally from the interior of the mind, and are they not first directed from there to nature? Therefore, it is also the mind to which religion actually looks and from which it takes intuitions of the world; the universe is portrayed in the inner life, and only through the internal is the external comprehensible. But even the mind, if it is to produce and sustain religion, must be intuited in a world.

Let me disclose to you a secret that lies concealed in one of the most ancient sources of poetry and religion.[26] As long as the first man was alone with himself and nature, the deity did indeed rule over him; it addressed the man in various ways, but he did not understand it, for he did not answer it; his paradise was beautiful and the stars shone down on him from a beautiful heaven, but the sense for the world did not open up within him; he did not even develop within his soul; but his heart was moved by a longing for a world, and so he gathered before him the animal creation to see if one might perhaps be formed from it. Since the deity recognized that his world would be nothing so long as man was alone, it created for him a partner, and now, for the first time, living and spiritual tones stirred within him; now, for the first time, the world rose before his eyes. In the flesh and bone of his bone he discovered humanity, and in humanity the world; from this moment on he became capable of hearing the voice of the deity and of answering it, and the most sacrilegious transgressions of its laws from now on no longer precluded him from association with the eternal being.

All our history is contained in this holy saga. Everything is present in vain for him who stands aloof; for in order to intuit the world and to have religion, man

---

[26] In turning to the biblical creation story of Genesis 2, a peopled garden is, as it were, substituted for a natural garden. The account of humanity's self-discovery illustrates Schleiermacher's dedication to the interhuman dimension of our experience. He does not recount the narrative of the fall and expulsion from paradise in Genesis 3; even in later years his theological orientation is more Johannine and incarnational, more focused on Christmas than on Good Friday. Yet pain and love go hand in hand in his basic view of religion; see "Sophie" in *Christmas Eve: Dialogue on the Incarnation*, trans. Terrence Tice (Richmond, VA, 1967), for whom joy and sorrow are often "strangely mixed up" (pp. 52, 56, 59).

must first have found humanity, and he finds it only in love and through love. This is why both are so deeply and indissolubly connected, longing for religion is what helps him to the enjoyment of religion. Each person embraces most ardently the one in whom the world is reflected most clearly and purely; each loves most tenderly the one in whom he believes he finds everything brought together that he himself lacks for the completion of humanity. Therefore, let us repair to humanity, that we may find the material for religion.

Here even you are in your most proper and beloved homeland. Your innermost life opens up in you. You see before yourselves the goal of all your striving and action, and simultaneously feel the inner drive of your powers, which constantly leads you toward that goal. Humanity itself is actually the universe for you, and you count everything else a part of this only to the extent that it comes into connection with humanity or surrounds it. I do not wish to lead you beyond this point of view; but it has often pained me deeply that, with all your love for humanity and all your zeal for it, you are nevertheless always embroiled and at odds with it. You labor to improve and educate it, each of you in his own manner, and in the end you disgruntledly leave behind whatever fails to produce the desired result. I may say, this also comes from your lack of religion. You wish to have an effect on humanity, and you look at individual persons. These displease you greatly; and among the thousand causes of your displeasure this is without doubt the most beautiful and one that belongs to the better among you: that in your own way you are entirely too moral. You take people individually, and thus you also have an ideal of an individual to which, however, they do not correspond. All of this together is a wrong beginning, and you will find yourselves far better off with religion. If you would only attempt to interchange the objects of your action and your intuition! Act on the individuals, but with your contemplation rise higher on the wings of religion to an infinite, undivided humanity. Seek it in every individual, look upon the existence of each as a revelation of it to you, and there can remain no trace of all that now oppresses you. I too, know how to pride myself on a moral disposition, I also know how to value human excellence, and, considered by themselves, common things can almost overwhelm me with the unpleasant feeling of disdain; but religion gives me an exceedingly great and splendid view of all.

Think of the genius of humanity as the most accomplished and universal artist. It can create nothing that would not have a unique existence. Living and significant features arise even where genius merely tests its colors or seems to sharpen its brush. The genius of humanity thus imagines countless forms and shapes them. Millions wear the garb of the age and are true images of its needs and its tastes; in others recollections of the prehistoric world or presentiments of a distant future are displayed. Some are the most sublime and striking reproductions of what is most beautiful and divine; others are grotesque products of the most original and fleeting mood of a virtuoso. It is irreligious to hold that humanity's genius prepares vessels of honor and vessels of dishonor;[27] you must consider nothing individually, but rejoice over each in the place where it stands. Everything that can be perceived simultaneously and, as it were, stands on one page belongs to a great historical picture that represents one moment of the universe. Would you despise that which elevates the main groups and gives life and fullness to the whole? Should individual heavenly forms not be exalted by having a thousand others bow down before them and by having someone see how everything looks to them and relates itself to them? There is actually something more than a trite simile in this notion. Eternal humanity is unweariedly busy in creating and in representing itself in the most varied ways in the provisional appearance of finite life.

What would be the point of the uniform repetition of a highest ideal whereby human beings, apart from time and circumstances, are after all actually identical, the same formula being merely combined with other coefficients? What would it be in comparison to this infinite variety of human appearances? Take whatever element of humanity you wish, and you will find each in every possible condition, from a nearly pure one – for nowhere will it be found completely pure – in every possible mixture with every other one, to nearly the most inseparable saturation with all the remaining elements – for this is also an unattainable extreme – with the mixture prepared in every possible way, in every variety and every rare combination. If you can still think of combinations you do not see, even this gap is a negative revelation of the universe, an indication that, given the requisite degree of the present temperature of the world, this mixture is not possible. Your imagination in this respect is a glimpse beyond the present limits of humanity, a truly divine inspiration, an involuntary and unconscious prophecy of what shall be in the future.

But just as this which is missing from the requisite infinite diversity is really not a deficiency, so also that which thus appears to you from your standpoint is not too much. Religion declares that oft-lamented abundance of the commonest forms of humanity, which always recur unchanged in a thousand copies, to be a sham. The eternal understanding dictates, and even the finite understanding can realize, that those forms in which the particular is most difficult to distinguish must stand most densely pressed upon one another. Yet each has something unique. None is like the other and in the life of each there is some moment, like the silvery flash in the melting process of baser metals, when, be it through the close approach of a higher being or through some sort of electrical shock, it is, as it were, raised out of itself and placed on the highest pinnacle of what it can be. For this moment it was created, in this it attended its definition, and after it the exhausted life force sinks back again. It is a special pleasure to help small souls to attain this moment or to observe them in it; but their whole existence must indeed appear superfluous and despicable to those who have never had this experience. Thus the existence of each one has a dual meaning in relation to the whole.

[27] Romans 9:21–2.

If I mentally halt the course of that restless bustle whereby everything human is intertwined and made dependent upon one another, I see that, according to their inner essence, all individuals are necessary supplements to the perfect intuition of humanity. One person shows me how every tiny fragment of humanity, if only the inner creative drive[28] that animates the whole can quietly progress in it, fashions itself into delicate and well-proportioned forms; another how, from want of a vivifying and unifying warmth, the hardness of the earthly material cannot be overcome or how, in an atmosphere that is too violently agitated, the innermost spirit is disturbed in its work and everything becomes insignificant and indiscernible. One person appears as the vulgar, animal portion of humankind, moved only by the first awkward stirrings of humanity;[29] another as the purest distilled spirit that, divorced from all that is base and unworthy, only hovers with a light step above the earth. All are there to show by their existence how these different parts of human nature work separately and in detail. Is it not enough if, among this countless multitude, there are yet always a few who, as the distinguished and higher representatives of humanity, strike one or another melodious chords that require no outside accompaniment and no subsequent resolution, but, through their inner harmony, enrapture and satisfy the whole soul in one tone? If I again observe the eternal wheels of humanity in their progress, then this vast interaction, where nothing movable is moved by itself alone and nothing moving moves only itself, must put me at considerable ease about your complaint that reason and soul, sensuality and ethical life, understanding and blind force appear in such separated proportions. Why do you see everything individually, which surely does not function individually and for itself? The reason of one person and the soul of another affect one another as deeply as could only happen in a single subject. Ethical life, which relates to our sensuality, is posited outside of it. Is its dominion, for that reason, more limited, and do you believe sensuality would be better ruled if ethical life were meted out to each individual in small, scarcely noticeable portions? The blind force that is attributed to the mass of humanity is, nevertheless, in its effect on the whole, not left to itself and to crude chance. Without being aware of it, understanding, which you find abundantly accumulated at other points, often directs this force, and force follows reason just as unknowingly in invisible bonds.

Thus the outlines of personality that appear so definite to you disappear from my

---

[28] The term "creative drive" (*Bildungstrieb*) had been used by Herder in a physical sense and by Schiller as an alternative to the more formal Kantian *Einbildungskraft* to designate the creative power of the human imagination.

[29] *Humanität*. The term, which appears once in the text as an alternative to the frequent use of *Menschheit*, here assumes the heightened meaning that was set forth in J. G. Herder's *Letters for the Advancement of Humanity* (1793–7), especially letters 27–9 (1794), *Sämtliche Werke* (Hildesheim, 1967), XVII, pp. 133–43, and his *Ideas toward a Philosophy of the History of Mankind* (1784ff.; Leipzig, 1841), pp. 125ff.; the subsequent argument of speech two qualifies his contemporaries' efforts to place *Humanität* at the center of the universe.

standpoint. The magic circle of prevailing opinions and epidemic feelings encompasses and plays upon everything. Like an atmosphere filled with dissolving and magnetic forces, this circle fuses and unites everything and, through a lively diffusion, places even what is most distant in active contact; it busily scatters the emanations of those in whom light and truth dwell independently so that they penetrate some people and illuminate the surface of others in a brilliant and striking manner. That is the harmony of the universe, the wondrous and great unity in its eternal work of art. But you blaspheme this splendor with your demands for a deplorable individualization because you, who are in the first forecourt of morality, and even there still occupied with the basics, despise a lofty religion. Your need is clearly enough indicated; would that you might only recognize and satisfy it! Look among all the occurrences in which this heavenly order is reflected to see if there is not one that reveals itself to you as a divine sign. Allow yourself to enjoy an old rejected concept,[30] and seek out among all the holy men in whom humanity is immediately revealed one who could be the mediator between your limited way of thinking and the eternal limits of the world; and when you have found him, go through all of humanity and let everything that heretofore appeared to you differently be illumined by the reflection of this new light.

From these wanderings through the whole realm of humanity, religion then returns to one's own self with sharpened meaning and better-formed judgment, and at last finds everything in itself that otherwise was gathered from most distant regions. When you have arrived there, you will find in yourselves not only the basic characteristics of what is most beautiful and vulgar, most noble and contemptible, which you have perceived in others as individual aspects of humanity. At various times not only will you discover in yourselves all the manifold levels of human powers, but all of the innumerable mixtures of different dispositions that you have intuited in the characters of others will appear to you as mere arrested moments of your own life. There were moments when, in spite of all distinctions of sex, culture, and external circumstances, you thought, felt, and acted this way, when you really were this or that person. You have really passed through all these different forms within your own order; you yourself are a compendium of humanity; in a certain sense your personality embraces the whole of human nature, and in all its versions this is nothing but your own self that is reproduced, clearly delineated, and immortalized in all its alterations. In whomever religion has thus worked back again inwardly and has discovered there the infinite, it is complete in that person in this respect; he no longer needs a mediator for some intuition of humanity, and he himself can be a mediator for many.

Yet you must intuit humanity not only in its being but also in its becoming; it too has a larger course that it does not retrace but on which it progresses; through

---

[30] An allusion to Christology, the human mediation of divinity, a theme that first comes fully to expression in the Fifth Speech.

its inner alterations it too is perfected into something higher and complete. By no
means does religion seek to hasten or direct this progress; it limits itself so that the
finite can work only on the finite. Rather, religion only wishes to observe and
perceive this progress as one of the great actions of the universe. To join the
different moments of humanity to one another and, from its succession, to divine
the spirit in which the whole is directed, that is religion's highest concern.

History, in the most proper sense, is the highest object of religion.[31] It begins
and ends with religion – for in religion's eyes prophecy is also history, and the two
are not to be distinguished from one another – and at all times all true history has
first had a religious purpose and proceeded from religious ideas. In its realm,
therefore, lies also the highest and most sublime intuitions of religion. Here you see
the transmigration of human spirits and souls, which otherwise seem like a delicate
literary creation, in more than one sense as a wondrous event of the universe for
comparing, with a sure standard, the different periods of humanity. Now after a
long interval in which nature could bring forth nothing similar, some distinguished
individual being returns who is just as he was before;[32] but only the seers recognize
this person, and only they shall judge the signs of different times by the effects of
this person. Soon a single moment of humanity returns just like its image that a
distant bygone time had left behind with you, and you shall recognize the path of
the universe and the formula of its laws from the various causes through which the
moment has now been produced. Soon the genius of some particular human
capacity, which here and there while rising and falling had already completed its
course, awakens from its slumber and appears to another place and under other
circumstances in a new life, and its quicker prosperity, its deeper action, its more
beautiful, more powerful form will indicate how much the climate of humanity has
improved and how much more suitable the soil has become for the nourishment of
nobler plants.

Here peoples and generations of mortals appear to you just as individual humans
appeared in our previous view.[33] Some peoples and generations are venerable and
spirited and powerfully and ceaselessly effective without regard to time and space.
Other peoples and generations are common and insignificant, only destined to give
a particular nuance to a single form of life or form of union, only really living and
noteworthy in one moment, only setting forth one thought, producing one concept,
and then rushing toward destruction so that this result of their most beautiful
flowering can be imprinted in another moment. Just as vegetable nature, through
the decline of whole species and from the ruins of whole generations of plants,

---

[31] "Gedanken I" (no. 85), *KGA* I.2, p. 25: "History is always religious and according to its nature
religion must be historical."

[32] The Platonic myth of the transmigration of souls (e.g., *Phaedrus* 256–7) reflects Schleiermacher's view
of the human soul as a microcosm of the universe.

[33] "Gedanken I" (no. 140), *KGA* I.2, p. 33: "The history of religiosity in the particular, compared with
that in the universal, as proof. Every search for truth in religion is blind faith, for it proceeds from the
premise that there is supposed to be belief."

brings forth and nourishes new ones, so you also see here how spiritual nature, from the ruins of a splendid and beautiful human world, produces a new one that absorbs its first life force from the decomposed and wonderfully transformed elements of the former.[34]

While intuiting a universal relationship your glance is so often led back and forth directly from the smallest to the greatest and from the latter back again to the former and moves between the two in living vibrations until it becomes dizzy and can distinguish neither great nor small, neither cause nor effect, neither preservation nor destruction any longer. There then appears to you the form of an eternal destiny whose features bear completely the mark of this condition, a strange mixture of inflexible obstinacy and deep wisdom, of vulgar, heartless force and heartfelt love, of which alternately sometimes the one seizes you and sometimes the other, while each in turn invites you to impotent defiance and childlike resignation. If you then compare the isolated striving of the individual, which has arisen from these contradictory views, with the calm and uniform progress of the whole, you see how the lofty world spirit smilingly strides across all that tumultuously opposes it. You see how the majestic Nemesis unweariedly follows its steps across the earth, how it administers chastisement and punishment to the haughty who resist the god, and how it mows down with an iron hand even the bravest and most excellent who, perhaps with laudable and admirable steadfastness, did not want to bow down before the gentle breath of the great spirit. If you finally want to grasp the actual character of all the changes and all the advances of humanity, religion shows you how the living gods hate nothing as much as death, how nothing but it shall be pursued and overthrown, the first and last enemy of humanity.[35] The vulgar, the barbaric, the misshapen shall be engulfed and transformed in an organic development. Nothing shall be a dead mass that is moved only by dead impact and resists only by unconscious friction. Everything shall be its own assembled, much intertwined, and elevated life. Blind instinct, unthinking habit, dead obedience, everything indolent and passive – all these sad symptoms of the asphyxia of freedom and humanity shall be annihilated. The work of the moment and of centuries points in this direction; that is the great, ever-continuous redemptive work of eternal love.

I have only lightly sketched some of the prominent religious intuitions from the realms of nature and humanity; but I have led you up to the final limit of your horizon. Here is the end of religion for those to whom humanity and the universe are of equal worth; from here I may only lead you back again to what is individual and smaller. Yet do not believe that this is at the same time the limit of religion. Rather, it cannot properly stop here, and only on the other side of this point does it gaze directly upon the infinite. If humanity itself is changeable and malleable, if it

---

[34] The depiction of the process of history as an organic unfolding of life, death, and rebirth is characteristic of the Romantic theory of history.

[35] 1 Corinthians 15:25: "The last enemy to be destroyed is death."

not only manifests itself differently in the particular but here and there also *becomes* different, do you not sense that it is impossible that humanity itself can be the universe? Rather, humanity itself is to the universe as individual persons are to humanity; it is only an individual form of the universe, a depiction of a single modification of its elements; there must be other such forms by which humanity is circumscribed and to which it is thus opposed. Humanity is only a middle term between the individual and the One, a resting place on the way to the infinite, and a still higher character would have to be found in the human being than our humanity in order to relate us and our appearance directly to the universe. All religion strives after such an intimation of something outside and above humanity in order to be seized by the common and the higher elements in both; but this is also the point where its outlines are lost to the common eye, where it removes itself ever farther from the individual objects by which it could cling to its way, and where its striving after the highest is regarded by most persons as folly.

This is sufficient reference to what lies so immeasurably far from you. Any further word about it would be an incomprehensible speech about which you would not know whence it came or where it was going. If only you had the religion you could have and only were conscious of what you already do have! In fact, if you just consider the few religious intuitions I have now lightly sketched, you will find that they are by far not all strange to you. Something like these intuitions has very likely entered your mind before. But I do not know which is the greater misfortune, to dispense with them altogether or not to understand them; for even then they completely fail to achieve their effect on your mind and you are thereby even deceived by yourselves.

Many among you are familiar with the retribution that strikes everything that tries to resist the spirit of the whole; with the hatred active everywhere toward everything haughty and insolent; and also with the continuous progress of all human things toward a goal. This progress is so certain that, even after many failed attempts, finally one day we nonetheless see each individual thought and plan succeed, which brings the whole closer to this goal. These are intuitions that catch the eye in such a way that they can be considered more an inducement to, than a result of, observation of the world. Many among you are also conscious of these, some even call them religion, but they want these to be religion exclusively; and thereby they want to repress everything else that nevertheless arises in the same way from the same operation of the mind.

How then have they arrived at these severed fragments? I want to tell you how. They do not at all consider this to be religion, which they despise in any case, but rather morals, and only want to slip in the term "religion" in order to give it – or what they consider to be religion – the final blow. If they do not wish to admit this, then ask them why, with an astonishing one-sidedness, they find all of this only in the realm of ethical life? Religion knows nothing of such partisan preference; for it the moral world is not the universe, and whatever would only be valid for morality would not be an intuition of the universe. In everything that belongs to human activity, in play as well as in seriousness, in the smallest things as well as in the greatest, religion knows how to discover and pursue the actions of the world spirit. What religion is supposed to perceive it must be able to perceive everywhere, for only thereby does religion acquire it as its own. And thus it also finds a divine Nemesis in the fact that the very people who, because they themselves are dominated by ethical life or legality, make religion into a mere insignificant appendage of morals, and only want to take from it whatever serves this end, thereby irretrievably ruin their morality, no matter how much it may already be purified, and thereby sow the seed of new errors. What they say sounds very beautiful; if someone succumbs while acting morally, it is the will of the eternal, and what may not come to pass through us will come into being another time. But even this sublime comfort is not necessary for ethical life; no drop of religion can be mixed with ethical life without, as it were, phlogisticating it[36] and robbing it of its purity.

This whole ignorance about religion reveals itself most clearly in their feelings, which are still most widely diffused among you. As deeply as such feelings are connected with those intuitions, as necessarily as they flow from them and can be explained only in terms of them, these feelings are nevertheless thoroughly misunderstood. When the world spirit has majestically revealed itself to us, when we have overheard its action guided by such magnificently conceived and excellent laws, what is more natural than to be permeated by a heartfelt reverence in the face of the eternal and invisible? And when we have intuited the universe and, looking back from that perspective upon our self, see how, in comparison with the universe, it disappears into infinite smallness, what can then be more appropriate for mortals than true unaffected humility? When we also perceive our fellow creatures in the intuition of the world and it is clear to us how each of them without distinction is his own representation of humanity just as we are, and how we would have to dispense with intuiting this humanity without the existence of each one, what is more natural than to embrace them all with heartfelt love and affection without any distinction of disposition and spiritual power? And when we look back from their connection with the whole to their influence on what happens to us, and then consider those who have diminished their own transient nature and the drive to enlarge and to isolate it in order to maintain ours, how can we refrain from feeling a special kinship with those whose actions once defended our existence and happily guided it through its dangers? How can we refrain from that feeling of gratitude that prompts us to honor them as people who have already united themselves with the whole and are conscious of the same in their lives?

When we, on the contrary, consider the normal drives of those who know

---

[36] The German *zu phlogistisieren* refers to the eighteenth-century scientific belief (disproved by Antoine Lavoisier [d. 1794]) in a subtle, inflammable substance called phlogiston.

nothing of this dependence,[37] we see how they seize and hold on to this and that in order to fortify and surround themselves with many external deeds, so that they might conduct their isolated lives according to their own free choice and so that the eternal stream of the world might not disturb any of it for them. We also see how fate then necessarily makes all of this hazy and wounds and tortures them in a thousand ways. What is more natural than the most heartfelt compassion toward all the pain and suffering that arise from this unequal battle and toward all the blows that dread Nemesis deals out on all sides? And when we have found out what is everywhere preserved and promoted in the course of humanity and must sooner or later inevitably be vanquished and destroyed if it cannot be transformed or changed, we regard our own action in the world in light of this law. What is more natural than overwhelming remorse over everything in us that is hostile to the genius of humanity; what is more natural than the humblest desire to be reconciled to the deity, than the most ardent longing to turn back and save ourselves, along with all that is ours, in that holy realm that alone is security against death and destruction?

All these feelings are religion, and likewise all others in which the universe is one pole and your own self is somehow the other pole between which consciousness hovers. The ancients certainly knew this. They called all these feelings "piety" and referred them immediately to religion, considering them its noblest part.[38] You also know them, but when you encounter something of this sort you wish to persuade yourselves that it is something moral, and assign these sentiments their place in morality; but it neither desires nor endures them. Morals do not like love and affection, but activity, which proceeds wholly from within and is not produced by considering its external object; they know no other awe than that for their own law;[39] they condemn as impure and self-seeking whatever can occur out of compassion and gratitude; they abase, indeed despise, humility; and if you speak of remorse, they think of lost time that you unprofitably prolong. Your innermost feeling must also assent to morality's view that all of these sentiments are not intended to produce action; as functions of your innermost and highest life they are self-contained in their own coming and going. Why do you contort yourselves, therefore, and ask mercy for them, if they do not belong there? If it should please you to realize that these sentiments are religion, you need ask nothing for them except their own strict right, and you will not deceive yourselves with unfounded

---

[37] The sole use of the term "dependence" (*Abhängigkeit*) in 1799 foreshadows Schleiermacher's mature definition of religion as "the feeling of utter dependence" in *The Christian Faith* (Edinburgh, 1928), proposition 4.

[38] See, e.g., Cicero, who distinguishes piety (*pietas*) and religion (*religio*) from superstition (*superstitio*) and defends the former beliefs and practices against atomism and astral determinism in *De natura deorum, De divinatione*, and *De fato*.

[39] An allusion to Kant's belief that "duty is the necessity of an action executed from respect for law" in *Foundations of the Metaphysics of Morals* (New York, 1959), p. 16, where respect (*Achtung*) is close to a sense of reverence or awe (*Ehrfurcht*).

46

claims that you are inclined to make in their name. But when you find similar feelings in morals or some other area, they have merely been usurped. Bring them back to religion, to which this treasure alone belongs; and as the possessor of the same, religion is not the servant of morals or anything else that is an object of human action, but the indispensable friend and their unexceptionable advocate and intermediary with humanity.

That is the level on which religion stands, especially that which is autonomous in it, its feelings. That religion alone gives universality to man I have already implied; now I can explain it more clearly. In all action, be it moral or philosophical or artistic, one is supposed to strive for virtuosity, and virtuosity always limits and makes things cold, one-sided, and hard. It directs the human mind first to one point, and this one point is always something finite. Can we, advancing from one limited work to another, really exhaust our whole infinite energy? Will not, rather, the greater part of it lie unused, and consequently turn against us and consume us? How many of you go to ruin simply because they are too great for themselves! An excess of energy and drive, which never results in a deed because none would be appropriate to it, drives these people restlessly about and is their destruction. Do you want to curb this evil again by having him, for whom one object is too great, unite all three of those objects of human striving or, if you know of still more objects, these also?[40] That would certainly be your old desire, to have humanity everywhere out of one mold that ever returns – yet if that were only possible! If only those pursuits, as soon as they individually catch our eye, did not stimulate the mind in the same way and strive to rule. Each of them wants to produce works, each has an ideal toward which it strives and a totality it wants to attain, and this rivalry cannot end except in the one suppressing the others.

To what end, therefore, is man supposed to use the energy that each regulated and expert application of his creative drive[41] leaves behind for him? He should not use it in such a way that he would want to shape something else again and actively work toward some other finite end, but so that, without definite activity, he would allow himself to be affected by the infinite and would reveal his reaction to this influence through every type of religious feeling. Whichever of those pursuits of your free and expert action you have chosen, it requires only a little thought to find the universe from each vantage point, and in this you also discover the rest as its command, inspiration, and revelation. Thus to contemplate and to consider them in the whole, not as something isolated and defined in themselves, is the only way in which, having already chosen a mental direction, you can also appropriate whatever lies outside that direction, not once again arbitrarily as art, but as religion, from an instinct for the universe. Because the pursuits again rival one another even in the form of religion, religion also appears more frequently isolated as natural poetry,

[40] The notion of unifying art, philosophy, and religion, here being criticized, was central to the new "poesie" of Friedrich Schlegel and Novalis.
[41] See n. 28 above.

natural philosophy, or natural morality, rather than completed in its whole form and unifying everything. Thus man posits an infinite beside the finite to which his free choice drives him, an expansive hovering in indeterminability and inexhaustibility alongside the contracting striving for something determinate and complete. Thus he creates an infinite release for his excess of energy and restores the equilibrium and harmony of his being that is irretrievably lost if he gives way to one particular direction without simultaneously having religion. A person's virtuosity is, as it were, merely the melody of his life; and it remains individual tones if he does not add religion to it. The latter accompanies the former in ever-richer variation with all the tones that are not fully repugnant to it, and thus transforms the simple song of life into a full-voiced and magnificent harmony.

If this, which I hope I have indicated clearly enough for all of you, actually makes up the essence of religion, then the question of the proper place of those dogmas and propositions that are commonly passed off as the content of religion is not too difficult to answer.[42] Some are merely abstract expressions of religious intuitions, and others are free reflections upon original achievements of the religious sense, the results of a comparison of the religious with the common view. To take the content of a reflection to be the essence of the action being reflected upon is such a common mistake that you must not wonder if it is also found here. Miracles, inspirations, revelations, feelings of the supernatural – one can have much religion without coming into contact with any of these concepts. But persons who reflect comparatively about their religion inevitably find concepts in their path and cannot possibly get around them. In this sense, all these concepts surely do belong to the realm of religion, indeed, belong unconditionally, without one being permitted to define the least thing about the limits of their application. The conflict about which event is actually a miracle and wherein the character of a miracle properly consists, over how much revelation there might be and the extent to which and the reasons why one might believe in it, and the obvious effort to deny and to push aside as much as may be done with propriety and discretion in the foolish opinion of thereby doing a service to philosophy and reason, all of these are the childish operations of the metaphysicians and moralists in religion. They confuse all points of view and bring religion into the disrepute of encroaching upon the totality of scientific and empirical judgments. I beg you not to let yourselves be confused, to the detriment of religion, by their sophistical disputations and their hypocritical secrecy about that which they would be all too pleased to make known. However loudly religion demands back all those defamed concepts, it leaves you, your physics, and, may it please God, your psychology inviolate.

What, then, is a miracle? Yet tell me in what language – I am indeed not talking about those which, like ours, have arisen after the decline of all religion – it means anything other than a sign, an indication. And so all these expressions indicate

---

42 "Gedanken I" (no. 86), *KGA* I.2, p. 25: "Dogmas – even original ones – are only born from the religious sense, and afterwards only the skull [*caput mortuum*] of the religious sense is left behind."

nothing else than the immediate relation of a phenomenon to the infinite or universe; but does that exclude just such an immediate connection to the finite and to nature? "Miracle" is merely the religious name for event, every one of which, even the most natural and usual, is a miracle as soon as it adapts itself to the fact that the religious view of it can be the dominant one. To me everything is a miracle, and for me what alone is a miracle in your mind, namely, something inexplicable and strange, is no miracle in mine. The more religious you would be, the more you would see miracles everywhere; every conflict as to whether individual events deserve to be so named only gives me the most painful impression of how poor and inadequate is the religious sense of the combatants. Some prove it by protesting against miracles everywhere, and others by thinking it all depends for them on this and that particular miracle and that a phenomenon must be shaped miraculously in order to be a miracle for them.

What is revelation? Every original and new intuition of the universe is one, and yet all individuals must know best what is original and new for them. And if something of what was original in them is still new for you, then their revelation is also one for you, and I advise you to ponder it well. What is inspiration? It is merely the religious name for freedom. Every free action that becomes a religious act, every restoration of a religious intuition, every expression of a religious feeling that really communicates itself so that the intuition of the universe is transferred to others, took place upon inspiration; for it was an action of the universe by the one on the others. Every anticipation of the other half of a religious event when the one half is given is a prophecy; it was very religious of the ancient Hebrews to measure the divineness of a prophet not by how difficult his prophecy was but quite simply by the outcome,[43] for one cannot know whether someone understands religion until one sees whether he has rightly conceived the religious view of this particular thing that affected that person. What are operations of grace? All religious feelings are supernatural, for they are religious only insofar as they are produced directly by the universe; whether they are religious in oneself, each person must judge best.

All these concepts are the first and most essential ones, if religion must indeed have some concepts. They indicate in a most characteristic manner human consciousness of religion; they are all the more important because they identify not only something that may be in religion universally, but precisely what must be in it universally. Indeed, a person who does not see his own miracle from his standpoint of contemplating the world, in whose interior his own revelations do not arise when his soul longs to drink in the beauty of the world and be permeated in its spirit; a person who does not now and again feel with vivid conviction that a divine spirit is driving him and that he speaks and acts out of holy inspiration; a person who is not at least – for this is actually the lowest level – conscious of his feelings as immediate influences of the universe and recognizes something characteristic in them that

---

[43] Deuteronomy 18:22.

cannot be imitated, but which guarantees the purity of their origin by his innermost being, such a person has no religion.

What one commonly calls belief, accepting what another person has done, wanting to ponder and empathize with what someone else has thought and felt, is a hard and unworthy service, and instead of being the highest in religion, as one supposes, it is exactly what must be renounced by those who would penetrate into its sanctuary. To want to have and retain belief in this sense proves that one is incapable of religion; to require this kind of faith from others shows that one does not understand it. You wish to stand on your own feet in all areas and go your own way, but this worthy intent should not frighten you away from religion. Religion is no enslavement and no imprisonment; even here you shall belong to yourselves; indeed this is even the sole condition under which you can share in it.

Except for a few chosen ones, every person surely needs a mediator, a leader who awakens his sense for religion from its first slumber and gives him an initial direction. But this is supposed to be merely a passing condition. A person should then see with his own eyes and should himself make a contribution to the treasures of religion; otherwise he deserves no place in its kingdom and also receives none. You are right to despise the paltry imitators who derive their religion wholly from someone else or cling to a dead document by which they swear and from which they draw proof. Every holy writing is merely a mausoleum of religion, a monument that a great spirit was there that no longer exists; for if it still lived and were active, why would it attach such great importance to the dead letter[44] that can only be a weak reproduction of it? It is not the person who believes in a holy writing who has religion, but only the one who needs none and probably could make one for himself. Exactly this contempt of yours for the miserable and powerless venerators of religion, in whom it already died from lack of nourishment before it was born, proves to me that there is a capacity for religion in you. The respect you always pay to its true heroes, and your rebellion against the way in which they have been misused and disgraced through idolatry, confirms me in this opinion.

I have shown you what religion actually is. Have you found anything therein that would be unworthy of your highest human formation? Must you not, in accord with the eternal laws of spiritual nature, yearn all the more anxiously for the universe and strive for a self-effected union with it the more you are separated and isolated by the most specific formation and individuality? And have you not often felt this holy longing as something unknown? Become conscious of the call of your innermost nature, I beseech you, and follow it. Dispel the false modesty in front of an age that is not supposed to define you but that is supposed to be defined and made by you! Turn back to what lies so close to you, especially to you, for whom a violent separation unfailingly destroys the most beautiful part of your existence.

[44] 2 Corinthians 3:6.

Yet it seems to me that many among you would not believe that I could wish to end my present business here, as if you were of the opinion that the essence of religion cannot really have been thoroughly addressed where nothing at all has been said about immortality and as good as nothing about divinity. Yet remember, I beg you, how from the beginning I have declared myself against these being considered the hinge and chief articles of religion; remember that when I sketched its outlines I indicated the way in which divinity is to be found. What then do you still stand to lose? And why should I do more for one kind of religious intuition than for others? But lest you think I am afraid to say a proper word about divinity because it would be dangerous to speak about it before a judicially valid definition of God and existence had been brought to light and sanctioned in the German empire;[45] or, on the other hand, lest you believe that I am perpetrating a pious fraud and, in order to be all things to all people,[46] wish to disparage with apparent indifference what must be for me of far greater importance than I am willing to admit, I want to explain myself a moment longer. I shall try to make clear to you that for me divinity can be nothing other than a particular type of religious intuition. The rest of the religious intuitions are independent of it and of each other. From my standpoint and according to my conceptions that are known to you, the belief "No God, no religion" cannot occur, and I shall also openly state my opinion to you concerning immortality.

Yet first tell me what they mean by divinity and what you intend it to mean. For that legal definition is still not available, and it is obvious that the greatest differences prevail concerning it. To most people God is obviously nothing more than the genius of humanity. Man is the prototype of their God, humanity is everything to them, and in accord with what they consider its events and directives they determine the dispositions and the essence of their God. But now I have told you clearly enough that humanity is not everything to me, that my religion strives for a universe of which humanity, with all that belongs to it, is only an infinitely small part, only one particular transient form. Can a God who would be merely the genius of humanity thus be the highest being of my religion? There may be minds that are more poetic, and I confess that I believe these stand higher, for whom God is an individual being wholly distinct from humanity, the single example of a particular type, and if they show me the revelations through which they know such a God – one or more revelations, for I despise nothing in religion as much as numbers – that will constitute a desired discovery for me, and certainly from this revelation several more will develop in me. But I strive for even more types of beings than one above and beyond humanity, and every class, with its individual being, is subordinated to the universe. Can God in this sense thus be for me anything else than an individual intuition? Yet these may be only incomplete

---

[45] Allusion is made to the "atheism controversy," which in March 1799 led to the dismissal of Fichte from his Jena professorship.

[46] 1 Corinthians 9:22.

concepts of God. If we immediately proceed to the highest concept, to that of a highest being, of a spirit of the universe that rules it with freedom and understanding, religion is still not dependent upon this idea. To have religion means to intuit the universe, and the value of your religion depends upon the manner in which you intuit it, on the principle that you find in its actions. Now if you cannot deny that the idea of God adapts itself to each intuition of the universe, you must also admit that one religion without God can be better than another with God.

To the unrefined person who has only a confused idea and only a dim instinct of the whole and of the infinite, the universe presents itself as a unity in which nothing manifold is to be distinguished, as a chaos uniform in its confusion, without division, order, and law, and from which nothing individual can be separated except by its being arbitrarily cut off in time and space.[47] For such an individual, who is without any impulse to animate this chaos, blind chance represents the character of the whole; with this impulse, his God becomes a being without definite qualities, an idol or a fetish, and if he accepts several of these, such beings can only be distinguished by the arbitrarily established limits of their realms. At another level of formation, the universe presents itself as a multiplicity without unity, as an indeterminate manifold of heterogeneous elements and forces whose constant and eternal conflict determines its manifestations. Blind chance denotes not its character but a motivated necessity in which one has the task of searching for its foundation and interconnection, with the consciousness of never being able to find it. If the idea of a God is added to this universe, it naturally disintegrates into infinitely many parts, and each of these forces and elements in which there is no unity becomes especially animated; gods arise in infinite number, differentiated by the various objects of their activity, by different inclinations and dispositions. You must admit that this intuition of the universe is infinitely more worthy than the former; do you not also have to admit that the one who has elevated himself to it, but who without the idea of gods bows down before eternal and unattainable necessity, still has more religion than the crude worshipper of a fetish? Now let us climb still higher to the point where all conflict is again united, where the universe manifests itself as totality, as unity in multiplicity, as system and thus for the first time deserves its name. Should not the one who intuits it as one and all thus have more religion, even without the idea of God, than the most cultured polytheist? Should Spinoza not stand just as far above a pious Roman, as Lucretius does above one who serves idols? But that is the old inconsistency that is the gloomy sign of a lack of cultivation, that they reject most vehemently those who stand on the same level as themselves, only at a different point on that level!

Which of these intuitions of the universe we appropriate depends on our sense of

[47] The rudimentary classification of philosophical and religious worldviews into the tripartite scheme of chaos, multiplicity, and unity in multiplicity (which in the history of religion correspond to animism, polytheism, and monotheism) recurs in the Fifth Speech; cf. his mature systematic theology in *The Christian Faith*, proposition 8, pp. 34–8.

the universe. This is the proper measure of our religiousness; whether we have a God as a part of our intuition depends on the direction of our imagination. In religion the universe is intuited; it is posited as originally acting on us. Now if your imagination clings to the consciousness of our freedom in such fashion that it cannot come to terms with what it construes as originally active other than in the form of a free being, then imagination will probably personify the spirit of the universe and you will have a God. If your imagination clings to understanding in such fashion that you always clearly see that freedom only has meaning in the particular and for the particular instance, then you will have a world and no God.

You will not consider it blasphemy, I hope, that belief in God depends on the direction of the imagination. You will know that imagination is the highest and most original element in us, and that everything besides it is merely reflection upon it;[48] you will know that it is our imagination that creates the world for you, and that you can have no God without the world. Moreover, God will not thereby become less certain to anyone, nor will individuals be better able to emancipate themselves from the nearly immutable necessity of accepting a deity because of knowing whence this necessity comes. In religion, therefore, the idea of God does not rank as high as you think. Among truly religious persons there have never been zealots, enthusiasts, or fanatics for the existence of God; with great equanimity they were aware of what one calls atheism alongside themselves, for there has always been something that seemed to them more irreligious than this. Even God cannot be imagined in religion except as active, and no one has ever denied the divine life and activity of the universe; religion has nothing to do with the existing and commanding God just as its God is of no use to the physicist or moralist whose sad misunderstandings these are and always will be. But this acting God of religion cannot guarantee our happiness; a free being cannot wish to affect another free being except by making itself known to the other, regardless of whether through pain or pleasure. He also cannot incite us to ethical life, for he is not considered other than as acting, and there can neither be any action upon our ethical life, nor can we conceive of any.

But concerning immortality, I cannot conceal that the way in which most people take it and their longing after it is completely irreligious, exactly contrary to the spirit of religion. Their wish has no other basis than their aversion to that which is the goal of religion. Recall how in religion everything strives to expand the sharply delineated outlines of our personality and gradually to lose them in the infinite in order that we, by intuiting the universe, will become one with it as much as possible. But they resist the infinite and do not wish to get beyond themselves; they wish to be nothing other than themselves and they are anxiously concerned about their individuality. Recall how it was the highest goal of religion to discover a universe beyond and above humanity, and its only complaint was that this goal

[48] The centrality of imagination (*Fantasie*) in Schleiermacher reflects its pivotal position in contemporary philosophy and aesthetic theory.

would not properly succeed in this world. But they do not want to seize the sole opportunity death affords them to transcend humanity; they are anxious about how they will take it with them beyond this world, and their highest endeavor is for further sight and better limbs. But the universe speaks to them, as it stands written: "Whoever loses his life for my sake, will find it, and whoever would save it will lose it."[49] The life they would keep is lamentable, for if it is the eternity of their person that concerns them, why do they not attend just as anxiously to what they have been as to what they will be? How does going forward help them if they cannot go backward? In search of an immortality, which is none, and over which they are not masters, they lose the immortality that they could have, and in addition their mortal life with thoughts that vainly distress and torment them. But try to yield up your life out of love for the universe. Strive here already to annihilate your individuality and to live in the one and all; strive to be more than yourselves so that you lose little if you lose yourselves; and if you have fused with as much of the universe as you find here and a greater and holier longing has arisen in you, then we will want to speak further about the hopes death gives to us and concerning the infinity to which we unerringly soar through it.[50]

That is my sentiment concerning these matters. God is not everything in religion, but one, and the universe is more; furthermore, you cannot believe in him by force of will or because you want to use him for solace and help, but because you must. Immortality may not be a wish unless it has first been a task you have carried out. To be one with the infinite in the midst of the finite and to be eternal in a moment, that is the immortality of religion.

[49] Matthew 10:39; Mark 8:35; Luke 9:24; 17:33; John 12:25.
[50] Cf. the function of night, darkness, and death as metaphors of infinity, and especially the final hymn, "Longing for death," in Novalis's *Hymns to the Night*, trans. Charles E. Passage (New York, 1960), which was completed in December 1799–January 1800 and appeared in the *Ath.* III, p. 188; John Neubauer, *Novalis* (Boston, 1980), p. 90, observes that "Schlegel's urging that Novalis make use of his 'artistic sense for death' was probably prompted by conversations with the theologian Friedrich Schleiermacher, who was at the time finishing his speeches."

Third Speech
On Self-Formation[1] for Religion

What I myself have freely confessed as deeply lodged in the character of religion, the endeavor to make proselytes out of unbelievers, is nevertheless not what impels me to speak to you now about the formation of humans toward this sublime capacity and about its conditions.[2] Religion knows no other means to that final goal than that it expresses and imparts itself freely.

When religion stirs with all its own power, when in the flow of this movement it sweeps along with it every faculty of one's mind into its service, it thus also expects to penetrate to the innermost being of every individual who breathes its atmosphere. Every homogeneous particle will be touched and, seized by the same vibration, the awaiting ear of a seeker will rejoice upon attaining consciousness of its existence through an answering, kindred tone. Only in this way, through the natural expressions of its own life, does religion wish to arouse what is similar. Where this is not successful, it proudly disdains every external attraction, every violent procedure, calmed in the conviction that the hour is not yet present in which something congenial to itself could stir. This unsuccessful outcome is not new to me. How often have I struck up the music of my religion in order to move

---

[1]   The task of finding adequate equivalents for the German *Bildung* (which is variously rendered by "education," "cultivation," "conscious development," "development," and "formation") is daunting. "Self-formation" echoes the German *Selbstbildung*, which is used in the First Speech, and the idea of forming oneself (*um sich zu bilden*) used in this speech; it captures the notion of "form" of *bilden*, while the addition of "self" connects the idea of development with the immediacy of self-discovery that features prominently in German philosophy and literature of the period.

[2]   On the theme of *Bildung* in the era, see J. G. Herder, *Letters for the Advancement of Humanity* (1793–7), especially letter 27 (1794), "That which is divine in our species is thus *Bildung*, aiming at humanity," *Sämtliche Werke* (Hildesheim, 1967), XVII, p. 138; the impact of Goethe's *Wilhelm Meister* and the genre of the *Bildungsroman* is seen in *Ath.* I in Novalis's "Blütenstaub," p. 78 ("The highest task of *Bildung* is to take possession of one's transcendental self, to be the self of one's self") and in Schlegel's review, "Über Goethe's Meister," pp. 323–54; cf. F. Schiller, *On the Aesthetic Education of Man*, trans. Reginald Snell (New York, 1954 [original 1795]), on the artistic formation of selfhood as the central task of the age.

those present, beginning with soft individual tones and longingly progressing with youthful impetuosity to the fullest harmony of religious feelings? Yet nothing stirred and responded in them! From how many of them will even these words, which I entrust to a greater and more versatile atmosphere, with all the good things they ought to offer, sadly return to me without being understood, without even having aroused the slightest inkling of their purpose? How often shall I, and all proclaimers of religion, still repeat this fate, which was allotted to us from the beginning? Nevertheless, it will never distress us, for we know that fate must not happen differently; and we shall never attempt to impose our religion in some other way, either upon this or upon a future generation.

Since I find missing in myself not a little what belongs to the whole of humanity and since so many are lacking so much, is it any wonder if the number of those to whom religion is denied is great? And it must necessarily be great, for how else would we come to an intuition of religion itself and the boundaries for the other human capacities that it stakes out in all directions? How else would we know how much a person can achieve here and there without religion and where it holds up and furthers him? How else would we surmise that religion is active in him even without his knowing it? It is especially in keeping with the nature of things that in these times of universal confusion and upheaval its slumbering spark will not flare up in many people and no matter how lovingly and patiently we might tend it, it will not be brought to life, while under more fortunate circumstances, the spark would have worked its own way in them through all obstacles. Where nothing among all human things remains unshaken, each of us sees that precisely what determines our place in the world and binds us to the earthly order of things is every moment on the verge not only of eluding us and of allowing itself to be seized by something else but of sinking in the universal maelstrom.[3] Some people spare no exertion of their powers and call for help in all directions in order to retain what they regard as the hinges of the world and of the society of art and science, which now lift themselves up by an incomprehensible fate as if by themselves from their innermost roots and let fall what had revolved around them for so long. Other people, with equally restless zeal, are busy clearing the rubble of collapsed centuries out of the way in order to be among the first to settle on the fruitful ground that forms underneath them from the rapidly cooling lava of the dread volcano. Individual persons, even without leaving their places, are so powerfully affected by the violent convulsions of the whole that, in the universal vertigo, they must be happy to fix their eye on any one particular object firmly enough to hold on to it and to be able gradually to convince themselves that something may still be standing after all. In such a situation it would be foolish to expect that many could be sufficiently deft to perceive the infinite. Its appearance is, to be sure, more majestic and sublime than

---

[3] Like his contemporaries, Schleiermacher had keenly observed the course of the French Revolution by which the Directory (1795–9) succeeded the Reign of Terror (1793–4); by 1799 his view of the revolution had become increasingly skeptical.

ever, and there are moments when one can discern more significant characteristics than have appeared in centuries. But who can save himself in the face of the universal activity and pressure? Who can escape the power of a more limited interest? Who has enough calm and stability to stand quietly and intuit?

But even in the happiest of times, even with the best intent, where is the person who can arouse through communication the capacity for religion not only where it already is, but also implant it and inculcate it on every path that could lead to that? The only thing you can effect in other people through art and external activity is to communicate your thoughts to them and make them a storehouse of your ideas, and interweave them so closely with their ideas until they recall them at an opportune time. But you can never cause them to bring forth from themselves those ideas that you wish.[4]

You see the contradiction that already cannot be eliminated from the words. You cannot even accustom another person to have a particular reaction each time a particular impression may occur; much less could you bring anyone to transcend this connection and thereby to produce freely an inner activity. In brief, you can affect the mechanism of the spirit, but you cannot penetrate into its organization, into this holy workshop of the universe, according to your own whim. There you are not able to alter or displace some part of it, to delete from or add to it; you can only retard its development and forcibly stunt a part of its growth. But everything that belongs to a truly human life and that should be an ever more active and effective drive in us must proceed from the innermost part of our constitution. Religion is of this nature. In the mind in which it dwells it is uninterruptedly active and living, making everything into an object for itself and every thought and action into a theme of its heavenly imagination. Everything that, like religion, is supposed to be a continuum in the human mind lies far beyond the realm of teaching and inculcating. To everyone who views religion in this fashion, "instruction" in it is therefore a tasteless and meaningless word. We can, to be sure, communicate our opinions and doctrines to others; for that we need only words and they need only the comprehending and imitative power of the spirit. But we know very well that our words are only shadows of our intuitions and feelings, and without sharing these with us they would not understand what they say and what they believe they think.

We cannot teach them to intuit. We cannot transfer from ourselves to them the power and knack of absorbing everywhere the original light of the universe into our senses, no matter which objects we nevertheless find before ourselves. Perhaps we can arouse the mimetic talent of their imagination to the extent that it becomes easy

---

[4] The hermeneutical reflection anticipates Schleiermacher's recognition of the need for an active, "rigorous art of interpretation," which "presupposes that the speaker and hearer differ in their use of language and in their ways of formulating thoughts, although to be sure there is an underlying unity between them" (*Hermeneutics: The Handwritten Manuscripts*, ed. Heinz Kimmerle, trans. James Duke and Jack Forstman [Missoula, MT, 1977], p. 110).

for them, when intuitions of religion are painted for them in bold colors, to produce in themselves some stirrings that remotely resemble those they see filling our souls. But does that penetrate to their being? Is that religion? If you want to compare the sense for the universe with an artistic sense, you must not compare these possessors of a passive religiousness – if one still wishes to call it religiousness – with persons who, without themselves bringing forth works of art, are nevertheless touched and seized by everything that strikes their intuition. For religious works of art are always exhibited everywhere; the whole world is a gallery of religious views, with each individual being placed in the midst of them. You must rather compare them to those who have no sensation until one prescribes for them commentaries and imaginative interpretations of works of art like medicine and who even then, in an artificial language that is poorly understood, only stammer a few inappropriate words that are not their own. That is the goal of all teaching and intentional formation in these things.

Show me someone in whom you have inculcated or implanted the power of judgment, the spirit of observation, aesthetic feeling, or morality and I shall then pledge myself also to teach religion. In religion there is, of course, a mastership and discipleship. There are individuals to whom thousands attach themselves, but this attachment is no blind imitation and they are not disciples because their master has made them into this; he is rather their master because they have chosen him as that. He who, by expressing his own religion, has aroused it in others no longer has it in his power to keep them for himself; their religion is also free as soon as it lives and goes its own way. As soon as the holy spark flares up in a soul, it expands into a free and living flame that draws its sustenance from its own atmosphere. It more or less illuminates for the soul the whole extent of the universe, and by its own choice this soul can settle even far away from the point at which it first beheld itself. Forced to alight in some particular region only by the feeling of its incapacity and its finitude and without being ungrateful to its first guide, it chooses every climate that pleases it best; there it seeks a center for itself, moves in its new path through free self-limitation, and calls that person its master who first took this up as its favorite region and presented it in its splendor, becoming a disciple as a matter of choice and free love.

It is not, therefore, as though I wanted to cultivate you or others for religion or teach you how to form yourselves intentionally and skillfully to that end. I do not want to go beyond the sphere of religion, which I would thereby do; I wish rather to tarry with you a little longer within its sphere. The universe creates its own observers and admirers, and we only wish to intuit how that happens as far as it allows itself to be intuited. You know that the manner in which each single element of humanity appears in an individual depends upon the manner in which it is limited or set free by the rest; only through this general conflict does each element in each individual attain a definite form and magnitude, and this conflict is sustained, in turn, only through the community of individuals and the movement of the whole. Hence everything is a work of the universe and only thus can religion regard humans. I would like to lead you back to this basis of our limited existence and to the religious limitation of our contemporaries; I would like to make clear to you why we are this way and not different and what would have to happen if our limits in this regard were now to be expanded. I wish you could become conscious of how even you, through your being and acting, are at the same time instruments of the universe and of how your action, which is directed toward wholly different things, has an influence on religion and its immediate condition.

A person is born with the religious capacity as with every other, and if only his sense is not forcibly suppressed, if only that communion between a person and the universe – these are admittedly the two poles of religion – is not blocked and barricaded, then religion would have to develop unerringly in each person according to his own individual manner. But unfortunately that blocking is just what happens in our age to such a great extent from earliest childhood on. With anguish I see daily how the rage of the understanding does not allow this sense to arise at all and how everything unites to bind us to the finite and to a very small spot of it, so that the infinite is removed from our view as far as possible. Who hinders the vitality of religion? Not the doubters and scoffers; even though these gladly communicate their desire to have no religion, they do not disturb the nature that wishes to bring it forth; not even immoral people, as one supposes, for their efforts and actions are opposed to a wholly different power than this. But in the present condition of the world prudent and practical people are the counterbalance to religion, and their great preponderance is the reason why it plays such a scant and insignificant role. From tenderest childhood on, they mistreat human beings and suppress their striving for something higher.

With great attentiveness I can observe the longing of young minds for the miraculous and supernatural. Already along with the finite and determined, they seek something different that they can oppose to it; they grasp in all directions after something that reaches beyond the sensible phenomena and their laws; and however much even their senses are full of earthly objects, it is always as if they had besides these yet other objects that would have to waste away without sustenance. That is the first stirring of religion. A secret, uncomprehended intimation drives them beyond the riches of this world; therefore every trace of another world is so welcome to them; thus they take delight in the stories of superterrestrial beings, and everything about which it is most clear to them that it cannot exist here, they embrace with all the zealous love one dedicates to an object to which one has an obvious right that one, however, cannot assert. Of course, it is an illusion to seek the infinite precisely outside the finite, to seek the opposite outside that to which it is opposed; but is it not highly natural for those who do not yet know the finite itself? Is it not the illusion of whole peoples and whole schools of wisdom? If there were guardians of religion among those who care for human development, how easily would the error that was brought about by nature itself be corrected and in more lucid times how eagerly would young souls relinquish themselves to impressions of the infinite in its omnipresence. Formerly, one allowed youth to do as it pleased; it was thought that a taste for grotesque figures suited the young imagination in religion as in art; one satisfied this taste in rich measure, and indeed the serious and holy mythology that one considered religion was quite light-heartedly linked up with those airy games of childhood. God, the Savior, and angels were merely other types of fairies and sylphs. In this way, of course, the basis was laid early enough by poetic creation for the usurpation of religion by metaphysics. But man was nevertheless left more to himself; and an honest, uncorrupted mind, which knew how to keep itself free from the yoke of under-standing and disputation, in later years found the way out of this labyrinth more easily.

In contrast, this proclivity is now forcibly suppressed from the beginning.[5] Everything supernatural and miraculous is proscribed and the imagination is not to be filled with empty images. In the meantime one can just as easily get real things into it and make preparations for life. Thus poor souls that thirst after something entirely different become bored with moralistic stories and learn how beautiful and useful it is to be genteel and prudent; they gain concepts from ordinary things and, without regard for what they lack, are handed more and more of what they already have too abundantly. In order to protect the sensory receptivity to a certain extent against the pretensions of the other faculties, there is implanted in each person his own drive to allow every other activity to rest for a time and only to open all sense organs in order to let himself be penetrated by every impression. Through a secret, most beneficial sympathy, this drive is strongest when universal life reveals itself most distinctly in one's own breast and in the surrounding world. But if only it were not begrudged them to yield to this drive in comfortable inactive rest, for, from the standpoint of bourgeois life, this is indolence and laziness. Design and purpose must be in everything; prudent and practical people must always accomplish something, and when the spirit can no longer serve, they are fond of exercising the body; work and play, only no quiet, submissive contemplation.

But the important thing is that they are supposed to understand everything, and with understanding they are completely robbed of their faculty of sense; for the way in which understanding is pursued, it is absolutely opposed to sensory receptivity. Sense perception seeks objects for itself; it approaches them and offers itself to their embraces; the objects should bear something in themselves that characterizes them as its possession, as its work; in brief, sense wants to find and to let itself be found. For their understanding it does not depend on where these

---

[5]   The Romantic theory of early childhood with its natural goodness and free use of the imagination, influenced by Rousseau and Herder, was currently embodied in the theories of the Swiss educational reformer Johann Heinrich Pestalozzi (1746–1827), whose methods and ideas were introduced into Prussian schools in 1803; cf. Robert B. Downs, *Heinrich Pestalozzi: Father of Modern Pedagogy* (Boston, 1975), pp. 109f. and Karl Friedrich Klöden's *Von Berlin nach Berlin* (Berlin, 1976), the memoir of a Pestalozzian teacher in Schleiermacher's Berlin. See text pertaining to n. 16 below.

objects come from; my God! They are indeed there, a well-acquired, inherited possession; for how long now have these objects been enumerated and defined? Only take them as life brings them, for you must understand exactly those objects that it brings; to want to make and to seek some yourself is truly eccentric, an arrogant and a vain effort; for what fruit does it bear in human life? None at all! But without our faculty of sense no universe is found.

Sense strives to grasp the undivided impression of something whole. It wants to perceive what and how something is for itself and to recognize each in its unique character. Among prudent people of our age their understanding is not concerned with that; the what and the how are too remote for them, for they suppose understanding exists only in the whither and the wherefore in which they eternally rotate. This is their great goal, the place an object occupies in the series of appearances. Its beginning and ending is their everything. They do not even ask whether and how that which they want to understand is a whole – this would indeed lead them far, and with such a tendency they would not get away so completely without religion – but they want to dismember and dissect it apart from this. They even deal with that whose purpose it is to satisfy sense in its highest potency, which is, as it were, in spite of them, a whole in itself. By that I mean everything that is art in nature and in the works of man. They destroy it before it can have its effect; it is supposed to be understood singly and this or that thing be learned from torn-off pieces. You will have to admit that this is actually the practice of prudent people; you will confess that a rich and powerful abundance of sense is required, if even only a portion of it is to escape these hostile procedures and that already, for that reason, the number of those who rise as far as religion can only be small. But religion melts away even more because now, in addition, everything possible happens so that any sense that remained would by no means devote itself to the universe. They and all that is in them must be restricted within the bounds of bourgeois life. All action is supposed to refer to bourgeois life, and thus they believe that even the exalted inner harmony of man consists in nothing else than his having everything again relate to his action. They suppose that he has material enough right before him for his sense and for sumptuous paintings, even though he may never go beyond this perspective that serves both as his standpoint and focal point. Therefore, all sentiments that have nothing to do with bourgeois life are, as it were, useless expenditures by which one exhausts oneself and from which the mind must be restrained as much as possible through purposeful activity. Thus a pure love of poetry and of art is an extravagance one merely tolerates because it is not quite as bad as other extravagances. Thus even knowledge is pursued with wise and sober moderation so that it may not transgress these limits, and while not leaving out of view the smallest thing that has an influence in this realm, they decry the greatest because it aims at more than something sensual.

That there are things that must be exhausted to a certain depth is for them a necessary evil, and they thank the gods that there are still some who, out of an unassailable inclination, give themselves to this task. It is with holy compassion that they view these as willing sacrifices. That there are feelings that will not let themselves be bridled by these people's demands for practical necessity and that so many people in bourgeois life become unhappy or immoral in this way – for in this class I include even those who go somewhat beyond being purely industrious, for whom the moral part of bourgeois life is everything – that is the object of their most heartfelt lament, and they take it to be one of the deepest ravages of humanity that they would want to see remedied as soon as possible. That is the great evil, that good people believe their activity is universal and exhaustive of humanity and that if one would do what they do, one would then need to have no sense except for what one does. Therefore, they mutilate everything with their shears and they would not even like to have an original appearance occur that could become a phenomenon for religion; for whatever can be seen and comprehended from their point of view, that is, everything they consider valid, is a small and unfruitful circle without science, without morals, without art, without love, without spirit, and truly even without letters. In brief, it is without anything by which the world might disclose itself, although it makes many haughty claims to all of these things. Indeed, they think they have the true and real world and that they are actually the ones who take everything in its proper context.

But might they just once realize that in order to intuit each thing as an element of the whole, one must have necessarily considered it in its unique nature and in its highest perfection. For it can be something in the universe only through the totality of its effects and connections; everything depends on this totality, and to become aware of it one must have considered a thing not only from an external point of view but from its own center outward and from all sides in relation to the center, that is to say, in the thing's differentiated existence, in its own essence. To know of only one point of view for everything is exactly the opposite of having all points of view for each thing; it is the way to distance oneself directly away from the universe and to sink into the most wretched limitedness, to become a true serf,[6] bound to the place on which by chance one may be standing.

In our relationship to this world there are certain transitions into the infinite, vistas that are hewn through, before which each person is led so that his sense might find the way to the universe and upon whose sight feelings are stimulated that, to be sure, are not immediately religion, but that are, if I may say so, a schematism of the same.[7] The good and the prudent wisely obstruct even these vistas and place in the opening the sort of thing with which one might conceal an unsightly place, an inferior picture, or a philosophical caricature. And if, as

6   *Glebae adscriptus*: a person who is bonded to the land.
7   Schleiermacher makes a free use of the Kantian term "schematism," which in the critical philosophy designates "a universal procedure of imagination in providing an image for a concept" (*Critique of Pure Reason*, p. 182). As an abstract object of the understanding, which enables the intuited impressions to be subsumed under the categories of the understanding, it is difficult to see how, on Kant's terms, religion could constitute a schema.

sometimes happens, a beam of light falls upon their eyes now and then, so that the omnipotence of the universe may be evident even to them and their souls cannot ward off a weak stirring of those sentiments, yet the infinite is not the goal to which their souls flee for rest, but like the mark at the end of a race course, it is only the point around which it moves with greatest haste without touching in order to be able to return – the sooner, the better – to its old place.

Being born and dying are such points, when they are perceived, at which it cannot escape us how our own self is universally surrounded by the infinite and which always arouse a quiet longing and a holy awe. The immeasurability of sensible intuition is, after all, also at least a hint at a different and higher infinity. But nothing would please them more than to be able to use even the greatest diameter of the cosmic order to measure and weigh everyday life as they now use the meridian of the earth;[8] and if the intuition of life and death once grasps them, believe me, however much they may speak about religion because of it, nothing is closer to their hearts than to use every occasion of this sort to win some of the young people for Hufeland.[9] They are, to be sure, punished sufficiently; for since they stand on no higher vantage point from which at least to shape by themselves this worldly wisdom to which they cling according to principles, thus they move slavishly and deferentially in old forms or amuse themselves with petty improvements. That is the extreme of practicality[10] to which the age has rushed with rapid steps from the useless scholastic quibbling about words; it is a new barbarism as a worthy counterpart of the old; it is the lovely fruit of the paternalistic, eudaimonistic politics that has taken the place of crude despotism. We all came about in the process, and the capacity for religion has suffered in early bloom so that it cannot maintain the same pace in its development as the rest.

These people – I cannot associate them with you to whom I speak because they do not despise religion, even though they annihilate it, nor are they to be termed "cultured" even though they shape the age and enlighten people and would like to do this to the point of tiresome transparency – these are always the dominant part; you and I are but a tiny crowd. Whole cities and countries are brought up on their principles; and when this education has been withstood, one finds them again in society, in the sciences and in philosophy; yes, even in the latter, for not only is

[8] An allusion to the fact that the meter measure was legally introduced in France on 7 April 1795 as the forty-millionth part of the earth's meridian which runs through the Paris Observatory (*KGA* I.2, p. 256).

[9] Christoph Wilhelm Hufeland (1762–1836), professor of medicine in Jena, became chief of medicine at the Charité, where Schleiermacher served as hospital chaplain, in 1800 (*Allgemeine Deutsche Biographie* [1881], XIII, pp. 186–96). In 1806 the text was changed to read, "to win some of the young people for the art of prolonging life," thus alluding to Hufeland's book, *Kunst, das menschliche Leben zu verlängern* (1796), which, in promoting macrobiotics and dietetics, went through eight editions and all major European languages.

[10] "Practicality" (*das Nützliche*). Schleiermacher's critique is aimed at the dominance of practical and utilitarian concerns in Prussia, even though he especially identifies this tendency with Britain where Jeremy Bentham's *Principles of Morals and Legislation* had appeared in 1789.

ancient philosophy their actual abode – as you know, one now divides philosophy with much historical spirit only into ancient, recent, and most recent – but they have even taken over recent philosophy. Through their powerful influence on every worldly interest and through the false appearance of philanthropy[11] with which it blinds the social inclination as well, this style of thinking always holds religion under pressure and resists every movement through which it wants to reveal its life somewhere with full power.

Only with the strongest spirit of opposition to this general tendency can religion therefore now work its way upward, and it can never appear in any other form than that which must be most distasteful to those people. For just as everything follows the law of association,[12] so also can sense gain the upper hand only where it has taken possession of an object to which the understanding, which is inimical to sense, only loosely clings, and which it can appropriate to itself most easily and with an excess of free power. But this object is the inner world, not the outer; explanatory psychology,[13] this masterpiece of that type of understanding, having exhausted itself by immoderation and having made itself almost disreputable, was the first to leave the field to intuition again.

Therefore, a religious person has surely turned inward with his sense in the process of intuiting himself, while for now leaving everything external, the intellectual as well as the physical, to people of understanding as the great goal of their investigations. Likewise, according to the same law, those individuals find the passage to the infinite most readily whose nature drives them furthest away from the central point of all opponents of the universe. This is the reason why truly religious minds have distinguished themselves through the ages by a mystical tinge and why all imaginative natures who are not fond of concerning themselves with what is real in worldly affairs have outbursts of religion.

This is the character of all religious phenomena of our time. These are the two colors from which it is always composed, even though in the most varied mixtures.

[11] Johann Bernhard Basedow (1724–90), the leading figure in German Enlightenment pedagogy, established a special school, the Philanthropin, at Dessau in 1774, which was based on the practical formation of the human will, and incorporated modern languages, physical education, and handwork into the curriculum, while resisting religious and church influences. Although both claimed to be followers of Rousseau, the rigid methods and materialism of the Philanthropin movement were opposed by the newer religious and humanistic pedagogy of Pestalozzi.

[12] *Gesetz der Verwandschaft*. The allusion here, and in the following note, is to pioneer work in German experimental psychology that antedates Wilhelm Wundt's laboratory in Leipzig by more than one hundred years; J. G. Krüger had published an *Attempt at an Experimental Psychology* in 1756 that was associationistic and hedonistic. Renewed interest in "associationist" psychology in Germany from 1770 to 1795 opposed the rational psychology of Kant and prepared for the turn to empirical psychology in J. F. Herbart (1776–1841) and F. E. Beneke (1798–1854) and the rise of experimental psychology in later nineteenth-century Germany.

[13] *Erklärende Psychologie*. Schleiermacher refers to early exponents of the "physicalist" school of genetic-causal psychological explanation, whose approach came to fruition in the work of Gustav Fechner (1801–89); on explanatory psychology see Dilthey's 1894 work, *Descriptive Psychology and Historical Understanding*, ed. Rudolf A. Makkreel, trans. Richard M. Zaner and Kenneth L. Heiges (The Hague, 1977), chapters 2, 3, and 5.

I purposely say phenomena, for more is not to be expected in this state of things. Imaginative natures are lacking in penetrating spirit, in the capacity to lay hold of the essential. An easy alternating play of beautiful, often enchanting, but always merely incidental and completely subjective combinations satisfies them and is their highest end; a deeper and more inward connection offers itself in vain to their eyes. They actually only seek the infinity and universality of enticing appearance – which is far less or even far more than sense really attains – which they are accustomed to attach themselves, and thus all their views remain fragmented and fleeting. Their mind is readily set on fire, but merely with an unsteady and, as it were, fickle flame; they only have outbursts of religion as they have outbursts of art, of philosophy, and of everything great and beautiful whose surface engrosses them.

In contrast, that person to whose inner essence religion belongs, but whose sense always remains turned inward because he does not know how to cope with more than just that in the present state of the world, too quickly runs out of the material needed to become a virtuoso or hero of religion. There is a great, powerful mysticism that even the most frivolous man cannot regard without deference and devotion, which wrings admiration from the most rational of people by virtue of its heroic simplicity and its proud contempt for the world. This person is not exactly satiated and overwhelmed by external intuitions of the universe, but is driven back upon himself by each individual intuition through a mysterious attraction and finds himself to be the foundation and key of the whole. He is convinced by a great analogy and a bold faith that it is not necessary to forsake oneself, but that spirit has enough within itself to become aware of everything that could be given to it externally. Thus, it is through a free decision that he closes his eyes forever to all that is not himself; but this contempt does not rest on ignorance, nor this obstructing of sense on incapacity.

So it is with our people. They have learned to see nothing beyond themselves because everything has only been more sketched in the base manner of common knowledge than actually shown to them. They have neither sense nor light enough left from their self-contemplation to penetrate this ancient darkness and, being angry with the age for which they have reproaches, they would rather have nothing to do with that which is its work in them. Therefore, the universe is unformed and paltry in them; they have too little to intuit and, being alone as they are with their sense, forced to move but eternally in all-too-narrow a circle, their religious sense expires from lack of stimulation, from indirect weakness after a sickly life.[14]

But for those whose sense of the universe, with greater power but equally little culture, turns boldly outward and likewise seeks there more and new material, there is another end that reveals only too clearly their incongruity within the age. Theirs is a violent death, if you will, euthanasia, but a horrible one: It is the suicide of the spirit. Not knowing how to grasp the world, whose inner essence and greater

---

[14] "Gedanken I" (no. 112a), *KGA* 1.2, p. 29: "The religious sense usually dies from indirect weakness."

sense remained unfamiliar to the spirit among the petty views of its upbringing, they are deceived by confused appearances, abandoned to unrestrained fantasies; they seek the universe and its traces where it never was, and in the end indignantly rend wholly asunder the connection between internal and external. They put the helpless understanding to flight and end in a holy madness whose source almost no one recognizes, a loudly protesting and misunderstood victim of the universal contempt and mistreatment of what is innermost in a person. But yet only a victim and not a hero, for whoever succumbs, usually in the final test, cannot be counted among those who have received the innermost mysteries.

This complaint that there are no permanent representatives of religion among us who are acknowledged by the whole world is, however, not intended to take back what I earlier, quite knowingly, said when I claimed that our age is no less propitious for religion than any other.[15] Certainly the quantity of religion in the world has not decreased, but rather is fragmented and driven too far apart. It reveals itself by a powerful force only in small and fleeting but frequent appearances that enhance the variety of the whole and delight the eye of the beholder more than they could make a great and noble impression. The conviction that there are many who exhale the freshest aroma of young life in holy longing and love for the eternal and imperishable and who have only recently, perhaps never wholly, been over-come by the world; that there is no one to whom the lofty world spirit would not have appeared at least once, and to whom, ashamed of oneself, blushing over one's unworthy limitation, it has not cast one of those piercing glances that the downcast eye feels without seeing it – here religion still stands and lets the consciousness of each of you judge it. Only the heroes of religion, the holy souls such as one formerly saw, to whom religion is everything and whose whole being is permeated by it, are lacking in this generation and must be lacking in it. And as often as I reflect upon what must happen and what direction our culture must take if religious people are to appear again in a more exalted style, albeit rare but natural products of their age, I find that you, through your whole striving – whether consciously or not you yourselves may decide – are no little help to a rebirth of religion and that in part your general work, in part the efforts of a narrower circle, and in part the sublime ideas of a few extraordinary spirits in the course of humanity shall serve this end.

The extent and truth of intuition depend on the sharpness and breadth of one's sense, and the wisest person without sensibility is no nearer to religion than the most foolish who has a proper view. Everything, therefore, must begin by putting an end to the bondage in which human sense is held for the purpose of those lessons of the understanding through which nothing is learned, those explanations that make nothing clear, and those analyses that resolve nothing. This is a goal toward which you will soon work with united powers. Improvements of instruction

---

[15] In the First Speech Schleiermacher remarks: "I would not know what other age may have accommodated it better than the present."

have gone the way all revolutions go that were not begun from the highest principles; they have gradually slid back again into the old course of things, and only some external changes preserve the memory that which at the beginning was held to be a marvelous as well as a great occurrence; prudent and practical instruction differs only a little – this "little" lies neither in its spirits nor in its effect – from the old rote learning. This has not escaped you. To a great extent it is already just as detested by you and a purer idea is spreading itself abroad about the sanctity of childhood and the eternity of inviolable free choice, the expressions of which we shall have to await and listen for among people now developing.[16] Soon these barriers will be broken, the intuitive power will take possession of its whole domain, every sense will open itself, and objects will be able to put themselves in touch with human beings in myriad ways.

A limitation and firm guidance of activity is, however, very compatible with this unlimited freedom of sensibility. This is the great demand with which the better among you now approach contemporaries and posterity. You are tired of watching a barren, encyclopedic dashing about; you have become what you are only by way of this self-limitation, and you know that there is no other way to form oneself. Thus you insist that individuals should seek to become something definite and should pursue something with steadfastness and with the whole soul. No one can perceive the truth of this advice better than someone who has already matured to that universality of sense, for such a person must know that there would be no objects if everything were not separate and limited. Thus I also delight in these efforts and wish they were already more successful. They would be of excellent help to religion. For just this limitation of power, provided only that sense is not limited along with it, prepares for it the way to the infinite all the more surely and reopens the community that was obstructed for so long. A person who has intuited and known much, and can then resolve to do and to further some individual thing for its own sake with all his power, can do nothing else than acknowledge that other things are also supposed to be there and be done for their own sake, because otherwise he would contradict himself. And when such a person has gone as far as he can with what he chose, it will scarcely escape him at the peak of perfection that the object of his choice is nothing without the rest. This acknowledgment of another realm and the annihilation of what is one's own, which everywhere forces itself upon a thoughtful person, and this simultaneously demanded love and contempt of everything finite and limited, are not possible without a dim presentiment of the universe and must necessarily precipitate a purer and more definite longing for the infinite, for the one in the all. Each individual knows from his own consciousness three different orientations of sense, the one directed inward to one's own self, another directed outward toward the indeterminate in the intuition of the world, and a third that connects both in which sense, suspended

---

[16] An allusion to the educational theories of Pestalozzi; see n. 5 above.

between them in a constant to-and-fro movement, finds peace only in the unconditional assumption of their innermost union; this last orientation is toward that which is completed in itself, toward art and its works. Only one among them can be the dominant tendency for a person, but there is a way from each to religion, and religion takes a characteristic form according to the variety of the way in which it was found.

Observe yourselves with unceasing effort. Detach all that is not yourself, always proceed with ever-sharper sense, and the more you fade from yourself, the clearer will the universe stand forth before you, the more splendidly will you be recompensed for the horror of self-annihilation through the feeling of the infinite in you. Look outside yourself to any part, to any element of the world, and comprehend it in its whole essence, but also collect everything that it is, not only in itself but in you, in this one and that one and everywhere; retrace your steps from the circumference to the center ever more frequently and in ever-greater distances. You will soon lose the finite and find the infinite. Were it not wanton to wish to go beyond oneself, I should wish that I could intuit ever so clearly how the artistic sense,[17] by itself alone, changes into religion, how in spite of the calm into which the mind is submerged by every individual enjoyment, it nevertheless feels driven to make the advances that can lead it to the universe. Why do those who are inclined to go this way have such reticent natures? That I am not acquainted with this path is my most acute limitation; it is the breach that I feel deeply in my being, but also treat with respect. I resign myself to not seeing, but I believe;[18] the possibility of the matter stands clearly before my eyes, but it must remain a secret from me. Indeed, if it is true that there are quick conversions, occasions by which, for someone who thought of nothing less than rising above the finite, the sense of the universe opens up, in a moment as if through an immediate inner illumination, and surprises a person with its splendor, then I believe that more than anything else the sight of great and sublime works of art can achieve this miracle. But I shall never grasp it. Yet this belief is directed more to the future than to the past or present. To find the universe on the path of the most abstract self-contemplation was the business of ancient oriental mysticism, which, with admirable boldness, joined the infinitely great directly to the infinitely small and found everything bordering on nothingness.[19]

I know that every religion whose schematism was either the heavens or organic nature proceeded from the intuition of the world. Polytheistic Egypt was for a long

---

[17] *der Kunstsinn*. While acknowledging that an "artistic sense" and religion are intimately related, Schleiermacher claims no personal knowledge of the way the two are related. Contrary to René Wellek (*A History of Modern Criticism:* II. The Romantic Age [New Haven, CT, 1955], p. 304), his argument cannot be taken as propounding a "religion of art" (*Kunstreligion*).

[18] John 20:29: "Blessed are those who have not seen and yet believe."

[19] *an der Grenze des Nichts*. On the image of India and Asian religions among the German Romantics, see René Gérard, *L'Orient et la pensée romantique allemande* (Paris, 1963) and A. Leslie Willson, *A Mythical Image: The Ideal of India in German Romanticism* (Durham, 1964).

time the most perfect guardian of this disposition in which – it can at least be surmised – the purest intuition of the original infinite and living being may have wandered in humble toleration close beside the darkest superstition and most absurd mythology. I have never heard anything about a religion of art[20] that has dominated peoples and ages, but I do know that an artistic sense has never approached those two types of religion without showering them with new beauty and holiness and pleasantly softening their original limitedness. Through the older sages and poets of the Greeks natural religion was thus transformed into a fairer and more joyful form, and their divine Plato thus raised the most holy mysticism to the highest pinnacle of divinity and of humanity. Let me pay homage to the goddess unknown to me for the fact that she cared for him and his religion so painstakingly and unselfishly. I marvel at the most beautiful self-forgetfulness in everything he says against her in holy zeal, like a just king who does not even spare his too tenderhearted mother, for everything he said was aimed at the voluntary service she rendered to the imperfect natural religion. Now she serves no religion, and everything is different and worse. Religion and art stand beside one another like two friendly souls whose inner affinity, whether or not they equally surmise it, is nevertheless still unknown to them. Friendly words and outpourings of the heart[21] always hover on their lips and return again and again because they are still not able to find the proper manner and final cause of their reflection and longing. They hope for a fuller revelation and, suffering and sighing under the same pressure, they see one another enduring, perhaps with inner sympathy and deep feeling, but yet without love. Will this common burden alone bring about the happiest moment of their union? Or if you should soon execute a bold stroke for the one of them that is so dear to you, it will thus surely hasten, at least with sisterly devotion, to aid the other.

For now, however, not only do both types of religion lack the help of art, but even in itself their condition is worse than before. Both sources of intuition[22] of the infinite streamed forth in great and splendid fashion at a time when scientific quibbling without true principles had not yet by its meanness done injury to the purity of sense, even though neither was rich enough by itself to produce the highest. Moreover, they are now dimmed by the loss of simplicity and by the destructive influence of presumptuous and false insight. How is one to purify them? How is one to provide them with enough power and fullness to make the soil fertile for more than ephemeral products? To bring them together and to unite

---

[20] The contrast is drawn between a "religion of art" (*Kunstreligion*) and an "artistic sense" (*Kunstsinn*) of the next sentence.

[21] *Ergiessungen des Herzens*. An ironic play on the *Herzensergiessungen eines kunstliebenden Klosterbruders* (*Confessions from the Heart of an Art-loving Friar*) by W. H. Wachenroder, published in 1797. Wachenroder epitomized the "religion of art" aspect of Romanticism by seeking to elevate art to religion.

[22] Reference is made back to Schleiermacher's fundamental contrast between self-contemplation (*Selbstbeschauung*) and intuition of the world (*Weltanschauung*).

them in one bed is the only thing that can bring religion to completion on the path on which we are headed; that would be an event from whose womb religion, soon in a new and splendid form, would face better times. Look there, the goal of your present highest endeavors is at the same time the resurrection of religion! It is your efforts that must bring about this event, and I celebrate you as the rescuers and guardians of religion, even though unintentionally so. Do not retreat from your posts and your works until you have unlocked the innermost element of knowledge and, in priestly humility, opened the sanctuary of true science where, to everyone who enters and even to the sons of religion, everything is replaced that superficial knowledge and arrogant boasting caused them to lose.

In its chaste, heavenly beauty, far from jealousy and despotic conceit, morality itself will hand them the heavenly lyre and the magic mirror upon entering, so that they may accompany its earnest, quiet creating with divine tones and may view it as ever the same through the whole of eternity in countless forms. By making him aware of the concept of his reciprocal action with the world and teaching him to know himself not only as creature but also as creator, philosophy will no longer tolerate the person under its purview who, turning his gaze steadfastly to his own spirit in order to seek the universe there, should miss the mark and pine in poverty and need. The anxious wall of division[23] will be torn down; everything external to him is merely an other within him; everything is the reflection of his spirit, and his spirit is the reproduction of everything. The human spirit will dare to seek itself in this reflection without losing itself or going out of itself; it can never be exhausted while intuiting itself, for everything lies within it. Physics will boldly put into the center of nature a person who looks around himself in order to perceive the universe, and will no longer tolerate his amusing himself fruitlessly and dwelling upon individual, small features.[24] He will only pursue the play of nature's forces into the most secret territory, from the inadequate storehouses of movable matter to the artistic workshops of organic life; he will grasp nature's power from the limits of space that gives birth to worlds to the center of his own self, and will find himself everywhere in eternal conflict and in the most indissoluble union with it, with his own being as its innermost center and its outermost boundary. Appearance will have fled, and being will be attained; sure is his glance and clear his view, which recognizes being under all its disguises, while resting nowhere except in the infinite and One.

Already I see some significant forms initiated in these mysteries returning from the sanctuary, who only have yet to purify and adorn themselves in order to go

---

[23] Ephesians 2:14.

[24] The passage reflects Schleiermacher's keen interest in 1799 in the emerging natural philosophy of Schelling, whose *Ideas for a Philosophy of Nature* (1797) and *On the World Soul* (1798), argue boldly for a reconceptualizing of human life amid the reciprocal natural philosophical forces of the universe. In *Br.* III, pp. 151, 154, Schlegel chides Schleiermacher for declining to do a review of *On the World Soul* on grounds of insufficient knowledge, after having advocated Schelling's philosophy of nature in the present book.

forth in priestly robes. Even if the one goddess should tarry long with her helpful manifestation, time will bring us a great and rich compensation for that. The greatest work of art is that whose material is humanity that the universe forms directly and the sense for this must soon open up in many. For even now it is creating with bold and powerful art, and you will be the modern Caryatides[25] when new structures are set up in the temple of time. Interpret the artist with power and spirit; explain the later works on the basis of earlier and the earlier on the basis of the former. Let past, present, and future surround us, an endless gallery of the most sublime works of art eternally reproduced by a thousand brilliant mirrors.[26] Let history, as it becomes one who has worlds at its command, reward religion with rich gratitude as its first nurse and awaken true and holy worshipers of eternal power and wisdom. See how the heavenly growth flourishes in the midst of your plantings without your aid. Neither disturb it nor pluck it out! It is a proof of the approval of the gods and of the imperishability of your merit; it is an ornament that adorns it, a talisman that protects it.

---

[25] *Neokoren*. Schleiermacher suggests that the new pillars of religion should be like the Caryatides, the six elegantly draped female figures who hold up the entablature of the porch of the Erechtheum in the Athenian Acropolis.

[26] An allusion to F. Schlegel's famous *Athenaeum* fragment 116 on *romantische Poesie*: "Romantic poetry is a progressive, universal poetry . . . It alone can become, like the epic, a mirror of the whole circumambient world, an image of the age. And it can also – more than any other form – hover at the midpoint between the portrayed and the portrayer, free of all real and ideal self-interest, on the wings of poetic reflection, and can raise that reflection again and again to a higher power, can multiply it in an endless succession of mirrors" (Peter Firchow, [ed.], *Friedrich Schlegel's Lucinde and the Fragments* [Minneapolis, 1971], p. 175).

Fourth Speech
On the Social Element in Religion; or, On Church and Priesthood

Those among you who are accustomed to regarding religion merely as a disease of the mind no doubt also entertain the idea that it is an evil that is easier to tolerate, indeed, perhaps to subdue, so long as only isolated individuals here and there are afflicted. But you think the common danger soars to its highest and everything is lost as soon as an all-too-close community should exist among several such unfortunates. In the former case, you think one can weaken the paroxysms through purposeful treatment, as it were, through a diet that counteracts the inflammation and through healthy air, and at least render the characteristic contagious element harmless where it is not fully conquered. But in the latter case you believe one must abandon every hope of deliverance. You fear the evil will become far more devastating and accompanied by the most dangerous symptoms, if each individual's disease is fostered and intensified by too close proximity to the others. You say the whole atmosphere will be poisoned by a few, even the soundest bodies will be contaminated, all channels in which the process of life is to take place destroyed, all fluids broken down, and, seized by the same feverish delirium, whole generations and peoples irretrievably affected. For this reason, your opposition to the church, to every event aimed at the communication of religion, is still greater than your opposition to religion itself; for this reason, priests, as the pillars and the really active members of such institutions, are for you the most despised of persons.

But even those among you who have a somewhat more moderate opinion of religion and consider it more as an oddity than as a derangement of the mind, more as an insignificant than as a dangerous phenomenon, have equally derogatory concepts of all social institutions of religion. They imagine that slavish sacrifice of everything characteristic and free and that lifeless mechanism and empty customs are the inseparable consequences of such institutions and the ingenious work of those who, with unbelievable success, make great profit from things that either are

72

nothing or are something any other person could have accomplished equally well. I would have poured out my heart to you very imperfectly on this topic, which is so important to me, if I had not likewise taken pains to put you in the right frame of mind on this matter. How many of the misguided efforts and the sad destinies of humanity you blame on religious associations I have no need to repeat; it is clear in a thousand utterances of the most esteemed among you. Nor shall I pause to refute these accusations individually or to shift blame for this evil back onto other causes. Let us rather subject the whole concept to a new consideration and create it anew from the center of the matter, unconcerned about what has been real until now, and what experience makes available to us.

Once there is religion, it must necessarily also be social. That not only lies in human nature but also is preeminently in the nature of religion. You must admit that it is highly unnatural for a person to want to lock up in himself what he has created and worked out. In the continuous reciprocity, which is not only practical but also intellectual, in which he stands with the rest of his species, he is supposed to express and communicate all that is in him. The more passionately something moves him, and the more intimately it penetrates his being, the stronger is the urge also to glimpse its power outside himself in others, in order to prove to himself that he has encountered nothing other than what is human. You see that nothing at all is said here about the endeavor to make others like ourselves, or about the belief in the indispensability for everyone of what is in us, but only about becoming conscious of the relation of our particular events to our shared nature. But the most proper object of this desire for communication is unquestionably that where man originally feels himself to be passive, his intuitions and feelings; there he has to ask whether it might not be an alien and unworthy power to which he must submit.

Therefore, we see that even from childhood on, man is primarily concerned to communicate these intuitions and feelings. He willingly lets his concepts, about whose origin no doubts can in any case arise, rest in themselves. But he wants to have witnesses for and participants in that which enters his senses and arouses his feelings. How should he keep to himself the influences of the universe that appear to him as greatest and most irresistible? How should he wish to retain within himself that which most strongly forces him out of himself and which, like nothing else, impresses him with the fact that he cannot know himself in and of himself alone. Rather, his first endeavor, when a religious view has become clear to him or a pious feeling penetrates his soul, is also to direct others to the object and, if possible, to communicate the vibrations of his mind to them. If, therefore, urged by his own nature, religious man necessarily speaks, it is this very nature that also provides hearers for him. With no type of thinking and sentiment does man have such a vivid feeling of his complete incapability ever to exhaust its object as with religion. His sense of it has no sooner opened up than he also feels its infinity and his limitations; he is conscious of encompassing only a small part of religion, and what he cannot attain immediately he wants at least to perceive through another medium. Therefore, every expression of religion interests him, and seeking his complement he listens attentively to every tone that he recognizes as religious. This is how mutual communication organizes itself; thus speaking and hearing are equally indispensable for everyone. Unlike other concepts and perceptions, religious communication is not be sought in books. Too much of the original impression is lost in this medium in which everything is slurred over that does not fit into the uniform signs in which it shall go forth again, where everything needs to be presented two or three times, while the original act of presenting ought to be re-presented. Yet the effect on the whole of humanity in its great unity could only be poorly reproduced by manifold reflection. Only when religion is expelled from the society of the living must it hide its varied life in the dead letter.[1]

This communication with the innermost part of humanity also cannot be carried on in common conversation.[2] Many who are full of goodwill toward religion have reproached you because you speak about all important subjects in friendly company, except God and divine things. I would like to defend you against that charge by suggesting that this view at least expresses neither contempt nor indifference, but a fortunate and very correct instinct. Where joy and laughter also dwell and seriousness is supposed to be compliantly joined to jest and wit, there can be no place for what must forever be encompassed by holy reserve and awe. People cannot toss religious views, pious feelings, and serious reflections upon them to each other in small snatches, like the ingredients of a light conversation; if the conversation were about such holy objects, it would be more an outrage than ingenuity to have an answer ready immediately for every question and a response for every address. Divine things do not permit themselves to be treated in the manner of a quick and easy exchange of well-aimed wit. The communication of religion must occur in a grander style, and another type of society, which is especially dedicated to religion, must arise from it. It is proper that the whole fullness and magnificence of human speech be expended on the highest which speech can attain, not as if there were some ornament with which religion could not dispense, but because it would be unholy and thoughtless not to show that everything is summoned to represent religion in appropriate power and dignity. Thus it is impossible to express and communicate religion other than verbally with all the effort and artistry of language, while willingly accepting the service of all skills that can assist fleeting and lively speech. Thus the mouth of the one whose heart is full[3] of religion is not opened except before an assembly where that which comes forth so magnificently endowed can have diverse effects.

---

[1] 2 Corinthians 3:6.

[2] The passage alludes to Schlegel's theory of ironic communication, which requires "circumspection" and "self-restraint," but also "wit" as its central feature; see the aphorisms from the *Lyceum* (9, 34, 37, 42, 108) and the *Athenaeum* (29, 32, 37, 220) in *Friedrich Schlegel: Dialogue on Poetry and Literary Aphorisms*, ed. Ernst Behler and Roman Struc (University Park, PA, 1968).

[3] Luke 6:45: "Out of the abundance of the heart his mouth speaks."

I wish I could draw you a picture of the rich, luxuriant life in this city of God[4] when its citizens assemble, all of whom are full of their own power, which wants to stream forth into the open, all full of holy passion to apprehend and appropriate everything the others might offer them. When a person steps forth before others, it is not an office or an appointment that empowers him to do so, not pride or ignorance that fills him with presumption. It is the free stirring of the spirit, the feeling of most cordial unanimity of each with all and of the most perfect equality, a mutual annihilation of every first and last and of all earthly order. He steps forth to present his own intuition as the object for the rest, to lead them into the region of religion where he is at home and to implant his holy feelings in them; he expresses the universe, and the community follows his inspired speech in holy silence. If he should now disclose a hidden miracle or, in prophetic confidence, link the future to the present, if he should confirm old perceptions by new examples, or if his fiery imagination should transport him in sublime visions into other parts of the world and another order of things, a practiced sense of community accompanies him everywhere; and when he returns to himself from his wanderings through the universe, his heart and the heart of each are but the common stage for the same feeling.

Then the audible confession of the accord of his view with what is in them answers him. And holy mysteries, which are not merely meaningful emblems, but, rightly viewed, are natural intimations of a definite consciousness and definite feelings, are thus discovered and celebrated; a higher choir, as it were, answers the summoning voice in a sublime language of its own. But not only "as it were": For just as such a speech is music even without song and tone, so is there also a music among the saints that becomes speech without words, the most definite, most understandable expression of what is innermost. The muse of harmony, whose intimate relation to religion still belongs to the mysteries, has from time immemorial offered the most splendid and most perfect works of her most dedicated pupils on the altars of religion. In holy hymns and choruses, to which the words of the poet cling only loosely and lightly, that is exhaled which definite speech can no longer comprehend, and thus the sounds of thought and feeling support one another and alternate until everything is saturated and full of the holy and infinite. That is how religious people influence one another in their natural and eternal association. Do not find fault with them if this heavenly bond, the most complete result of human fellowship to which religion can attain only when it is recognized from the highest standpoint in its innermost essence, is of more value to them than your earthly political bond, which is only a forced, transitory, and provisional work.

Where, then, in all that, is the opposition between priests and laity that you are accustomed to label as the source of so much evil? A false appearance has deceived you; this is not at all a distinction between people, but merely a distinction of

---

[4] *Stadt Gottes* recalls Augustine's *The City of God* as well as Revelation 3:12: "The city of my God, the new Jerusalem."

situation and functions. Each person is a priest to the extent that he draws others to himself in the field that he has specially made his own and in which he can present himself as a virtuoso; each is a layperson to the extent that he follows the art and direction of another where he himself is a stranger in religion. There is none of that tyrannical aristocracy you describe so maliciously; this society is a priestly people, a perfect republic[5] where each alternately leads and is led; each follows in the other the same power that he also feels in himself and with which he rules others.

Where is the spirit of discord and dissension that you consider the inevitable consequence of all religious associations? I see nothing except that all is one and that all distinctions that really exist in religion flow smoothly into one another through the social association. I have drawn your attention to various degrees of religiousness; I have referred to two differing types of sense and to differing orientations according to which the imagination individualizes the highest object of religion.[6] Do you suppose that sects necessarily would have to arise from these and this would have to hinder free sociability in religion? At an ideal level of thinking it is true that everything posited outside each other and treated under different categories must also be opposed and in contradiction. But you free yourselves from that notion when you intuit reality itself where all things flow into each other. To be sure, those who are most similar in one of these respects will also attract one another the most strongly. But they cannot on that account make up a separate whole. For the degrees of this relatedness imperceptibly wax and wane, and with so many transitions there is no absolute repulsion or complete separation even between most remote elements. Take whichever you wish of these substances that individually form themselves chemically; if you do not forcibly isolate them through some mechanical operation, none will be a true individual. Its outermost parts will at once be connected with other individuals who actually already belong to another group.

If those who stand on a lower level of the same group are more closely united, there are still some among them who have an intimation of something better, and a person who is really higher placed understands them better than they understand themselves. He is conscious of the meeting point that is hidden from them. If those in whom the one type of sense is dominant draw together, there will be some who understand both types and belong to both types; and a person whose nature leads him to personify the universe is in the essence and matter of religion no different from an individual who does not do this, and there will never be a lack of those who are able to think their way into the opposed form with ease. If unlimited universality of sense is the first and original condition of religion, and is therefore naturally also its most beautiful and ripest fruit, you can surely see that nothing else is feasible than that the further you progress in religion the more the whole religious world must appear to you as an indivisible whole. Only in the lower

---

[5] An allusion to Exodus 19:6; 1 Peter 2:5, 9.
[6] See the Third Speech, n. 22 on "self-contemplation" and "intuition of the world."

regions, perhaps, can a certain drive for separation be perceived; the highest and most cultivated see a universal association, and simply by seeing it, they also establish it. Insofar as everyone stands only in contact with the closest person, but also has a closest person on all sides and in all directions, each is, in fact, inseparably bound up with the whole. Mystics and empiricists in religion, theists and pantheists, those who have raised themselves to the systematic view of the universe, and those who still intuit it merely in its rudiments or in dark chaos should all, however, be only one; one bond encloses them all, and they can only be separated forcibly and arbitrarily; each act of individual union is merely a flowing, integrating part of the whole that loses itself to the indefinite outlines of the whole and perceives itself only in this manner.

Where is the infamous mania for converting everyone to individual definite forms of religion, and where is the horrible motto "Outside of us, no salvation"?[7] In the way I have presented the society of religious people to you and as it has to be by its very nature, it is only meant for mutual communication and exists only among those who already have religion, whatever sort it may be. How could it thus be their business to change the minds of those who already confess a definite religion or to induct and initiate those who still lack it completely? The religion of a society taken together is the entire religion, religion in its infinity, which no individual can completely comprehend, and to which none can be educated or elevated. If a person has already chosen for himself a portion of religion, whatever sort it may be, would it not be an absurd procedure for the society to wish to wrest from him that which accords with his nature, since the religious society is supposed to include this element in itself and it therefore must necessarily be possessed by someone?

And to what purpose should the society cultivate those for whom religion is still quite foreign? Even the society itself cannot impart its possession, the infinite whole, to them. Shall it then communicate something general, something indefinite that would perhaps result if anyone sought out whatever is shared by all its members? But you know of course that nothing at all can be given and communicated anywhere in the form of something general and indeterminate, but only as something individual in a thoroughly determined form. Otherwise it would not be something, but actually nothing. In this endeavor the society would consequently lack every standard and every measure. And how would the society come to reach beyond itself, since the need from which it arose, the principle of religious sociability, hints at nothing of this sort? Therefore, whatever thing of this kind occurs in religion is always merely a private affair of the individual. If a person is required to withdraw from the circle of religious union into the lower regions of life, although he must leave the region where an intuition of the universe affords him the most sublime enjoyment, and where his spirit, permeated by holy feelings,

---

[7] An allusion to the motto of St. Cyprian (bishop of Carthage 248–58): *extra eccclesiam nulla salus.*

hovers above the highest pinnacle of life, he is consoled by the fact that he can immediately relate everything that necessarily concerns him there to whatever remains highest in his mind.

As he descends among people who restrict themselves to some earthly aspiration and activity, he easily believes – pardon him for it – he has been transplanted from the company of gods and muses to a race of crude barbarians. He feels himself to be a steward of religion among unbelievers, a missionary among savages. Like a new Orpheus,[8] he hopes to win many among them through heavenly tones. He presents himself among them as a priestly figure who expresses his higher sense clearly and brightly in every action of his whole being. If the impression of the holy and the divine arouses something similar, how gladly he nurses the first intimations of religion in a new disposition, a beautiful proof of his prospering even in a foreign and severe climate, and how triumphantly he raises the novice with himself into the sublime assembly! This zeal about the extension of religion is only the pious longing of the stranger for home, the endeavor to carry one's fatherland with one and everywhere to intuit its laws and customs, its higher, more beautiful life, while the fatherland, which is blessed and perfect enough in itself, knows nothing of this aspiration.

After all this you will perhaps say that I seem to be completely at one with you; that I have construed the church from the concept of its purpose; and that by denying all the qualities that now characterize it, I have condemned its present form just as strongly as you yourselves. But I assure you that I have been speaking not of what is supposed to be but of what is, unless you wish to deny that that is already real which is only hindered by limitations of space from also appearing to a less refined eye. The true church has in fact always been this way and still is; and if you do not see it, the blame is actually your own and has its basis in a rather obvious misunderstanding. Only consider, I beg you, that I have availed myself of an old but very meaningful expression, not of the church militant, but of the church triumphant, not of the church that still struggles against all the hindrances of religious culture that the age and the condition of humanity place in its way, but of the church that has already overcome everything that was opposed to it and has established itself.

I have presented to you a society of those who have become conscious of their religion and for whom the religious view of life has become one of the dominant ones. Since I hope to have convinced you that such people must have some cultivation and much strength and that, therefore, there can always be only very few of them, you must certainly not seek their union where many hundreds are assembled in great temples and where their song already shocks your ear from afar; you certainly know that people of this type do not stand so closely to one another. Perhaps something similar is to be found concentrated only in a particular space in

---

8   The allusion is ironic in view of Orpheus's inability to raise his wife, Eurydice, from the underworld and his dismal end in the traditional Greek tale.

individual communities that are, as it were, cut off from the great church, but it is certain that all truly religious people, as many as there have ever been, have carried about not merely the belief but the living feeling of such a union and have actually lived in it. They all knew how to esteem what one commonly calls the church at its real value, that is to say, not particularly highly.

This great association to which your harsh accusations actually refer is far removed from being a society of religious people. Rather, it is merely an amalgamation of people who are only just seeking religion, and thus I find it very natural that it contrasts with the religious society in nearly all respects. Unfortunately, if I am to make this as clear to you as it is to me, I must descend into a welter of earthly, worldly things and wend my way through a labyrinth of most wondrous aberrations. It is not done without repugnance, but it is done so that you might yet agree with me. Perhaps the wholly different form of sociability, if I draw your attention to it, will basically convince you of my opinion. I hope that from the previous discussion you are in agreement with me that in true religious fellowship all communication is mutual;[9] the principle that prompts us to express what is our own is closely connected with that which inclines us to join what is unfamiliar, and thus action and reaction are inseparably bound up with one another. In contrast, here in the common church you find a thoroughly different form: All people want to receive, and there is only one who is supposed to give. Completely passive, they allow themselves to be influenced in one and the same way through all their senses. At best, they themselves thereby assist from within to the extent that they have power over themselves without even thinking of a countereffect on others. Does that not show clearly enough that even the principle of their fellowship must be a completely different one? It certainly cannot be said of them that they only wish to supplement their religion through that of others, for if what dwells in them were in fact religion, it would demonstrate some type of action upon others, for this is in its nature. They produce no countereffect because they are capable of none, and they can only be incapable of one for the reason that no religion dwells in them. If I may use an illustration from science, from which I like best to borrow expressions in matters of religion,[10] then I would like to say that they are negatively religious and press in great crowds toward the few points where they surmise the positive principle of religion in order to unite with this principle. But having assimilated this into themselves, they again lack the capacity to retain the new product; their finer element that, as it were, was able merely to hover around their atmosphere escapes them, and they now proceed for a while with a certain feeling of emptiness until they have again filled themselves up negatively.

[9] Earlier in this address Schleiermacher states: "this society is a priestly people, a perfect republic where each alternately leads and is led."

[10] The appeal to natural scientific imagery reflects Schleiermacher's admiration of the early Schelling's effort to integrate chemical and organic processes into a new philosophical physics.

In a few words, this is the history of their religious life and the character of the social inclination that is woven into it. Not religion but merely a little taste for it, and a laborious but lamentably futile effort to attain it for themselves, is all that one can grant even to the best among them, who pursue it with spirit and zeal. In the course of their domestic and civil life, in the greater arena of occurrences where they are spectators, much is naturally encountered that must affect even a slight portion of religious sense. But it remains only an obscure presentiment, a weak impression on a substance that is too soft and whose outlines likewise flow into indefiniteness. Everything is soon swept away by the waves of practical life into the most unfrequented region of memory, and even there it is soon overwhelmed by worldly things. Nevertheless, a need finally arises from the frequent repetition of this tiny stimulus; the dim appearance in the mind, which always recurs, finally wants to be made clear. The best means to that end, one surely ought to think, would be for them to take the time to consider calmly and closely that which thus has influence on them. But what is active is the universe, and therein exists, among other things, all the individual things they have to think about and with which they are concerned in the remaining parts of their lives. From old habit their sense would automatically turn to these particulars, and the sublime and infinite would again be broken up before their eyes into nothing but particulars and trivialities. They feel this, and therefore they do not trust themselves and seek outside help; in the mirror of someone else's representation they wish to intuit what they would only ruin in immediate perception.

Thus they seek religion. But in the end they misunderstand this whole endeavor. For if the utterances of a religious person have awakened all those memories and, jointly affected by them they now go away with a stronger impression, they think their need is satisfied, that enough has transpired for the intimation of nature, and that they now have religion itself within them. Yet it has come to them – exactly as before, only in a higher degree – merely as a fleeting appearance from outside. They remain ever subject to this illusion because they have neither a concept nor an intuition of true and living religion, and in the vain hope of finally coming to the correct one, they repeat the same operation a thousand times, while always remaining where and what they have been. If they progressed, if religion would in this way be spontaneously and vivaciously implanted in them, they would soon leave that religion whose one-sidedness and passivity would thereupon no longer be suited to their condition or could even be tolerable. They would at least seek alongside it another circle in which their religion could also show itself as actively working beyond itself, and this circle would soon have to become their chief work and their exclusive love. Thus, in fact, people become all the more indifferent to the church the more they increase in religion, and the most pious sever themselves from it proudly and coldly. Nothing can in fact be clearer than that seekers of religion are in this association only because they have no religion; they persevere in it only so long as they have none.

But this situation arises directly from the manner in which such seekers treat religion. For even supposing a one-sided communication and a condition of voluntary passivity and renunciation were possible among the truly religious, the religious seekers' communal actions are dominated throughout by the greatest wrongheadedness and ignorance of the subject. If they knew religion well, their chief concern would then be that the one whom they have made their spokesman of religion would communicate the clearest, very individual intuitions and feelings to them. Yet they do not want that, but rather place limitations on all sides to expressions of his individuality, and demand that he illuminate concepts, opinions, and doctrines for them – in short, in place of the actual elements of religion, the abstractions about it. If they knew religion well, they would know from their own feelings that those symbolic actions I have said are essential to true religious fellowship can by their very nature be nothing but signs of the equality of the result that has arisen in everyone, the hint of a return to a shared center, nothing but the most full-voiced refrain after everything individuals have communicated in a pure and artistic manner. But of this they know nothing, for such actions are taken by them as existing for themselves and as requiring specific times. What is the consequence of this except that their communal action has nothing of the character of high and free enthusiasm that is thoroughly proper to religion, but instead is a juvenile, mechanical thing? Again, what does this mean except that they would first like to get their religion from outside? They want to attempt that by all means. Therefore they are so attached to dead concepts, to the results of reflection about religion, and eagerly absorb them, hoping that these will retrace the way of their actual genesis inside them and will again be transformed back into the living intuitions and feelings from which they were originally derived. Therefore they need the symbolic actions, which actually are last in religious communication, as stimulants to arouse what properly ought to precede them.

If I have spoken of this great and widespread association only very disparagingly and as something vulgar and base in comparison with the more excellent association that alone accords with my idea of the true church, that is certainly substantiated by the nature of the case, and I was not able to conceal my opinion concerning it. But I most solemnly protest against any conjecture you could entertain that I would concur with the desire that is becoming ever more general of preferring wholly to destroy this institution. No, if the true church will always stand open only to those who already possess religion, then there must be some binding agent between it and those who are still seeking religion. That is what this institution is supposed to be, for it must, by its very nature, always take its leaders and priests from the true church. Or shall religion be the sole human affair in which there are no institutions for the benefit of pupils and novices? Yet, to be sure, the whole style of this institution ought to be different, and its relationship to the true church must assume a different appearance. I am not permitted to keep silent on this matter. These wishes and views are too closely tied to the nature of religious fellowship, while the better state of things that I envisage contributes so much to its glorification that I must not keep my presentiments a secret.

At least this has been gained through the sharp distinction we have made between the two: We are able to reflect with one another very calmly and peaceably upon all the abuses that prevail in the ecclesiastical society and upon their causes. For you must admit that religion, since it has not produced such a church, must be provisionally acquitted of all blame for every ill this church supposedly has produced and for the abominable condition in which it may find itself, acquitted so completely that one cannot even reproach religion for being capable of degenerating into something of this sort, for it cannot possibly deteriorate where it has never even been. I grant that there is, and would have to be, a ruinous sectarian spirit in this society. Where religious opinions are used, as it were, as methods for the attainment of religion, they must certainly be brought into a determinate whole, for a method must by all means be determinate and also finite; and where religion is something that can be given only from outside, being accepted on the authority of the giver, then those who think differently must be viewed as disturbers of calm and sure progress, for by their mere existence and the claims connected with it, they weaken this authority.

I even confess that in ancient polytheism, in which the whole of religion did not purport to be one and more willingly submitted to every division and separation, this sectarian spirit was far milder and more humane. It organized itself and demonstrated its full power only in the otherwise better times of systematic religion; for where all individuals each believe they have a whole system with a center, there the work that is assigned to every individual detail must be incomparably greater. I grant both these things. But you will concede that the former is no reproach to religion at all and that the latter can prove nothing against the claim that the view of the universe as a system would be the highest level of religion. I grant that there is more support in this society for understanding or belief and for action and observance of customs than for intuition and feeling and that, therefore, however enlightened its doctrine may be, this society always verges on superstition and clings to some kind of mythology; but you will admit that it is so much the more removed from true religion. I grant that this association cannot exist without a permanent distinction between priests and laity, for those among them who might possibly succeed in being priests themselves, that is, have true religion, could not possibly remain laypeople, and even less could they comport themselves as if they had no religion. Rather, they would be free and compelled to leave this society and to seek the true church; but it remains certain that this separation, with all that is unworthy in it and with all the bad consequences possibly inherent in it, does not proceed from religion, but rather is itself completely irreligious.

Just now, however, I hear you raise a new objection, which seems once again to shift all these reproaches back onto religion. You will remind me that I myself have said that the great ecclesiastical society, I mean that institution for novices in religion, would in accord with the nature of the case have to take its leaders, the priests, only from the members of the true church because it lacks in itself the true principle of religion. If this is the case, you will ask how then can the virtuosos of religion tolerate, indeed more than tolerate, so much that would be contrary to the spirit of religion right where they are to rule, where all listen to their voice, and where they themselves should only hear the voice of religion. For to whom does the church owe all its regulations unless to the priests? Or if it is not as it should be, if perhaps they let the government of their filial society be wrested from them, where then is the lofty spirit we rightly seek in them? Why have they administered their important province so badly? Why have they permitted base passions to make what would have remained a blessing in the hands of religion into a scourge of humanity? And these are people, as you yourself confess, for whom the guidance of those needing their help so very much must be at once their most joyful and sacred duty.

Unfortunately, it is certainly not as I have maintained it is supposed to be. Who would wish to say that all of those, even the better part, – that after such groupings are once made, even the first and foremost among those who have ruled the great ecclesiastical society – were virtuosos of religion or even merely members of the true church? Only do not, I beg you, take what I must say to excuse them as a deceitful retort. When you declaim against religion, you do so usually in the name of philosophy; when you reproach the church, you speak in the name of the state; you want to defend the artists of politics of all eras by asserting that their handiwork has acquired so many imperfect and ill-advised positions by virtue of the intervention of the church. Now if I, speaking in the name of and for the religious virtuosos, blame their failure to conduct their business with better results on the state and on artists of politics, will you not suspect me of that same trick? Nevertheless, I hope you will not be able to deny my correctness if you listen to me concerning the actual origin of all this malady.

Every new doctrine, revelation, or view that awakens the sense of the universe in a respect in which it had not previously been stirred also wins some minds for religion, for whom exactly this aspect was the only one through which they were able to be introduced to the new and infinite world. For most of them this intuition naturally remains the focal point of religion. They form around their master a school of their own, a detached fragment of the true and universal church, which is just maturing quietly and slowly toward its union in spirit with this great whole. But before this results, when the new feelings have first permeated and satisfied their whole spirit, they are usually vehemently seized by the need to express what is in them lest the inner fire consume them. Thus they each proclaim, wherever and however they can, the new salvation that has awakened in them; from each object they find the transition to the newly discovered infinite; every conversation turns into a sketch of their particular religious view; every counsel, every wish, every friendly word into an enthusiastic commendation, which is the only way they know to the temple of religion.

Anyone who knows the effect of religion finds it natural that they should all speak, lest they fear that the stones would surpass them.[11] Anyone who knows the effect of a new enthusiasm finds it natural that this living fire vigorously gains ground, consuming some, warming many, and imparting to thousands the false superficial gleam of an inner glow. Precisely these thousands are the corruption. The youthful fire of new saints also takes them, too, to be true brethren. "What hinders them," they say all too rashly, "also from receiving the Holy Spirit?" They take themselves to be true brethren and allow themselves to be introduced into the bosom of the pious society in joyful triumph. But when the intoxication of first enthusiasm has passed, when the glowing surface has burned out, it is clear that the newer saints are not able to endure and share the condition in which the others find themselves; these latter mercifully descend to them and renounce their own higher and more intimate pleasure in order to help them again, and thus everything assumes an imperfect form. In this way, without external causes, a false and depraved church develops around each fragment of the true church that arises in isolation somewhere in the world, not separated from the true church but in and with it; this occurs through the corruption common to all human things, conforming to the eternal order by which this corruption most quickly seizes precisely the most fervid and active life. In this way it has happened in all times, among all peoples, and in every particular religion.[12]

But if everything were left to itself, this condition could not possibly have continued anywhere for long. Pour liquids of different weights and densities that have little internal attraction to one another into a container, shake them most vigorously together so that all appear to be one, and you will see how, if you only let it stand, everything gradually separates again and only like associates with like. Thus would it have happened here too, for that is the natural course of things. The true church would quietly have separated out again in order to enjoy the more intimate and higher fellowship of which the others were not capable; the bond among the latter would then have been as good as dissolved and their natural passivity would have had to await something external to determine what should become of them. But they would not have remained forsaken by the members of the true church. Who, aside from these members, would have had the least interest in them? What kind of an inducement would their condition have offered to the intentions of anyone else? What would there have been to gain or what sort of fame would there have been to achieve with them?

---

[11] Luke 19:40: "He answered, 'I tell you, if these were silent, the very stones would cry out.' "

[12] The analysis of the institutionalization of religious communities points to what Max Weber has identified as the "routinization [*Veralltäglichung*] of the charisma," the transformation of vivid, prophetic religion into more permanent institutional forms. See Weber, *The Sociology of Religion* (Boston, 1963), pp. 46–59, and 6off.

The members of the true church would thus have remained undisturbed in their possession, resuming their priestly office among these others in a new and better arranged form. These members would have each gathered around them exactly those who understood them best, who could be most affected in accordance with their individual way. Instead of the monstrous association whose existence you now bemoan, there would have arisen a great number of smaller and less definite societies in which people would, in all sorts of ways and places, have examined themselves regarding religion. The sojourn in those societies would have only been a transitory condition, preparatory for those in whom the sense of religion had arisen and decisive for those who had found themselves incapable of being stirred by religion in any way. O golden age of religion, when will the revolutions of human things give rise to you by artful means after they have failed to find you on the simple path of nature! Hail to those who shall then be called! The gods are gracious to them, and a rich blessing follows the endeavors of their mission to help beginners and to smooth the way to the temple of the eternal for dependents, endeavors that brings us present-day people so little fruit under the most adverse circumstances.

It is an unholy wish, but one I can hardly deny myself. Would that even the most distant inkling of religion had ever remained foreign to all heads of state, all virtuosos and artists of politics! Would that not one had ever been seized by the force of that epidemic enthusiasm, if they did not know how to separate their individuality from their profession and their public character! For that has become for us the source of all corruption. Why did they have to bring along into the assembly of the saints the petty vanity and strange presumption that the advantages they would be able to impart are everywhere important to the same degree? Why did they have to bring back from that assembly into their palaces and courts of justice the reverence due to servants of the sanctuary? You are right to wish that the hem of a priestly garment might never have touched the floor of a royal chamber; but let us only wish that the purple might never have kissed the dust on the altar, for had the latter not happened, the former would not have resulted. Indeed, if only no prince had ever been allowed in the temple before he had laid down in front of the portal the most beautiful royal ornaments, the rich cornucopia of all his favors and tokens of honor! But they have taken it with them; they have presumed they could decorate the simple nobility of the heavenly edifice with the tatters of their earthly splendor, and instead of a sanctified heart they have left behind worldly gifts as offerings to the highest being.

As often as a prince declared a church to be a corporation, a community with its own privileges, a notable personage of the civil world – this never occurred otherwise than when that unfortunate circumstance had already transpired whereby the society of believers and the society of those who desired faith, the true and the false church, which might have soon separated forever, were already mixed; for before that there was never a religious society large enough to arouse the attention of the ruler – as often as a prince, I say, permitted himself to be misled into this most dangerous and pernicious of all deeds, the ruin of this church was irrevocably decided and commenced. Such constitutional charter of political existence affects the religious society like the terrible head of Medusa: Everything turns to stone as soon as it appears. All things not belonging together, which were intertwined for only a moment, are now inseparably chained together; everything accidental, which might easily have been cast off, is now established forever; the garment is of one piece with the body, and every unbecoming fold is fixed for eternity. The larger and inauthentic society can now no longer be separated from the higher and smaller as it ought to be separated; it can no longer be divided or dissolved; it can change neither its form nor its articles of faith; its views, its customs, everything is condemned to remain in the condition in which it was just then found. But that is still not all: The members of the true church who are included in the false church are from now on as good as excluded by force from any part in its governance and are prevented from doing the little for it that might still be done. For there is now more to govern than they are able or wish to govern; there are now worldly things to order and care for, and even if they are immediately expert at worldly things in their domestic and civil affairs, they still cannot treat them as a matter of their priestly office. That is a contradiction that does not enter their mind and with which they can never reconcile themselves; it does not match their high and pure concept of religion and religious fellowship. Neither for the true church to which they belong nor for the greater society they are supposed to lead can they comprehend what they are now to do with the houses and lands they can acquire and with the riches they are able to possess, or how that is supposed to help them toward their goal. They are quite disconcerted and confused by this unnatural condition.

And if now, as a result of all this, all those are also attracted who would otherwise have ever remained outside, if it has now become the interest of all the proud, the ambitious, the covetous, and the schemers to press into the church in whose community they would otherwise have experienced only the most bitter boredom – if these now begin to feign participation in and knowledge of holy things in order to carry off the worldly reward, how shall the members of the true church not succumb to them? Who bears the blame, then, if unworthy people take the place of the virtuosos of holiness and if, under their supervision, everything that is most opposed to the spirit of religion is allowed to creep in and establish itself? Who but the state with its ill-considered generosity? But in a still more immediate way it is the cause of the dissolution of the bond between the true church and the external religious society. For after the state had conferred that fatal kindness upon this society, it thought it had a right to its active gratitude, and invested it with three highly important commissions in its affairs. The state more or less transferred to the church the care and oversight of instruction; under the auspices of religion and in the form of a congregation, it desires that the people be instructed in the duties its laws do not cover and be induced to moral sentiments; and through the power of religion and the teachings of the church, the state demands that its citizens be made truthful to it in their utterances. And as recompense for the services it demands, the state now robs the church of its freedom, as is the case in almost all parts of the civilized world where there is a state and a church; it treats it as an institution it has established and invented, and indeed the church's defects and abuses are almost all of the state's invention. The state alone presumes to decide who is fit to come forward in this society as model and priest of religion. And yet you still call religion to account if the religious society is not composed entirely of holy souls.

But I am not yet at the end of my indictment. The state even imports its interests into the innermost mysteries of the religious fellowship and defiles them.[13] When the church, in prophetic devotion, consecrates newborns to the deity and to striving for the highest, then the state wants to receive them at the same time from the church's hands into the list of its own charges; when the church gives an adolescent the first kiss of brotherhood as one who has now taken a first look into the sanctuaries of religion, that is also supposed to be the sign for the state of the first stage of his civil independence; if, with communal, pious wishes, the church sanctifies the union of two persons whereby they become instruments of the creative universe, that is simultaneously supposed to be its sanction for their civil bond; and the state will not even believe that a human being has disappeared from the arena of this world until the church has assured it that the church has given back his soul to the infinite and enclosed his dust in the bosom of the holy earth. It shows reverence for religion and an endeavor to keep it ever conscious of its own limits, that the state bows down so before it and its worshipers each time it receives something from the hands of the infinite or delivers it again unto the same. But the way in which all of this brings about the corruption of the religious society is clear enough. Now there is nothing in all its manifestations that would be directed to religion alone or in which religion by itself would be the main affair; in sacred speech and teachings as well as in secret and symbolic actions, everything is full of moral and political references, everything is diverted from its original purpose and concept. Hence, there are many among its leaders who understand nothing of religion and many among its members to whom it does not occur to want to seek it.

I think it is obvious that a society to which something of this sort can occur, a society that accepts with humility kindnesses that in no way serve it and with groveling readiness takes on burdens that hurl it into ruin, that allows itself to be abused by an alien power, that abandons the freedom and independence that are its birthright for an empty pretense, that gives up its high and noble purpose in order

---

[13] The sharp critique of political intrusion into religion is missed in the criticism of Schleiermacher as a "cultural accommodationist" in Dieter Schellong, *Bürgertum und christliche Religion: Anpassungsprobleme der Theorie seit Schleiermacher* (Munich, 1975) and Frederick Herzog, *Justice Church* (Maryknoll, NY, 1980); see Richard Crouter, "Schleiermacher and the Theology of Bourgeois Society: A Critique of the Critics," *Journal of Religion*, 66 (July 1986), 302–23.

to pursue things that lie completely off its path, cannot be a society that has a definite aim and knows exactly what it wants. And this brief reference to the circumstances of ecclesiastical society is, I think, the best proof that it is not the actual society of religious people, that at best a few particles of this were intermingled with it and overwhelmed by external elements, and that the whole, in order to absorb the first substance of this immeasurable corruption, already had to be in a state of unhealthy ferment in which the few sound parts soon completely disappeared. Full of holy pride, the true church would have refused gifts it could not use, knowing well that those who have found the deity and rejoice in their community, in their pure fellowship in which they would exhibit and communicate only their innermost being, actually have nothing in common whose possession would have to be protected for them by a worldly power, knowing that they need nothing on earth and can use nothing except a language in order to understand one another and have a space to be together, things for which they need no prince and his favor.

But if there is supposed to be a mediating institution through which the true church comes into a certain contact with the profane world with which it has nothing to do directly, an atmosphere, as it were, through which it simultaneously purifies itself and also draws to itself and shapes new material, what form shall this society then take, and how might it be freed from the corruption it has absorbed? Let the last question be left for time to answer. For everything that must happen sometime there are a thousand different ways, and for all diseases of humanity there are manifold methods of healing; each will be tried in its place and will lead to the goal. Only allow me to indicate this goal in order to show you all the more clearly that here too it has not been religion and its endeavor upon which you have vented your wrath.

The actual fundamental concept of that mediating institution is that those who have a certain degree of sense for religion, but who, because religion has not yet burst out or become conscious in them, are not yet capable of being incorporated into the true church, be intentionally shown so much religion that their capacity for it must necessarily be developed. Let us see what really hinders this from being able to happen in the present state of affairs.

I do not want to recall once again that the state at present selects, according to its own wishes, those who are now the leaders and teachers in this society – only reluctantly and under duress do I avail myself of the word "teacher," which is not suited for this business – who are oriented more toward the furtherance of the extraneous affairs to which the state has bound this institution. Nor shall I recall that one can be a highly intelligent pedagogue and a very sound, first-rate moralist without understanding the least thing about religion, and that hence there are many, whom the state numbers among its most estimable servants in this institution, who may easily be wholly wanting in it. If I assume that everyone the state appoints were really a virtuoso of religion, then you would nevertheless have to grant that no artist can communicate his art to a school with any success unless a certain similarity of prior knowledge obtains among the pupils; and yet this is less necessary in every art where the student progresses through practice and the teacher is useful primarily through criticism than in religion where the master can do nothing except to demonstrate and to illustrate. Here all his work must be in vain if the same thing is not only understandable to all but also appropriate and beneficial. The sacred orator must thus obtain his hearers, not by rank and file as they are counted out to him according to an old distribution, not by how their houses stand beside one another or how they are noted in the records of the police,[14] but by a certain similarity of capability and type of sense.

But even if you let only such as are equally close to religion assemble around one master, they are not all close in the same way. It is a serious mistake to want to limit any pupil to a particular master, because there can be no one such virtuoso in religion who would be able, through exposition and speech, to coax the hidden bud of religion to light for each of those who come before him. Its domain is far too encompassing. Recall the different ways in which a person makes the transition from the intuition of the finite to the intuition of the infinite and how his religion thereby assumes its own distinct character. Think of the different modifications by which the universe can be intuited and of the thousand individual intuitions and the different ways in which these intuitions might be put together in order to illumine one another. Consider that each one who seeks religion must encounter it under the specific form appropriate to his talents and his standpoint if his own religion is really supposed to be aroused by it. Thus you will find that it must be impossible for each master to be all things to everyone[15] and to be for all what they need, because no one can possibly be at the same time mystic, empirical theologian, and holy artist, at the same time deist and pantheist, at once master in prophecies, visions, and prayers, in presentations from history and from sentiment and much else besides. If only it were possible to enumerate all the splendid branches into which the heavenly tree of priestly art divides its crown. Master and disciple must be allowed to seek out and choose one another in perfect freedom, otherwise one is lost for the other; one must be permitted to seek what is beneficial to all individuals, and no persons must be compelled to give more than they have and understand.

But if all are supposed to teach only what they understand, then they cannot do even that if at the same time they are supposed to do yet something else in the same action. There can be no question about whether priestly individuals are able to present their religion with diligence and ingenuity as befits it and simultaneously perform some civil activity faithfully and with considerable perfection. Why, therefore, if circumstances permit, should the one who makes a profession of

---

[14] The age-old German practice of registering one's domicile with local police authorities, which is akin to basing the church on a residential parish system, is contrasted with Schleiermacher's idea of religious community as consisting of freely selected, mutual relationships.

[15] 1 Corinthians 9:22.

priesthood not also be permitted to be simultaneously a moralist in the service of the state? There is nothing against it. Only he must be both alongside each other and not in and through each other; he must not burden himself with both dispositions at the same time and should not discharge both responsibilities in the same action. If it deems it proper, let the state be satisfied with a religious morality. But religion rejects every moralizing prophet and priest; whoever would proclaim religion should do it purely. It would contradict all the ambition of a virtuoso if a true priest would want to engage in such unworthy and inconsistent arrangements with the state. When the state hires other artists, be it to take better care of their talents or to draw students, it removes all extraneous business from them and indeed even makes it a duty for them to refrain therefrom; it urges them to devote themselves primarily to the particular part of their art in which they believe they are able to achieve most, and then allows their genius full freedom; only with the artists of religion does it do precisely the opposite. They are supposed to embrace the whole domain of their subject, and in addition it prescribes for them the school to which they are to belong and further lays inappropriate burdens upon them. Either it should also give them the leisure to develop in particular some single part of religion for which they believe themselves most qualified and release them from everything else, or after it has set up for itself its institute for moral cultivation, which it must indeed do in that case, it should likewise allow the institute to pursue its essence for its own sake and should not worry at all about the priestly works that are completed in its domain, since the state needs them neither for show nor for utility as it does with other arts and sciences.

Away, therefore, with every such union of church and state! That remains my Cato's counsel to the end, or until I experience seeing every such union actually destroyed.[16] Away with everything that even looks like a closed union of laity and priests under or with one another! Apprentices are in any case not supposed to form a body, for one sees how little this avails in the mechanical trades and among the pupils of the Muses; but I also mean that the priests as such are not to form a brotherhood among themselves; they shall divide neither their business nor their clientele according to guild practices, but without being concerned about the others or without being bound any closer in this matter to one than to the others, each should do his own task; and even between teacher and congregation let there be no fixed bond. According to the basic principles of the true church, the mission of a priest in the world is a private affair; let the temple also be a private chamber where his voice rises to proclaim religion; let there be an assembly before him and not a congregation; let him be a speaker for all who will hear, but not a shepherd for a particular flock.

Only under these circumstances can truly priestly souls assist those who seek

---

[16] Marcus Porcius Cato Censorius (234–149 BC), a determined advocate of old Roman customs against Hellenistic corruption, ended his senate speeches with the words *Ceterum censeo Carthaginem esse delendam* (I am also of the opinion that Carthage ought to be destroyed).

religion. Only thus can this preparatory union really lead to religion and make itself worthy of being regarded as an appendage of the true church and as its vestibule, for only thus will everything disappear that is unholy and irreligious in its present form. Through universal freedom of choice, of recognition, and of judgment, the all too hard and fast distinction between priests and laity will be softened until the better among the laity arrive at the point where they are at the same time priests. Everything that was held together by the unholy bonds of symbols will be scattered and dispersed. The only means of finally ending this nonsense is for there to be no more point of union of this sort, for no one to offer the seekers a system of religion, but each to offer only one part. It is only a poor remedy of earlier times to carve up the church (using this word in this worst of all senses); it is in the nature of a polyp, each piece of which grows again into a whole, and if the concept contradicts the spirit of religion, more individuals of it are not better than fewer. The external society of religion will be brought closer to the universal freedom and the majestic unity of the true church only by becoming a flowing mass where there are no outlines, where each part is found, now here and now there, while all mingle peacefully with one another. The malicious spirit of sectarianism and proselytizing, which always leads further away from the essence of religion, will be annihilated only when people can no longer feel that they belong to one distinct circle and believe differently from someone else.

You see that in regard to this society, our wishes are completely identical. What is offensive to you also stands in our way, only that – always permit me to say this – the course of things would not at all have come to this if we had been left alone to be busy with what was actually our work. That this offense might again be removed is our common interest. How this will happen among us, whether only after a great convulsion as in the neighboring country,[17] or whether the state, by amicable agreement and without both first dying in order to be resurrected, will terminate its unsuccessful marriage with the church, or whether the state will only allow another, more virginal institution to appear beside the one that has been sold out to it, I know not. But until something of this sort does happen a hard fate will humble all holy souls who, permeated by the ardor of religion, exhibit their most holy possession even in the greater circle of the profane world and want to accomplish something with it. I do not want to tempt those who have been admitted to the order favored by the state to speculate about what they might be able to accomplish in this relationship for the innermost wish of their heart by speaking. Let them be on their guard about always or even quite frequently speaking only about religion and never purely, except on ceremonial occasions in order not to be untrue to their moral profession in which they are placed. But one will have to grant them that they are able to proclaim the spirit of religion by a priestly life, and let this be their consolation and their most beautiful reward. Everything about a holy person is significant; everything about an

17 An allusion to the French Revolution.

acknowledged priest of religion has a canonical meaning. Thus, let them exhibit the essence of religion in all their movements; let nothing of the expression of a pious sense be lost, even in the common relationships of life. Let the holy intimacy with which they treat everything show that even with trivialities over which a profane mind skims thoughtlessly, the music of sublime feelings might resonate in them; let the majestic calm with which they equate great and small demonstrate that they relate everything to the immutable and see the deity in everything in the same manner; let the bright cheerfulness with which they pass over every trace of transitoriness reveal to each how they live above time and above the world; let the most adroit self-denial indicate how much they have already annihilated the barriers of personality; and let the ever-active and open sense that does not overlook what is rarest or most common show how tirelessly they seek the universe and search out its expression. If their whole life and every movement of their inner and outer form are thus a priestly work of art, then perhaps, by this mute speech, the sense of what dwells in them will open up in many.

Not satisfied, however, to express the essence of religion, they must likewise also annihilate its false appearance. With childlike ingenuousness and the lofty simplicity of a complete unawareness that sees no danger and believes it needs no courage, they pass over everything that gross prejudice and subtle superstition have surrounded with an inauthentic glory of divinity. Indifferent as the infant Heracles, they let themselves be hissed at by the snakes of holy slander, which they can suffocate quietly and calmly in a moment.[18] Let them devote themselves to this holy service until better times, and I think that you yourselves will have respect for this unassuming dignity and will prophesy good things for its effect upon others.

But what shall I then say to those to whom you refuse the priestly robe because they have not run through a particular course of vain sciences in a certain manner?[19] Whither shall I direct them with the social drive of their religion inasmuch as that drive is oriented not only toward the higher church but also toward the world? Since they lack a greater arena where they could appear in a distinguishing manner, let them be satisfied with the priestly service of their household gods. A family can be the most cultivated element and the truest picture of the universe; if everything cooperates calmly and powerfully, then all powers that animate the infinite are here operative; if everything progresses quietly and surely, then the lofty world spirit rules here as well as there; if sounds of love accompany all movements, the family has the music of the spheres in its domain. They may cultivate, order, and cherish this sanctuary; they may represent it clearly

[18] Heracles was fathered by Zeus, who in the form of Amphitryon, had relations with his wife Alcmene. The jealous Hera wanted to destroy Heracles and his twin brother, Iphicles, whom Amphitryon had fathered on the same night, and for this purpose sent two giant poisonous snakes to the nursery of the boys. Heracles effortlessly strangled both of the reptiles.

[19] "Gedanken I" (no. 155), *KGA* 1.2, p. 36: "Concerning the scholarly preparation of priests and their preparation in Switzerland. From this one can determine what idea about religion seems to rule a people."

and distinctly in moral power; they may expound it with love and spirit; thus many of them and among them will learn to intuit the universe in its small, hidden dwelling; it will be a most holy place in which many will receive the consecration of religion. This priesthood was the first in the holy and childlike primeval world, and it will be the last when no other is any longer necessary.

Indeed, we await a time at the end of our artful cultivation when no other preparatory society for religion will be needed except pious domesticity. Now millions of persons of both sexes and all estates groan under mechanical and unworthy labors. The older generation cowardly succumbs and, with pardonable laziness, almost abandons the younger generation to chance in all things, except that they must likewise imitate and learn the same humiliation. This is the reason why they do not attain the free and open view with which alone one finds the universe. There is no greater hindrance to religion than that we must be our own slaves, for everyone is a slave who performs something that should be accomplishable by dead forces. One thing we hope for from the perfection of the sciences and arts is that they will make these dead forces subject to us, that they might turn the corporeal world and everything of the spiritual world that can be regulated into a fairy palace where the god of the earth needs only to utter a magic word or to press a button to have his commands done. Then, for the first time, everyone will be freeborn; then every life will be at the same time practical and contemplative; the rod of the taskmaster will be raised over no one, and all people will have peace and leisure to contemplate the world in themselves. Only for the unfortunates who lacked this leisure, whose senses were deprived of their powers, whose muscles had to be expended unceasingly on a taskmaster's service, was it necessary that more fortunate individuals stepped forth, and gathered them around themselves, in order to be their eyes while, in a few fleeting moments, imparting to them the intuitions of a lifetime. In that happy time when each person can freely exercise and use his senses, everyone, at the first awakening of the higher powers in holy youth under the care of paternal wisdom, will take part in religion who is capable of it. All one-sided communication will then cease, and the rewarded father will lead the powerful son not only into a more joyful world and into an easier life but also immediately into the holy assembly of the worshipers of the eternal who will now be increased in number and activity.

In the grateful feeling that when this better time has come one day, however distant it may still be, even the endeavours to which you devote your days will have contributed something to its coming, permit me once more to draw your attention to the beautiful fruit of your labor. Allow yourselves to be led once more to the sublime community of truly religious minds that, to be sure, is now scattered and almost invisible, but whose spirit nevertheless reigns everywhere, even where only a few are gathered in the name of the deity.[20] What is there here that should not fill

---

[20] Matthew 18:20: "For where two or three are gathered in my name, there am I in the midst of them."

you with admiration and respect, you friends and admirers of everything beautiful and good!

Together they are an academy of priests. Religion, which is for them the highest, is treated by each of them as art and object of study, and in addition it grants each person his own lot out of its infinite richness. As befits artists, each person joins the endeavor to complete himself in some particular aspect with the general sense for all that belongs in its holy realm. A noble rivalry prevails, and the longing to produce something worthy of such an assembly permits each person to absorb faithfully and diligently everything that belongs to his particular realm. It is preserved in a pure heart, arranged by a composed mind, adorned and perfected by heavenly art, and thus praise and knowledge of the infinite resound in every way and from every source inasmuch as every individual, with a joyful heart, produces the ripest fruits of his sense and vision, of his comprehension and feeling.

Together they are a choir of friends. Each person knows that he is also a part and a creation of the universe, that its divine work and life reveals itself also in him. He thus looks on himself as an object worthy of the intuition of others. With holy reserve but with a ready openness he lays bare everything he perceives in himself of the relations of the universe, all of the elements of humanity that take shape in him in order that everyone may enter and observe. Why should they also hide something from one another? Everything human is holy, for everything is divine.

Together they are a band of brothers. Or do you have a more intimate expression for the complete blending of their natures, not as regards their existence and volition, but as regards their sense and understanding? The more each person approaches the universe, the more he communicates himself to others, and the more perfectly do they become one; none is conscious of himself alone, but each is simultaneously conscious of the other. They are no longer merely people, but also humanity; going out beyond themselves, triumphing over themselves, they are on the way to true immortality and eternity.

If you have discovered something nobler in another realm of human life or in another school of wisdom, then impart it to me; I have given you mine.

Fifth Speech
On the Religions

It is beyond all doubt that a human being, engaged in the intuition of the universe, must be an object of esteem and veneration for all of you. No one who is still capable of understanding something of that condition can, upon considering it, withhold these feelings. You may despise anyone whose mind is readily and completely filled up with petty things, but you will try in vain to scorn the person who absorbs the greatest in himself and sustains himself by it.

You may love or hate each individual according to whether he moves with you or toward you on the limited path of activity and culture. But even that fairest feeling among those who are rooted in equality will no longer remain in you in relation to someone who is raised as far above you as the contemplator of the universe stands above anyone who is not in the same condition. Your wisest people say you must honor, even against your will, the virtuous individual who according to the laws of moral nature tries to determine the finite in conformity with infinite demands. But even if it were possible for you to find virtue itself somewhat ludicrous in the contrast of finite forces with an infinite undertaking, you would still be unable to deny esteem and reverence to that person whose senses are open to the universe. Such a person is far from every conflict and contrast and elevated above every endeavor; he is permeated by the influences of the universe and has become one with it; and when you observe him in this exquisite moment of human existence, he reflects the heavenly beam purely upon you. Therefore, I shall not inquire whether the idea I have given you about the soul of religion has wrung from you the esteem that, in consequence of your false representations and because you tarried with accidental things, has so often been denied by you. Nor shall I ask whether my thoughts concerning the connection of this capacity dwelling within us all with whatever else splendid and divine has been allotted to our nature have roused you to a more intimate intuition of our being and becoming. I have shown you a higher standpoint in that so much misunderstood, more sublime community of spirits,

95

which is where we, caring nothing for the renown of free choice or the exclusive possession of our innermost uniqueness and its secret, freely surrender ourselves so that we may be intuited as a work of the eternal and all-fashioning world spirit; yet I shall not inquire whether you now admire in that community the holy sanctity of fellowship that is incomparably higher than every earthly association, holier than even the tenderest bonds of friendship of moral minds. Whether, therefore, the whole of religion in its infinity, in its divine power, has carried you off to adoration – about all of that I do not inquire, for I am certain of the force of the object that was allowed to be set free only in order to work upon you. But now I have a new business to carry out and a new opposition to vanquish. I wish to lead you, as it were, to the God who has become flesh;[1] I want to show you religion as it has divested itself of its infinity and appeared, often in paltry form, among human beings; in the religions, you are to discover religion; in what stands before you as earthly and impure, you are to seek out the individual features of the same heavenly beauty whose form I have tried to reproduce.

When you cast a glance at the present condition of things, where churches and religions encounter one another nearly everywhere in their plurality and seem to be inseparably united in their isolation, and where there are as many doctrinal edifices and confessions of faith as churches and religious communities, you might easily be misled to believe that in my judgment about the plurality of the churches I have simultaneously expressed my judgment concerning the plurality of religions. But in this you would misunderstand my opinion completely. I have condemned the plurality of the churches; but just by showing from the nature of the matter that here all outlines are lost, all definite divisions disappear, and all is supposed to be one undivided whole, not only in spirit and sympathy but also in real connection, I have at all times presupposed the plurality of religions and their most distinct diversity as something necessary and unavoidable.[2] For why should the inner, true church be one? It is so that each person may intuit and let the religion of another be imparted to him that he cannot intuit as his own and that was thought to be wholly different from it. Why should the external and inauthentic, so-called church also be one? It is so that each person may seek out religion in a form that is congenial to the slumbering bud that lies in him, and thus this bud has to be of a specific kind because it can be stimulated and awakened only by the same specific kind. These manifestations of religion could not be intended merely as complements that differ only in number and size, which, if one had brought them together, would only then have made up a uniform and perfected whole. For in that case, each of us would arrive by his own natural progress at the same religion everyone else has; the religion he allows to be imparted to himself would change into his own and become

---

[1] John 1:14: "And the Word became flesh and dwelt among us, full of grace and truth." By presenting the essence of religion in particular, embodied form the final speech assumes a decidedly Johannine cast.

[2] See the Introduction, p. xxxv n. 66 on Gerardus van der Leeuw.

one with it. And the church, this community with all believers, which according to the accepted view presents itself as indispensable to every religious person, would only be an interim institution that abolishes itself all the more quickly through its own action. I have in no way wanted to entertain or represent this institution in this way. Thus I have presupposed the multiplicity of religions, and I likewise find them rooted in the essence of religion.

Everyone can easily see that no one can possess religion completely, for the human being is finite and religion is infinite. But it also cannot be strange to you that religion is not able to be only partially parceled out among people, as much as each can grasp, but that it must organize itself in manifestations that are rather different from one another. Only remember the several levels of religion to which I have drawn your attention. The religion of a person who considers the universe a system cannot merely be a continuation of the view of someone who only intuits religion in its apparently contradictory elements. In turn, those for whom the universe is still a chaotic and undifferentiated representation cannot arrive on their path at the place where the latter stands. Now you may call these differences types or degrees of religion; consequently you will, however, have to admit that everywhere else where there are such classifications individual people are also customarily found.

Each infinite force, once it divides and separates itself in its manifestations, also reveals itself in unique and varied forms. Hence the plurality of religions differs completely from that of churches. In their plurality the churches are, to be sure, merely fragments of a particular individual entity that is defined utterly as one by the understanding and whose unity is unattainable only at the level of sensory presentation. Whatever moved these individual fragments to view themselves as distinct individuals was always only a misunderstanding that had to be based on the influence of an extraneous principle. Yet in accord with its concept and essence religion is infinite and immeasurable, even for the understanding; it must therefore have in itself a principle of individualization, for otherwise it could not exist at all and be perceived. Thus we must postulate and seek out an infinite number of finite and specific forms in which religion reveals itself. Where we find something that claims to be such, as each separated religion purports to be, we must examine it to see if it is designed in accord with this principle and must clarify for ourselves the determinate concept it is supposed to exhibit, under whatever strange trappings this concept may be hidden, and how much it may also be distorted by the transient influences to which the imperishable has lowered itself and by the unholy hand of humankind.

If you do not want to have only a general concept of religion, and it would indeed be unworthy if you wished to be content with such an incomplete knowledge; if you also want to understand it in its reality and in its manifestations; if you want to intuit these even with religion as a work of the world spirit progressing into infinity – then you must abandon your vain and futile wish that there might be only one religion, lay aside your loathing of its plurality, and, as impartially as possible, approach all those that have already developed out of the eternally rich womb of the universe in the changing forms during the course of humanity, which is also progressing in this respect.

You call these existing determinate religious manifestations "positive religions," and under this name they have long been the object of a quite exquisite hatred. But in spite of all your aversion to religion generally, you have always endured ever more easily and have even spoken with esteem of something else, which is called "natural religion."[3] I shall not hesitate to allow you a glimpse of my inner convictions on this matter, since I for my part protest most vehemently against this preference. In consideration of all those who generally purport to have and to love religion, I declare this preference for natural religion to be the grossest inconsistency and the most obvious self-contradiction on grounds of which you will certainly approve, once I am able to explain them. In contrast to you, to whom any religion whatever was offensive, I have always found it very natural to make this distinction. So-called natural religion is usually so refined and has such philosophical and moral manners that it allows little of the unique character of religion to shine through; it knows how to live so politely, to restrain and accommodate itself so well, that it is tolerated everywhere. In contrast, every positive religion has exceedingly strong features and a very marked physiognomy, so that it unfailingly reminds one of what it really is with every movement it makes and with every glance one casts upon it. If this is the true and internal reason for your aversion, as well as being the only one that concerns the subject itself, then you must now liberate yourselves from it; and I should actually have no more quarrel with it. For if you now, as I hope, pass a more favorable judgment on religion, if you realize that a special and noble human capacity lies at its core, which must consequently also be cultivated wherever it shows itself, then it cannot be offensive to you to intuit it in the determinate forms in which it has already actually appeared. Rather, you must deem these all the more worthy of your contemplation, the more the unique and distinguishing features of religion are formed in them.

But not admitting these arguments, you will perhaps heap all the old reproaches, which you were otherwise accustomed to make against religion, upon the individual religions, while maintaining that these reproaches are occasioned and justified anew by the element that you call positive in religion. You will deny that they can be manifestations of true religion. You will draw my attention to the way in which all of them without exception are full of what, on my own testimony, is not religion and conclude that, therefore, a principle of corruption must lie deep in their constitution. You will remind me of how each of them proclaims itself as the only true religion and just declares its particular characteristic to be the highest; of how

---

[3]   In contrast with popular deism of the eighteenth century and its philosophical critics (e.g., David Hume in *Dialogues Concerning Natural Religion*, 1776), Schleiermacher appeals to his Romanticist contemporaries to turn back to the historical particularity of religious tradition.

they distinguish themselves from one another precisely by something that purports to be essential but that each should get rid of as much as possible; and of how, wholly against the nature of true religion, they prove, contradict, and quarrel, whether with the weapons of art and of the understanding or with still more unusual and more unworthy means. You will add that, since you esteem religion and acknowledge it as something important, you just now have to take a lively interest in seeing that it is everywhere afforded the greatest freedom to fashion itself in the most manifold ways in all directions and that, therefore, you have to hate all the more vividly the determinate forms of religion that bind all who confess them to the same form, withdraw from them the freedom to follow their own nature, and constrain them in unnatural limits. And in all these points you will energetically commend to me the superiority of natural over positive religion.

I declare once more that I will not deny these distortions and that I find nothing to object to in the repugnance you feel toward them. Indeed, I recognize in all of them that much lamented degeneration and deviation into a foreign region; the more divine religion itself is, the less do I wish to adorn its corruption and admiringly care for its wild aberrations. But forget for once this quite one-sided view and follow me to another. Consider how much of this corruption is attributable to those who have forced religion out of the depths of the heart and into the civil world; admit that much corruption is generally unavoidable as soon as the infinite takes on an imperfect and limited raiment, and descends into the realm of time and the universal sway of finite things to let itself be dominated by it. But however deep this corruption may be rooted in these religions, and however much they may have suffered under this, yet consider also that it is the properly religious view of all things to seek every trace of the divine, the true, and the eternal, even in what appears to us to be vulgar and base, and to worship even the most distant trace. Why should what has the most just claims to be directed religiously be deprived of the benefit of such contemplation? And yet you will still find more than distant traces of divinity.

I invite you to consider every faith humanity has confessed, every religion that you designate with a definite name and character and that has perhaps long since degenerated into a code of empty customs and a system of abstract concepts and theories. If you investigate them at their source and their original components, you will find that all the dead slag was once the glowing outpouring of the inner fire that is contained in all religions, and is more or less of the true essence of religion as I have presented it to you. Each religion was one of the particular forms eternal and infinite religion necessarily had to assume among finite and limited beings. However, you must not grope about by chance in this infinite chaos – although I must forgo leading you around in it in systematic and complete fashion, for that would be the study of a lifetime and not the task of an address. So that you are not misled by vulgar concepts, you should survey the true content and the actual essence of the individual religions according to a correct standard, and should learn

99

to distinguish the inner from the outer, the native from the borrowed and foreign, the holy from the profane according to determinate and firm ideas. In order to do this, forget for the present each individual religion and what is taken to be its individual characteristic and first seek from inside out to attain a general idea of what actually makes up the essence of a determinate form of religion. You will find that precisely the positive religions are these determinate forms in which infinite religion manifests itself in the finite, and that natural religion cannot claim to be something similar inasmuch as it is merely an indefinite, insufficient, and paltry idea that can never really exist by itself. You will find that in these positive religions alone a true, individual development of the religious capacity is possible and that by their very essence they do no injury at all to the freedom of their confessors.

Why have I assumed that religion cannot be completely given except in an unending multitude of thoroughly determinate forms? Only on grounds that were explained when I spoke about the essence of religion.[4] These are that every intuition of the infinite exists wholly for itself, is dependent on no other, and has no other as a necessary consequence; they are infinitely many and have no reason in themselves why they should be related to one another in one way and not in some other, and yet each appears completely different if it is viewed from another point or related to another intuition; thus the whole of religion cannot possibly exist otherwise than when all these different views of each intuition that can arise in such a manner are really given. This is not possible except in an infinite multitude of various forms, each of which is thoroughly determined by the different principle of relation in it and in each of which the same object is quite differently modified; that is to say, that are all true individuals. By what are these individuals determined and how do they differentiate themselves from one another? What is the common element in their components that holds them together or the principle of attraction they follow? How does one decide to which individual a given religious datum must belong?

Something cannot be a determinate form of religion simply because it contains a determinate quantity of religious material. Precisely this is the complete misunderstanding about the essence of individual religions that is frequently disseminated among their adherents themselves and has laid the foundation for their corruption. They just supposed that because so many people adhere to the same religion they would also have to have the same religious views and feelings, the same opinions and beliefs, and that this common element would have to be the essence of their religion. It is not readily possible to find the truly characteristic and individual element of a religion everywhere with certainty, if one abstracts it thus from the individual; but no matter how general the concept is, surely this individuality can least of all be found there; and if you perhaps also believe that the positive religions are for that reason disadvantageous to a person's freedom to develop his religion

---

[4]   See the Second Speech, p. 26.

because they demand a certain number of religious intuitions and feelings and exclude others, you are in error.

Individual intuitions and feelings are, as you know, the elements of religion, and only to observe these in a quantitative fashion, such as asking how many of them are present and what kinds for whom, cannot possibly lead us to the character of an individual instance of religion. If religion has to individualize itself because different views of every intuition are possible depending on the way it is related to the rest, we would certainly not be helped at all by such an exclusive condensing of several among them, whereby none of those possible views is defined. If the positive religions are distinguished from one another merely by such an act of exclusion, they would certainly not be the individual manifestations we seek. That this is really not their character becomes clear from the fact that it is impossible to attain a specific concept of them from this point of view; yet this concept must be their foundation, because they would otherwise very soon flow into one another. We have considered it part of the essence of religion that there is no definite inner connection between the various intuitions and feelings of the universe, and that each individual intuition and feeling exists for itself and can lead to every other one through a thousand accidental combinations.

Nothing is therefore already more accidental in the religion of every individual person as it forms in the course of his life than the particular quantity of his religious material. Individual views may be obscured for him, others may open up for him and form themselves clearly, and his religion is, in this regard, ever in motion and flowing. It is impossible, therefore, that this flowing quality can be a permanent and essential element in the religion common to several individuals; for it must be a highly accidental and rare occurrence, and then only briefly, when several persons stop in the same precise circle of intuitions and proceed along the same path of feelings. Among those who determine their religion in this way, there is therefore a standing conflict about what is essential to it and what is not; they do not know what they are supposed to establish as characteristic and necessary, what they are to separate as free and accidental. They do not find the point from which they can survey the whole and do not understand the religious manifestation in which they themselves live, for which they presume to fight, and to whose degeneration they contribute, in that they do not know where they stand and what they are doing. But the instinct they do not understand guides them more correctly than their understanding, and nature holds together what their false reflection and their actions based thereon would annihilate. Whoever posits the character of a particular religion in a specific quantity of intuitions and feelings must necessarily assume an inner and objective connection that binds just these intuitions and feelings to one another and excludes all others; and this delusion is precisely the principle of building systems and sects that is so completely opposed to the spirit of religion. The whole they strive to create in this way would not be a whole such as we seek, whereby religion in all its parts attains a specific form, but it would be a violent excision out of the infinite, not a religion, but a sect, the most irreligious concept one can want to realize in the realm of religion.

But the forms that the universe has brought forth and that are really present are not totalities of this type. All sectarianism, be it now speculative, which brings individual intuitions into philosophical coherence, or ascetic, which insists on a system and a certain succession of feelings, works for a uniformity of the greatest possible completeness of all who want to participate in the same fragment of religion. If those who are infected by this mania and who certainly do not lack activity still do not succeed in bringing some positive religion to such a state, you will admit that these sects, since they were, after all, generated at one time, and insofar as they still exist in spite of those attacks, must have been formed according to another principle and must have another character. Indeed, if you think of the time when they originated, you will realize this even more clearly, for you will recall that every positive religion, during the time of its formation and its flowering, when its peculiar life force has the freshest and most youthful effect and thus can be recognized most assuredly, moves in a completely opposite direction, not concentrating itself and excluding much from itself, but growing towards the outside, ever sprouting new shoots and appropriating more religious material to itself and fashioning it according to its particular nature. Thus religions are not formed according to that false principle; it is not one with their nature; it is an external, intruding corruption, and since it is just as hostile to them as to the spirit of religion generally, their relationship to this principle, which is a perpetual warfare, can sooner prove than contradict the fact that they are the individual appearances of religion that we seek.

All the variations of religion, to which I have previously drawn your attention here and there, are just as insufficient to produce a form of religion that is a thoroughly defined individual. Those three so frequently adduced ways of intuiting the universe as chaos, as system, and in its elementary multiplicity are far removed from being just so many individual and specific religions.[5] You know that if we divide a concept as much as we want and continue ad infinitum, we still never arrive at individuals by this means but always only at less universal concepts that are contained under the earlier concepts as divisions and subdivisions, and which in turn can encompass a multitude of very different individual instances among themselves. To find the particular essential character itself, we must proceed from the universal concept and its attributes. But those three differences in religion are in fact nothing else than a customary and universally recurring division of the concept of intuition. They are, therefore, types of religion but not determinate forms, and the need motivating our search for them would also not be at all satisfied by the fact that religion is present in this threefold manner. Certainly each

---

[5]   On the typology which sees intuition occurring as chaos, system, and in elementary multiplicity, see the Second Speech, n. 47, and related text.

individual intuition has its own character, and thus each specific form of religion must rely on one of these types. But a special relation and orientation of the various intuitions to one another is by no means exclusively determined by them, and in this respect everything remains, according to this division, just as infinite and ambiguous as before.

It might have more the appearance that in religion personalism and the pantheistic type of representation opposed to personalism present us with two such individual forms of religion. But it is also merely appearance, after all. Indeed, these types of representation run through all three types of religion, and already for that reason they cannot be individual instances, since it is impossible for an individual to unite in itself three different special characters. Upon more rigorous observation you must, however, also see that they likewise provide no specific relation of the several religious intuitions to one another. Indeed, if the idea of a personal deity were a separate religious intuition, then personalism would certainly be a wholly distinct form in each of the three types of religion, for all religious material in personalism is related to this idea. But is this the case? Is this idea a separate intuition of the universe, a separate impression of the universe that something certain and finite produces in me? If so, would pantheism, which is contrasted with personalism, also have to be one? Thus there would have to be certain specific perceptions out of which both personalism and pantheism would be created. And where have these perceptions ever been exhibited? There would have to be particular intuitions of religion that are mutually opposed, which cannot be the case. Moreover, these two types of representation are by no means different intuitions of the universe in the finite, not elements of religion, but different ways of simultaneously conceptualizing the universe, while being intuited in the finite, as an individual, since the one intuition then attributes a specific consciousness to it and the other does not.

In respect to their reciprocal situation, all single elements of religion likewise remain undefined, and none of the many views of these elements is made real by the fact that the one or the other thought accompanies them. As you can see everywhere, whenever something is presented as being simultaneously religious and deistic, you will find that all intuitions and feelings, and especially – which is the point around which everything in this sphere is accustomed to turn – intuitions about the movements of humanity in the particular, and of the unity in that which lies beyond its free choices, hover indeterminately and ambiguously in their reciprocal relationship. Both personalism and pantheism are thus only more general forms, whose realm is to be filled up first with what is individual and determinate; and if you further restrict this realm by combining them individually with one of the three specific types of intuition, then these forms, which are pieced together from different principles of dividing the whole, are for all that merely special subdivisions, but in no way are they thoroughly defined and closed wholes. Therefore neither naturalism – which I understand to be the intuition of the universe in its elementary multiplicity, without the idea of personal consciousness and will of individual elements – nor pantheism, neither polytheism nor deism, is an individual and determinate religion such as we are seeking, but each is merely a type within whose realm many actual individuals have already developed and still more will develop. In trying to assign your natural religion its proper place, note well that pantheism and deism are not determinate forms of religion, if it by chance turns out that natural religion is nothing but these types.

Let me say it briefly: An individual instance of religion such as we are seeking cannot be established other than through free choice by making a particular intuition of the universe the center of the whole of religion and relating everything therein to it. It cannot happen otherwise, since every single intuition would have similar claims to be established. Thereby the whole suddenly takes on a determinate spirit; everything that was previously ambiguous and indeterminate is fixed; of the infinitely varied views and relationships of individual elements, all of which were possible and all of which should be presented, a single one is thoroughly realized through every such formation; all individual elements now appear from a perspective of the same name that is turned toward that center, and just in this way all feelings receive a common tone while becoming livelier and more engaged in one another. Only in the totality of all forms that are possible according to this construction can the whole of religion really be expressed. It is, therefore, exhibited only in an infinite succession of waxing and waning forms, and only what lies in one of these forms contributes something to its completed presentation. Every such formation of religion, where everything is seen and felt in relation to a central intuition, wherever and however it is formed, and whatever this preferred intuition may be, is a truly positive religion. In respect to the whole of religion, it is a heresy – a word that should again be brought to honor – because something highly voluntary is the cause of its having arisen.[6] In regard to the community of all participants and their relationship to him who first founded their religion it is its own school and discipleship, because he first saw that intuition in the center of religion. And if religion is exhibited only in and through such determinate forms, then only the person who settles down in such a form with his own religion really establishes a firm abode and, might I say, an active citizenship in the religious world; only he can boast of contributing something to the existence and growth of the whole; only he is a truly religious person with a character and fixed and definite traits.

But, you will ask with considerable perplexity, must everyone in whose religion one intuition is dominant belong to one of the existing forms? By no means. Yet one intuition must be dominant in his religion or else it is as good as nothing. Have I then spoken of two or three determinate forms and said that they shall remain the only ones? Innumerable ones shall develop from all points, and a person who does

---

6 *eine Häresis*, literally, "choice" in Greek. Cf. the approach to religious traditions of Peter L. Berger, *The Heretical Imperative: Contemporary Possibilities of Religious Affirmation* (Garden City, NY, 1979), who cites this passage, p. 132.

not fit into one of those that are readily available, I might say, who would not have been in a position of making it himself if it did not already exist, will surely not belong to any of them, but make a new one. If he remains alone in it and without disciples, it does no harm. In every place there are always seeds of something that cannot attain a more widely diffused existence, yet they exist, and thus his religion also exists and has just as much definite form and organization, is just as much a truly positive religion, as if he had founded the greatest school.

You see that the prior existence of these available forms in no way prevents a person from cultivating a religion according to his own nature and sense. Whether he abides in one of them or constructs one of his own merely depends upon which intuition of the universe first seizes him with genuine vivacity. Dim presentiments that disappear unrecognized, without penetrating to the interior of the mind, that are known to hover around each person frequently and early on, and that might arise from hearsay and remain without any relatedness, are also nothing individual. But if the sense for the universe opens up permanently for him in a clear consciousness and a specific intuition, then he relates everything hereafter to this intuition, and everything takes shape around it; his religion is determined by this moment; and I hope you will not say that something natural or inherited could have an influence on that, and you will not suppose the religion of a person to be less unique and less his own if it is situated in a region where several are already gathered. For even if thousands before him, with him, and after him begin their religious life with the same intuition, would it for that reason be the same in all and would religion take shape in all alike? Remember that, in every specific form of religion, not only a limited number of intuitions to the same view and the same relationship to one of them should be allowed, but the whole unending multitude of intuitions; does that not accord sufficient room to move for every person? I would doubt that a single form of religion would have already succeeded in taking possession of its whole realm and in determining and exhibiting everything according to its spirit. It has been granted to only a few persons in the time of their freedom and their better life to form correctly and to complete only that which is closest to their center. "The harvest is great, and the laborers are few."[7] An infinite field is opened in each of these religions wherein thousands may scatter themselves; enough uncultivated regions come into the view of all individuals who are capable of creating and bringing forth something of their own, and holy blossoms give forth their fragrance and are resplendent in all regions into which no one has yet penetrated to observe and to enjoy them.

Yet your reproach that a human being could no longer properly develop his own religion within a positive religion is so weakly founded that not only, as you have just seen, does a positive religion allow enough room for everyone, but precisely insofar as a person enters a positive religion, and for this same reason, his own

---

[7] Matthew 9:37; Luke 10:2.

religion is able to be a particular individual as well as become one by itself. Consider once more the sublime moment in which man first enters into the realm of religion. The first specific religious view, which penetrates his mind with such force that his sense for the universe is brought to life through a singular stimulation and is now forevermore set in motion, certainly determines his religion; it is and remains his fundamental intuition in relation to which he will view everything, and it determines in advance in which form every element of religion must appear to him as soon as he perceives it. That is the objective side of this moment; look, however, also at the subjective side: His religion is determined by himself in that respect insofar as it belongs to an individual completely enclosed in regard to the infinite whole, but merely as an undetermined fragment of the same, for this individual can exhibit the whole only when united with several of them. Thus even his religiousness is brought into the world by this moment with respect to the infinite religious capacity of humanity as a wholly unique and new individual instance. That is to say, this moment is simultaneously a definite point in his life, a link in the series of spiritual activities that are wholly characteristic for him, an occurrence that, like every other, stands in a particular relationship with a before, a now, and an afterward; and since the before and now are completely unique in each individual, so also is the afterward.

Since the whole subsequent religious life attaches itself to the instant and situation when this moment surprised his mind as well as to his relationship with the earlier, more impoverished consciousness, and, as it were, develops from it genetically, there is in each individual a unique, thoroughly defined personality as well as his human life itself. Thus when a part of the infinite consciousness tears itself away and, as finite consciousness, attaches itself to a definite moment in the series of organic evolutions, a new man arises, a unique being whose differentiated existence is independent of the multitude of other persons and of the objective quality of his deeds and actions. This new being consists in the unity of the continuing consciousness joined to that first moment, in the unique relation of every later moment to a specific earlier one, and in the influence of this earlier of the formation of the later. Thus, in that moment in which a definite consciousness of the universe begins, a unique religious life also arises, unique, not by being irrevocably limited to a particular number and selection of intuitions and feelings, nor by the nature of the religious material occurring in it that he has in common with all who are spiritually born at the same time and in the same realm of religion, but by what he can have in common with no one, by the abiding influence of the situation in which his mind had first been greeted and embraced by the universe, by the unique way in which he assimilates contemplation of the universe and reflection upon it, by the character and tone in which this harmonizes the whole subsequent series of his religious views and feelings, all of which is never lost, however far he may hereafter move beyond that intuition of the universe that the early childhood of his religion offered him.

Every intelligent finite being verifies its spiritual nature and its individuality by leading you back to that marriage of the infinite with the finite as its origin, to that incomprehensible fact beyond which you are not able to pursue the finite series further, and in which your imagination fails you if you would explain it on the basis of something earlier, whether it be either free choice or nature. You must likewise concede a unique spiritual life to everyone who shows you as documentation of his religious individuality just such an incomprehensible fact about how, in the midst of the finite and the individual, the consciousness of the finite and the whole has developed for that person. You must also consider that each person who can thus specify the birthday of his spiritual life and relate a wondrous tale of the origin of his religion, which appears as an immediate influence of the deity and as a movement of its spirit, can be unique, through whom something special is supposed to be said. For such a thing does not happen in order to bring forth an empty doublet in the realm of religion. Each being that arises in that way can be explained only from itself and can never be completely understood, if you do not go back as far as possible to the initial expressions of free choice in earliest times. In the same way each religious personality is also a completed whole, and your understanding of it rests on your seeking to fathom its first revelations.

For that reason I also believe that you are not serious with this entire complaint against the positive religions. It is probably only a preconceived notion, for you are far too careless about the matter for your view of it to be justified. You have probably never felt the call to cling to the few religious people whom you can perhaps observe – even though they are always attractive and worthy enough of love – in order to investigate more closely, through the microscope of friendship or the closer knowledge that at least looks similar to it, how they are oriented to and by the universe. For my part I have diligently examined them. I seek them out just as assiduously and observe them with the same holy care you devote to the curiosities of nature; and it has often occurred to me that this might lead you to religion if you only paid heed to how almightily the deity quite specifically edifies even as its holiest and truest, apart from everything that is otherwise built and formed in man, the part of the soul in which it preeminently dwells, in which it reveals and contemplates itself in its direct workings, and how the deity therein exalts itself through the inexhaustible manifoldness of forms in its entire richness.

I, at least, am ever newly astonished by the many remarkable developments in the so sparsely populated realm of religion, at the way in which they differ from one another through the most varied levels of receptivity for the attraction of the same object, through the greatest variety that is operative in them, through the manifoldness of tone that the decisive superiority of one or the other type of feeling brings forth, and through all sorts of idiosyncrasies of sensitivity and peculiarities of temperament inasmuch as each soon has his own situation in which the religious view of things especially dominates him. Then again I am astonished by how the human religious character is often utterly unique, separate from all that we disclose in our other aptitudes; how the calmest and soberest mind is here capable of being affected by something resembling the strongest passion; how the dullest sense for vulgar and earthly things here feels deeply to the point of sadness and sees clearly to the point of rapture and prophecy, how the spirit that is most timid in all worldly affairs speaks boldly throughout the world and the age concerning and on behalf of holy things, often to the point of martyrdom. How amazingly often is this religious character formed and pieced together from cultivation and vulgarity, capability and limitation, tenderness and hardness, intermingled and interwoven with one another in each person in a unique way.

Where have I seen all these forms? In the actual realm of religion, in its particular forms, in the positive religions that you decry as merely negative, among the heroes and martyrs of a specific faith, among the enthusiasts of specific feelings, among the worshipers of a specific light and individual revelations; there I shall show them to you at all times and among all peoples. Moreover, it is only there, nowhere else, that they can be met. Just as no human being can come into existence as an individual without simultaneously, through the same act, also coming into a world, into a definite order of things, and being placed among individual objects, so also a religious person cannot attain his individuality without, through the same act, also dwelling in a determinate form of religion. Both are the effect of one and the same moment, and therefore one cannot be separated from the other. If a person's original intuition of the universe does not have enough strength to make itself the focal point of personal religion around which everything in religion moves, then neither is its attraction strong enough to initiate the process of a unique and vigorous religious life.

Now that I have given you this account, tell me how it is with this personal development and individualization in your celebrated natural religion. Show me among its adherents an equally great multiplicity of strongly delineated characters! For I must confess that I myself have never been able to find it among them; and if you boast that natural religion accords its adherents more freedom to form themselves religiously according to their own inclination, then I can imagine your boast meaning nothing else than – as the word is so often used – the freedom to remain unformed, the freedom from every compulsion to be, to see, and to feel something even remotely specific. Religion plays far too paltry a role in their mind. It is as if religion had no pulse of its own, no unique vascular system, no unique circulation, and thus also no temperature of its own and no assimilative power for itself and no character; it is everywhere intermingled with their ethical life and their natural sentimentality; in combination with these, or rather, meekly following them, religion moves indolently and sparingly and as a sign of its existence it is only occasionally separated out from them drop by drop. To be sure, I have encountered many a noteworthy and strong religious character whom the adherents of the positive religions, not without being astonished at the phenomenon, passed off as an adherent of natural religion. Yet upon closer inspection the adherents of natural religion no longer recognized this individual as one of their own; he had already swerved somewhat from the original purity of rational religion and had taken up something arbitrary and positive into his own religion, which the former adherents simply did not recognize because it was too very different from their own. Why do they immediately mistrust every person who brings something unique into his religion? They simply want them all to be uniform – I mean only contrasted to the extreme on the other side, the sectarians – uniform in indeterminacy. Particular personal development is so unthinkable in natural religion that its most authentic devotees do not even like the religion of a person to have its own history and begin with a notable event. That is already too much for them, for moderation is their chief interest in religion, and a person who is able to say such a thing about himself immediately comes under the suspicion of being disposed toward a loathsome fanaticism.

By and by, man is supposed to become religious just as he becomes clever and prudent and everything else he is supposed to be. All that is supposed to come to him through schooling and instruction; there must be nothing along with it that could be regarded as supernatural or even merely unusual. I do not wish to say that the fact that schooling and instruction are supposed to be everything arouses the suspicion in me that natural religion has been completely overtaken by that evil of an amalgamation, or even of a transformation, into philosophy and morals; but it is clear, however, that they have not proceeded from some living intuition and have no intuition as their stable center, because among themselves they do not know what might seize a person in a special way. The belief in a personal God, as they themselves know, is not the result of a specific, single intuition of the universe in the finite; therefore, they do not ask persons who have such a belief how they came to it; but rather just as they want to demonstrate faith, they also imagine it would have to be demonstrated to everyone. You would have difficulty pointing out any other and more specific central point that they would have. The little that their meager and lean religion contains stands there for itself in indefinite ambiguity; they have providence in general, justification in general, divine tutelage in general; all these intuitions they see in relation to one another, now in this, now in that perspective and abbreviated form, and they mean for them now this, now that. Or if one does encounter therein a common reference to one point, this point lies outside religion, and it is a reference to something foreign, to the end that ethical life would certainly not be hindered and that the drive for happiness receive some support – things about which truly religious people have never asked in constructing the elements of their religion, connections by which their scanty religious possessions are still more scattered and driven asunder.

This natural religion thus has no unity of a specific view for its religious intuition. It is therefore no determinate form, no truly individual presentation of religion; and those who confess only it have no specific dwelling in its realm, but are strangers whose home, if they have one (which I doubt), must lie elsewhere.

They remind me of the substance[8] that is supposed to be suspended, thin and dispersed, between the world systems, pulled a little bit here by the one, there by the other, but pulled by none strongly enough to be carried into its orbit. Why it is there the gods may know; it must be to show that even the indefinite can exist in a certain fashion. But it is actually only a matter of waiting for an existence they would not be able to achieve unless a force, stronger than every previous one and strong in a different way, seized them. I cannot grant more to the adherents of natural religion than the dim intimations that precede that living intuition that opens the religious life to a person. There are certain dim impulses and representations that are not at all connected with the human personality but that, as it were, merely fill up the empty spaces of it and are uniformly the same in all personalities. Thus it is with their religion.

At most their religion is natural religion in the sense that one otherwise applies the term "natural," when speaking of natural philosophy and natural poetry, to expressions of the unrefined instincts to distinguish them from art and cultivation. But they hardly await something better, esteem it more highly in the feeling of not being able to attain it; rather, they oppose something better with all their powers. The essence of natural religion actually consists wholly in the negation of everything positive and characteristic in religion and in the most violent polemic against it. Thus natural religion is also the worthy product of an age whose hobbyhorse was a lamentable generality and an empty sobriety, which, more than everything else, works against true cultivation in all things. There are two things that they especially hate: They do not want to begin with anything extraordinary or incomprehensible, and whatever they might be and do is in no way supposed to smack of a school. This is the decadence you find in all arts and sciences; it has also penetrated religion, and its result is this contentless, formless thing. They would like to be indigenous and self-taught in religion, but they have only the crude and uncultivated part of these qualities; they have neither the power nor the will to bring forth the unique. They resist every particular religion because it is at the same time a school; but if they encountered something through which a religion of their own was about to be formed in them, they would resist it just as violently because a school might arise from it. So their bristling against the positive and voluntary is simultaneously a bristling against everything definite and real. If a specific religion is not supposed to begin with a fact, it cannot begin at all; for there must be a basis, and it can only be a subjective one for why something is brought forth and placed in the center; and if a religion is not supposed to be a specific one, then it is not religion at all, but merely loose, unrelated material. Remember what the poets say about a state of souls before birth, if a soul wanted forcefully to resist coming into the world because it would not like to be this person or that, but a

---

[8] "The substance" (*die Masse*) refers to the common belief in Newtonian ether of eighteenth-century physics and natural philosophy.

human being generally; this polemic against life is the polemic of natural religion against positive religion, and this is the permanent condition of its adherents.

Thus if you are serious about considering religion in its determinate forms, turn back from these enlightened religions to the despised positive religions where everything real, powerful, and determinate appears, where every particular intuition has its specific content and its own relationship to the rest. Turn to the religions where every feeling has its own circle and its special connection; where you encounter every modification of religiousness somewhere and every state of mind into which only religion can transpose a person; where you find each part of religion formed somewhere and each of its effects completed somewhere; where all communal institutions and all individual expressions prove the high worth that is put on religion to the point of forgetting all the rest; where the holy zeal with which it is contemplated, communicated, and enjoyed and the childlike longing with which one looks forward to new revelations of heavenly powers guarantee for you that none of its elements that could already be perceived from this point has been overlooked and that none of its moments has disappeared without leaving a monument.

Consider all the manifold forms in which every single way of intuiting the universe has already appeared. Do not shrink back in fright either because of mysterious darkness or wonderfully grotesque traits, and fall victim to the delusion that everything is mere imagination and poetry; merely dig ever deeper where your magic rod[9] has once struck, and you will certainly unearth the heavenly. But so that you differentiate and analyze things properly, look to the human element that the divine had to take on; do not disregard how religion everywhere bears in itself the traces of the culture of every age, of the history of every human type, how it often had to go about in the form of a servant,[10] displaying the neediness of its pupils and its domicile by its surroundings and in its adornment; do not overlook how it has often been stunted in its growth because one did not allow it room to exercise its powers, how it has often lamentably perished in the first days of childhood, owing to bad treatment and atrophy. And if you would comprehend the whole, do not stop just with the forms of religion that have shone for centuries and ruled over great peoples and that have been glorified by poets and wise men in many ways; what was historically and religiously the most noteworthy is often distributed only among a few and remains hidden to the common view.

But even if, in this way, you wholly and completely fix your gaze on the right objects, it will always still be a difficult business to discover the spirit of religions and to understand them thoroughly. Once more I warn you not to want to abstract it from that which is common to all those who confess a specific religion; you stray into a thousand vain investigations on this path, and in the end you always come to a certain quantity of material instead of the spirit of religion. You must remember

---

[9] An allusion to the magic rod stories of Moses and Aaron, Exodus 4:1–5; 7:9–12, 17f.; Numbers 17:5–11.

[10] Philippians 2:7.

that no determinate religion has ever become completely real and that you are not acquainted with them until, far from seeking them in a limited space, you yourself are capable of completing them and determining how this and that would have had to develop if their horizon had only been wide enough. You cannot impress it upon yourselves strongly enough that everything depends only upon finding its basic intuition, that all knowledge of the particular avails you nothing so long as you do not have this, and that you do not have it until you are able to explain everything particular from this perspective. And even with this rule of investigation, which is only a touchstone, you will still be exposed to a thousand mistakes; much will approach you, as it were, intentionally to lead you astray; much will place itself in the way, as if to guide your eye in a false direction.

Above all, I beg you, do not lose sight of the difference between that which makes up the essence of an individual religion insofar as it is a determinate form and presentation of religion generally, and that which designates its unity as a school and holds it together as such. Religious people are thoroughly historical; that is not their least praise, but it is also the source of great misunderstandings. The moment in which they themselves have been filled by the intuition that has made itself the focal point of their religion is always sacred to them; it appears to them as an immediate influence of the deity, and they never speak of what, for them, is unique in their religion and of the form it has taken in them without reference to it. You can imagine, therefore, how much holier still must be the moment for them in which this infinite intuition was first established in the world as foundation and focal point of a unique religion, since the whole development of this religion in all generations and individuals is just as historically tied to this moment. Yet this whole of religion and the religious culture of a great mass of humanity is something infinitely greater than their own religious life and the small fragment of this religion they personally exhibit. They glorify this fact, therefore, in every way, heap upon it all ornaments of religious art, worship it as the richest and most beneficent miracle of the highest, and never speak of their religion, never exhibit one of its elements, without orienting and portraying it in connection with this fact. If, therefore, the continuous mention of this accompanies all expressions of religion and gives them their own coloring, nothing is more natural than to confuse this fact with the basic intuition of religion itself; not only has this misled nearly everyone, it has shifted the perspective of almost all religions. Never forget, therefore, that the basic intuition of a religion can be nothing other than some intuition of the infinite in the finite, some universal element of religion that may also occur in all other religions – and, should they be complete, must be present – but not placed in the center of them.[11]

I beg you not to consider as religion everything you find among the heroes of religion or in the holy documents and seek the distinguishing spirit therein. In this

[11] See Gerardus van der Leeuw, *Religion in Essence and Manifestations* (New York, 1963), II, pp. 645–6, who places the single, historical intuition of Christianity at the center of his phenomenology of religion, while acknowledging that a Buddhist would write a Buddhist phenomenology of religion.

I do not mean the trivialities you can readily imagine or such things as are wholly unfamiliar according to every estimate of religion, but something else that is often confused with it. Recall how unintentionally those documents were made and how impossible it was for their authors to see how to remove everything that is not religion. Consider how those people lived in the world under all sorts of circumstances and could not possibly say, with every word they uttered, "This is not religion." And if they, therefore, talk worldly wisdom and morals or metaphysics and poetry, do not suppose that these things also have to be forced into religion and that its character must also be sought therein. At least there should only be one morality everywhere, and the religions, which should not be the same anywhere, cannot distinguish themselves according to the variations of morality, which always exist but are something to be done away with.

But more than anything, I beg you, do not let yourselves be misled by the two hostile principles that have sought to distort and conceal the spirit of each religion everywhere, almost from earliest times. In all places there have soon been those who have circumscribed its spirit in individual dogmas and wanted to exclude from religion whatever was not yet formed in accord with this circumscribed spirit; and there have been such people who, whether from hatred of polemics or to make religion more agreeable to the irreligious, whether from misunderstanding and ignorance of the matter or from lack of sense, decry everything unique as dead letters in order to set off toward the indeterminate. Guard yourselves against both; you will find the spirit of a religion, not among rigid systematizers or superficial indifferentists, but among those who live in it as their element and move ever further in it without nurturing the illusion that they are able to embrace it completely.

Whether you will succeed in discovering the spirit of the religions with these precautionary measures I do not know. But I fear that religion can be understood only through itself and that its special manner of construction and its characteristic distinction will not become clear to you until you yourselves belong to some one or other of them. However fortunate you may be at deciphering the crude and undeveloped religions of distant peoples or at sorting out the many types of individual religions that lie enclosed in the beautiful mythology of the Greeks and Romans is all the same to me; may their gods guide you. But when you approach the most holy, where the universe is intuited in its highest unity, when you want to contemplate the different forms of systematic religions – not the exotic and strange but those that are still more or less present among us – then it cannot be a matter of indifference to me whether you find the right point from which you must view them.

I should, to be sure, speak of only one, for Judaism is long since a dead religion,[12]

---

12 The portrayal of Judaism as no longer a living tradition was dominant in Berlin Enlightenment (*Haskalah*) Jewish circles in which Schleiermacher moved. See Joseph W. Pickle, "Schleiermacher on Judaism," *Journal of Religion* 60 (April 1980), 115–37 and Gunter Scholtz, "Friedrich Schleiermacher über das Sendschreiben jüdischer Hausväter" in *Judentum im Zeitalter der Aufklärung* (Bremen, 1977), pp. 297–351, with an acknowledgment of "ambivalence" (Pickle) and "distance and tension" (Scholz); on Schleiermacher's part in Prussia's debates regarding Jewish emancipation see Michael A.

and those who at present still bear its colors are actually sitting and mourning beside the undecaying mummy and weeping over its demise and its sad legacy. Moreover, I speak of it, not because it was somehow the forerunner of Christianity; I hate that type of historical reference in religion. Its necessity is a far higher and eternal one, and every beginning in it is original. But Judaism has such a beautiful, childlike character, and this is so completely buried, and the whole constitutes such a remarkable example of the corruption and total disappearance of religion from a great body in which it was formerly found. Just take away everything political and, if God wills, everything moral by which it is commonly characterized; forget the whole experiment of joining the state to the religion (I shall not say "to the church"); forget that Judaism was to a certain extent simultaneously an order founded on an old family history and preserved by priests;[13] look merely to the properly religious element in it to which all this does not belong, and then tell me which is the idea of the universe that everywhere shines through. It is none other than that of a universal immediate retribution, of the infinite's own reaction against every individual finite form that proceeds from free choice by acting through another finite element that is not viewed as proceeding from free choice. Everything is considered this way; origin and passing away, fortune and misfortune; even within the human soul an expression of freedom and choice and an immediate influence of the deity always alternate. All other attributes of God that are also intuited express themselves according to this principle and are always seen in connection with this. The deity is thus portrayed throughout as rewarding, chastising, and punishing what is singled out in the individual person. When the disciples once asked Christ, "Who has sinned, these people or their parents?" and he answered them, "Do you think that these have sinned more than the others?"[14] that was religious spirit of Judaism in its sharpest form and that was his polemic against it.

For that reason one encounters in Judaism the ubiquitous interwoven parallelism that is no accidental form and the prominence of the dialogue that is in all that is religious.[15] The whole of history, as well as being an abiding interchange between this attraction and this repulsion, is presented as a conversation between God and man in word and deed, and everything that is united is united only by its uniformity in this treatment. This is the reason for the sacredness of the tradition in which the context of this great conversation was contained, and the impossibility

---

Meyer, *The Origins of the Modern Jew* (Detroit, 1967), pp. 76–8, 93, 95–7, 104–7, and Jacob Katz, *Out of the Ghetto: The Social Background of Jewish Emancipation 1770–1870* (New York, 1978), pp. 118f.; and relevant texts in *KGA* I.2, pp. lxxviii–lxxxv, 327–61, 373–413.

[13] "Gedanken I" (no. 139), *KGA* I.2, p. 33: "Judaism was never a religion but an order with unknown superiors built on a family history."

[14] A conflation of John 9:2 and Luke 13:2.

[15] A belief in the dialogue as the highest form of discourse, which pervades Schleiermacher's work, is here associated with the stylistic features of parallelism and repetition as well as the covenantal and prophetic traditions of the Hebrew Bible.

of attaining religion except through the initiation into this context and, in still later times, the conflict among the sects as to which were in possession of this continuing conversation. It originates precisely from this view that the gift of prophecy was developed so perfectly in the Jewish religion as in no other; for in respect to prophecy, Christians are mere children compared to them. This whole idea is highly childlike, intended only for a small arena without complications where, in a simple entity, the natural consequences of actions are neither disturbed nor hindered.

But the further the adherents of this religion advanced on the arena of the world in connection with other peoples, the more difficult it became to manifest this idea. The imagination had to anticipate the Almighty's word that he had just been about to speak, and from far away bring into view the second part of this same moment, while annihilating the intervening time and space. This is a prophecy, and striving after it necessarily had to be a principal manifestation as long as it was still possible to retain that idea, and with it religion. The belief in the messiah was its last fruit, engendered with great effort; a new ruler was supposed to come to restore the Zion[16] in its splendor where the voice of the Lord had grown silent, and by the subjugation of peoples under the old law that simple course was again supposed to become universal in the events of the world, that simple path that was interrupted by their unpeaceful community, by their energies being directed against one another, and by the difference of their customs. It has long persevered, as a single fruit, after all the life force has vanished from the branch, often remains hanging until the bleakest season on a withered stem and dries up on it. Its limited vantage point afforded this religion, as religion, a short duration. It died when its holy books were closed; then the conversation of Jehovah with his people was viewed as ended; the political association that was linked to it dragged on in an ailing existence, and its external parts were preserved even longer still, the unpleasant appearance of a mechanical movement after the life and spirit had long since departed.

The original intuition of Christianity is more glorious, more sublime, more worthy of adult humanity, more deeply penetrating into the spirit of systematic religion, and extending farther over the whole universe. It is none other than the intuition of the universal straining of everything finite against the unity of the whole and of the way in which the deity handles this striving, how it reconciles the enmity directed against it and sets bounds to the ever-greater distance by scattering over the whole individual points that are at once finite and infinite, at once human and divine. Corruption and redemption, enmity and mediation are two sides of this intuition that are inseparably bound to each other, and the shape of all religious material in Christianity and its whole form are determined through them. The physical world has departed from its perfection and imperishable beauty with ever

---

[16] Micah 4:7: "And the Lord will reign over them in Mount Zion from this time forth and for evermore."

more rapid steps; but all evil, even that which the finite must commit before it has completely run the course of its existence, is a consequence of the will, of the self-seeking endeavor of individual nature that everywhere tears itself loose from relationship with the whole in order to be something for itself; even death has come for the sake of sin.[17] The moral world is progressing from bad to worse; being incapable of producing something in which the spirit of the universe really would live, it darkens the understanding; having departed from the truth, it corrupts the heart; and, while being devoid of any praise before God, it has extinguished the image of the infinite in every part of finite nature. Even divine providence in all its expressions is intuited in relation to this condition, not aimed in its action at immediate consequences for our feeling, not having in view the happiness or suffering it produces, no longer hindering or promoting individual actions, but only concerned to regulate corruption in great masses, to destroy without mercy what can no longer be restored, and to beget from itself new creations with new powers. Thus providence works signs and miracles that interrupt and deeply affect the course of things; thus it sends ambassadors in whom more or less of its own spirit dwells in order to pour out divine powers among humanity.

In Christianity the religious world is also represented this way. Even while the finite wishes to intuit the universe, it strains against it, always seeking without finding and losing what it has found; ever one-sided, ever vacillating, ever halting at the particular and accidental, and ever wanting more than to intuit, the finite loses sight of its goal. Every revelation is in vain. Everything is swallowed up by earthly sense, everything is carried away by the indwelling irreligious principle, and the deity makes ever-new arrangements; through its power alone ever more splendid revelations issue from the womb of the old; it places ever more sublime mediators between itself and the human being; in every later ambassador it unites the deity more intimately with humanity so that through them and by them we might learn to recognize the eternal being; and yet the old lament is never lifted that we do not perceive what is of the spirit of God.[18] The fact that Christianity in its most characteristic basic intuition most frequently and best prefers to intuit the universe in religion and in its history, the fact that it treats religion itself as material for religion and thus is, as it were, raised to a higher power of religion, makes up its most distinctive character and determines its whole form.[19] Precisely because it

---

[17] Genesis 2:17; Romans 5:12.

[18] 1 Corinthians 2:14: "The unspiritual man does not receive the gifts of the Spirit of God, for they are folly to him, and he is not able to understand them because they are spiritually discerned."

[19] The principle articulated here of Christianity as "religion . . . raised to a higher power," where religion is used polemically to overcome and criticize religion, reflects the efforts of Romanticism to get at the roots of poetry as a creative act. Cf. F. Schlegel's view of hierarchically arranged "powers" (*Potenzen*) operating in the universe and of "poesie" as the highest power of the human imagination in mediating the finite and infinite; see Friedrich Schlegel, *Dialogue on Poetry and Literary Aphorisms*, ed. Ernst Behler and Roman Struc (University Park, PA, 1968), pp. 15f. and the multiple references to *Potenzierung* and cognate terms in his early philosophical notebooks, F. Schlegel, *Philosophische Lehrjahre 1796–1806* (Munich, 1971 [*Kritische Friedrich-Schlegel-Ausgabe XIX*]), p. 747. For the

presupposes an irreligious principle as widespread, and because this forms an essential part of the intuition to which everything else is related, it is thoroughly polemical.[20]

Christianity is polemical in its external communication, for in order to make clear its innermost nature it must everywhere disclose all corruption, be it in morals or in the manner of thinking, and above all in the irreligious principle itself. Without mercy it therefore unmasks every false morality, every inferior religion, every unfortunate mixture of the two whereby their mutual nakedness is supposed to be covered; it penetrates into the innermost secrets of the corrupted heart and illuminates every evil that lurks in the darkness with the holy torch of its own experience. Thus Christianity destroyed – and this was almost its first movement – the last expectation of its closest brothers and contemporaries and called it irreligious and godless to wish for or to expect some other restoration than the hope for a better religion, for a higher view of things, and for eternal life in God. It boldly led the heathen beyond the separation they had made between life and the world of the gods and of human beings. To the one who does not live, move, and have his being[21] in the eternal, God is completely unknown; no religion has yet come to the limited mind of the one who has lost this natural feeling, this inner intuition, among the mass of sensory impressions and desires. Thus everywhere they tore open the whitewashed sepulchres and brought the dead bones to light,[22] and if the first heroes of Christianity had been philosophers, they would have been just as polemical against the corruption of philosophy. Certainly nowhere did they misconstrue the basic characteristics of the divine image; in all distortions and degenerations they surely saw the heavenly seed of religion; but as Christians their chief concern was the distance from the universe, which needs a mediator, and as often as they proclaimed Christianity they aimed only at that.

But Christianity is just as sharply and bitingly polemical within its own borders and in its innermost communion of the saints. Nowhere is religion so completely idealized as it is in Christianity by means of its original presupposition; and just for that reason continuous polemicizing against everything real in religion is simultaneously posed as a task that can never be fully and adequately achieved. Just because the irreligious principle is everywhere present and operative, and because everything real appears at the same time to be unholy, an infinite holiness is the goal of Christianity. Never satisfied with its attainment, it seeks, even in the purest intuitions, even in its holiest feelings, traces of the irreligious and the tendency of

---

impact of Schleiermacher's idea in twentieth-century theology, see the formulation of "the Protestant principle" in Paul Tillich (1886–1965), *The Protestant Era*, (Chicago, 1948), pp. 161–81 and *Systematic Theology* I–III (Chicago, 1951–63), passim.

[20] "Gedanken I" (no. 141), *KGA* 1.2, p. 33: "The original presentation of Christianity is polemical and it must also remain this way, namely relatively polemical."

[21] Acts 17:28, citing Epimenides from Paul's Areopagus speech.

[22] Matthew 23:27: "Woe to you scribes and Pharisees, hypocrites! For you are like whitewashed tombs, which outwardly look beautiful, but within they are full of dead men's bones and all uncleanness."

everything finite to be turned away from and opposed to the universe. With the tone of highest inspiration one of the most ancient sacred authors criticizes the religious condition of the communities;[23] the lofty apostles speak of themselves with simple openness; thus each person is supposed to step into this holy circle, not only enthused and teaching, but also offering his own part in humility to universal testing; nothing is to be spared, even the dearest and most cherished; and nothing should be indolently put aside, not even that which is most generally recognized. The same thing that is publicly praised as holy and is set before the world as the essence of religion is still always inwardly subject to strict and repeated judgment in order that ever more impurities may be separated and that the splendor of the heavenly colors appear ever more clearly in all intuitions of the infinite. You see in nature that a compound substance, when it has had its chemical powers directed against something outside itself, as soon as it has overcome this or has produced an equilibrium, begins to ferment within itself and precipitates this or that element from itself. So it is with individual elements and with whole masses of Christendom; it finally turns its polemical power against itself, and always concerned that it has absorbed something extraneous through the struggle with external irreligion or even that it has a principle of corruption within itself, it does not shun even the most violent inner commotions in order to expel it. This is the history of Christianity that is rooted in its nature. "I have come not to bring peace, but a sword," said its founder;[24] and his gentle soul could not possibly have meant that he had come to provoke those bloody commotions that are so completely contrary to the spirit of religion or those wretched verbal disputes concerning the dead matter that living religion does not assimilate, but he foresaw only these holy wars that would necessarily arise from the nature of his teaching, and by foreseeing, he commanded them.

But not only is the quality of the individual elements of Christianity subjected to this constant sifting. The insatiable desire for religion is also aimed at its unbroken existence and life in the mind. In each moment when the religious principle cannot be perceived in the mind, the irreligious principle is thought to be dominant, for only through opposition can that which is be canceled and brought to naught. Every interruption of religion is irreligion; the mind cannot for a moment feel devoid of intuitions and feelings of the universe without at once becoming conscious of enmity and distance from it. Christianity has thus made first and essential the demand that religiousness shall be a continuum in human life, and it scorns being satisfied even with the strongest expressions of religiousness as soon as it is supposed to pertain to and govern only certain parts of life. Religion is never supposed to rest, and nothing is to be so absolutely opposed to it that it cannot also exist with it concurrently. From everything finite we are to look upon the infinite;

[23] An allusion to the inspired criticism of the life of early Christian communities in the letters of St. Paul.
[24] Matthew 10:34.

we are supposed to be capable of associating religious feelings and views with all sentiments of the mind, wherever they may have originated, and with all actions, whatever may be the objects to which they are related. That is the actual and highest goal of virtuosity in Christianity.

You will now easily discover how the original intuition of Christianity from which all these views derive determines the character of its feelings. What do you call the feeling of an unsatisfied longing that is directed toward a great object and of whose infinity you are conscious? What seizes you when you find the holy most intimately mixed with the profane, the sublime with the lowly and transitory? And what do you call the mood that sometimes forces you to presuppose the universality of this mixture and to search for it everywhere? This mood does not seize Christians now and then but is, rather, the dominant tone of all their religious feeling; this holy sadness — for that is the only name language affords me — accompanies every joy and every pain; every love and every fear accompanies it. Indeed, in Christians' pride as well as in their humility, it is the undertone to which all is related. If you know how to reproduce the interior of a mind from individual traits and do not allow yourself to be disturbed by the oddness that is intermixed with them from God knows where, you will find this feeling wholly dominant in the founder of Christianity. If a writer who has left behind only a few pages in a simple language is not too unimportant for you to turn your attention to him, then this undertone will speak to you from every word that is left to us by his bosom friend.[25] And if ever a Christian has permitted you to look into the holiest depth of his heart, it has certainly been just this one.

Thus is Christianity. I do not wish to gloss over its distortions and its manifold corruptions, for the corruptibility of everything holy, as soon as it becomes human, is a part of its original worldview. Nor do I wish to lead you further into its particulars; its proceedings lie before you, and I believe I have given you the thread that will lead you through all anomalies and, without being concerned for the outcome, will make the most precise overview possible for you. Only hold it fast, and from the very first look to nothing else than the clarity, variety, and richness with which that first basic idea developed. When I consider the holy image in the mutilated descriptions of the life of him who is the sublime originator of what has been the most majestic in religion even to now, I do not admire the purity of his ethical teaching, which only expressed what all persons who have become aware of their spiritual nature have in common with him, and which can have a greater value neither because of its utterance nor because of its being first. I do not admire the uniqueness of his character, the intimate marriage of higher power with touching gentleness — every noble, simple heart in a special situation must exhibit a great character in certain respects; these are all merely human things. But the truly divine is the splendid clarity with which the great idea he

---

[25] An allusion to the Fourth Gospel, that of the "beloved disciple," John 21:20.

had come to exhibit was formed in his soul, the idea that everything finite requires higher mediation in order to be connected with the divine. It is vain insolence to want to remove the veil that conceals and should conceal this idea's origin in him, because all beginning in religion is mysterious. The impertinent outrage that has dared to do this was able only to disfigure the divine,[26] as if he had proceeded from the ancient idea of his people, whose annihilation he only wanted to express and in fact had expressed in too glorious a form when he claimed to be the one whom they awaited.

Let us consider the living intuition of the universe that filled his soul only as we find it developed to perfection in him. If everything finite requires higher mediation in order not to stray even farther from the universe and become dispersed into emptiness and nothingness, in order to retain its connection with the universe and come to conscious awareness of it, then indeed what mediates cannot possibly be something merely finite that, in turn, itself requires mediation. It must belong to both; it must be a part of the divine nature just as much as and in the same sense in which it is part of the finite. But what did he see around himself except what was finite and in need of mediation, and where was there something better able to mediate than he himself? "No one knows the Father but the Son and any one to whom he chooses to reveal it."[27] This consciousness of the uniqueness of his religiousness, of the originality of his view, and of its power to communicate itself and arouse religion was at the same time the consciousness of his office as mediator and of his divinity. To say that he was confronted by the raw power of his enemy without hope of being able to live longer is unspeakably petty; but when he, forsaken, was at the point of becoming silent forever, without seeing any sort of institution really erected for community among his own people, facing the imposing ostentation of the old, corrupt religion that seemed strong and powerful, surrounded by everything that can instill awe and demand subjection, by everything he himself had been taught to honor from childhood on, he alone, supported by nothing but this feeling and without hesitation uttered that "yes" that is the greatest word a mortal has ever spoken.[28] This was thus the most glorious apotheosis, and no deity can be more certain than what thus posits itself. With this faith in himself, who can wonder that he was certain not only to be mediator for many but also to leave behind a great school that would derive its identical religion from his own; he was so certain that he instituted symbols for it before it yet

---

[26] Presumably an allusion to the essay, *On the Purpose of Jesus and His Disciples* (Braunschweig, 1778), in which Gotthold Ephraim Lessing (1729–81) anonymously published the longest and most formidable fragment of Hermann Samuel Reimarus (1694–1768), from the manuscript *Apology or Defence of the Rational Worshippers of God* during his controversy with the Hamburg pastor Johann Melchior Goeze (1717–86). The essay argues that Jesus never intended his disciples to break with Jewish ceremonial law and preached about the kingdom of God wholly within the Jewish apocalyptic expectation of a messianic deliverer from foreign domination.

[27] Matthew 11:27.

[28] Matthew 26:63f.; Mark 14:61f.; Luke 22:70.

existed[29] in the conviction that this would suffice to bring it into existence and that he had spoken even earlier with prophetic enthusiasm about the perpetuation in this school of his personal memorable occurrences.

But he never claimed to be the sole instance in the application of his idea, the sole mediator, and he never confused his school with a religion – he would tolerate leaving the judgment of the worth of his mediation undecided if only the spirit, the principle from which his religion developed in him and in others, was not reviled – and this confusion was remote even from his disciples. They immediately regarded the followers of John,[30] who participated only very imperfectly in the basic intuition of Christ, as Christians and included them among the active members of the same community. And it should be so even now: People who make the same intuition the basis of their religion are Christians without regard to the school, whether their religion be derived historically from themselves or from someone else. Never did he pass off the intuitions and the feelings he himself could communicate as the whole compass of religion that was to proceed from his basic intuition; he always pointed to the truth that would come after him.[31] Thus his disciples also never set limits to the Holy Spirit; its unlimited freedom and the thorough unity of its revelations were universally acknowledged by them. And later on, when the first season of its flowering was past and it appeared to be resting from its works, these works, so far as they were contained in the holy writings, were without authorization declared to be a closed code of religion. This was brought about only by those who took the slumber of the spirit to be its death, those for whom religion itself had died; and all who still felt its life in themselves or perceived it in others have always protested against this unchristian beginning. The holy writings have become Scripture by their own power, but they prohibit no other book from also being or becoming Scripture,[32] and whatever had been written with equal power they would gladly have associated with themselves.

By virtue of this unlimited freedom and this essential infinity, the fundamental idea of Christianity about divine mediating powers has developed in many ways, and all intuitions and feelings of the indwelling of the divine nature in finite nature have been brought to perfection within it. Thus holy Scripture, in which the divine nature dwelt in its own manner, was very soon considered a logical mediator for the knowledge of the divine to the finite and corrupted nature of the understanding, and the Holy Spirit – in a later sense of the term – was considered an ethical mediator for approaching the divine in practice. One numerous party of Christians now still declares its readiness to accept everyone as a mediating and divine being

---

[29] An allusion to the eucharistic elements of the Lord's supper, e.g., 1 Corinthians 11:23f.

[30] New Testament traditions bear out the inclusion of John the Baptist's followers in the earliest Christian communities, e.g., Acts 18:25.

[31] See, e.g., John 16:13.

[32] As part of their literary projects Friedrich Schlegel and Novalis independently hoped to produce a new scripture. For Schlegel this *progressive Universalpoesie* would reunite the literary genres, fuse philosophy and literature, and imbue the arts with learning.

who can prove himself, by a godly life or any other impression of divinity, to have been a connecting point to the infinite, even if only for a small circle. For others, Christ has remained one and all, and still others have declared themselves, or this or that other one, to be mediators for themselves. However often something may be formally or materially erroneous in all this, the principle is genuinely Christian so long as it is free. Thus other intuitions and feelings about which there is nothing in Christ or in the sacred books have been expressed in relation to the focal point of Christianity, and more will subsequently be expressed, because great territories in religion are not yet tilled for Christianity and because it will still have a long history in spite of all that is said of its imminent or already accomplished demise.

Just how is it supposed to perish? Its living spirit slumbers often and long, and in a state of torpidity it withdraws into the dead husk of the letter,[33] but it always awakens again as often as the changing climate in the spiritual world is favorable to its revival and sets its fluids in motion; and that will still occur often. The basic intuition of every positive religion is eternal in itself because it is a supplementary part of the infinite totality in which everything must be eternal, but it itself and its whole formation are transitory; for to view that basic intuition precisely in the center of religion requires not only a particular bent of mind but also a particular situation of humanity in which, indeed until now, the very universe can actually be intuited. If this situation has run its course, if humanity is so far advanced in its progress that it can never more return, then even that intuition is relieved of its value as a basic intuition and religion can no longer exist in this form. This has long since been true of all childish religions from that time when humanity lacked a consciousness of its essential powers; it is time to collect them as monuments to former ages and to deposit them in the storehouse of history, for their life is gone and will never return. Sublime above them all, more historical and humble in its splendor, Christianity has expressly recognized this transitoriness of its nature; there will come a time, it declares, when there will be no more talk of a mediator, but the Father will be all in all.[34] But when will this time come? I fear it lies beyond all time. The corruptibility of all that is great and divine in human and finite things is one half of the original intuition of Christianity. Might there really come a time when this – I shall not say would no longer be perceived at all, but only – would no longer obtrude, when humanity would advance so uniformly and calmly that it would hardly be noticeable how it is now and then somewhat driven back on the great ocean it traverses by a temporary adverse wind, that only the artist who reckons its course by the stars would be able to know it, and that it would never be a great and noteworthy intuition for the rest? I would desire it, and I would gladly stand on the ruins of the religion I honor. The other half of Christianity's original intuition is that certain brilliant and divine points are the source of every betterment of this corruption and of every new and closer union of the finite with

[33] 2 Corinthians 3:6.
[34] 1 Corinthians 15:28.

the divine. Might there ever come a time when this power that draws us to the universe would be so evenly distributed among the great mass of humanity that it would cease to be mediating for them? I would desire it, and I would gladly help to level every great thing that thus exalts itself, but this equality is probably less possible than any other. Times of corruption await everything earthly, even if it be of divine origin; new messengers of God are becoming necessary in order to attract what has withdrawn with enhanced power and to purify the corrupt with heavenly fire; and every such epoch of humanity becomes the rebirth of Christianity and awakens its spirit in a new and more beautiful form.

But now, if there will always be Christians, will Christianity for this reason also be infinite in its universal dissemination and rule humanity as the only form of religion? Christianity disdains this despotism; it esteems every one of its own elements enough to want to intuit it as the focal point of its whole; it wishes not only to produce within itself a multiplicity extending to infinity but also to intuit it outside itself. Never forgetting that it has the best proof of its eternalness in its own corruptibility, in its own sad history, and always expecting salvation from the misery by which it is at the moment oppressed, it gladly watches other and younger forms of religion arise from all points outside this corruption, from close beside itself, even from those regions that appear to it as the very outermost and most dubious limits of religion. The religion of religions cannot gather enough material for the truest aspect of its innermost intuition, and just as nothing is more irreligious than to demand uniformity in humanity generally, so nothing is more unchristian than to seek uniformity in religion.

Let the universe be intuited and worshiped in all ways. Innumerable forms of religion are possible, and if it is necessary that each become real at some time, then it would at least be desirable that one could have an intimation of many at all times. The great moments must be rare when everything coincides to ensure one among them a widely disseminated and enduring life, when the same view develops simultaneously and irresistibly in many and they are permeated by the same impression of the divine. Yet what is not to be expected from a time that is so obviously the boundary between two different order of things? Only when the intense crisis is past can it produce such a moment, and a sensitive soul turned toward creative genius could now already adduce the point that, for future generations, must become the center of the intuition of the universe. But however that may be and however long such a moment may still tarry, new formations of religion must appear and soon, even though for a long time they may be perceived only in individual and fleeting manifestations. A new creation[35] always arises out of nothing, and religion is virtually nothing in all members of the present age when their intellectual life opens up for them in power and fullness. In many persons it will develop from one of countless occasions, and in new soil it will grow into a new

---

[35] 2 Corinthians 5:17.

form. If only the time of reservation and timidity were past! Religion hates to be alone; and most of all in its youth, which is the hour of love for all things, it perishes in desirous longing. When it develops in you, when you realize the first traces of its life, then enter at once into the one and indivisible communion of saints that embraces all religions and in which alone each can prosper. Do you imagine that because this community is scattered and distant you would then also have to address profane ears? You ask which language is secret enough – speech, writing, deeds, or the quiet imitation of the spirit. "Each one," I answer, and you see that I have not shunned the most public. In each, the holy remains secret and hidden from the profane. Let them gnaw at the shell as they may, but do not prevent us from worshiping the God that is within you.

Index

aesthetic, *see* art

Arendt, Hannah xxxvii

art, humanity as greatest work of 71; *Kunstreligion* (religion of art) 68, 69; and religion xxxiv–xxxv, 69

Asian religions xxxv; and mysticism bordering on nothingness 68; *see also* Judaism *and* religious pluralism

atheism xvii, xxiv

Athenaeum xvi, xxviii; fragment 116 of xxv, 71

Australia xvii–xviii

Bahrdt, Karl Friedrich xiii

Bamberger, Johann Peter xvii

Barth, Karl xi, xxxii

Basedow, Johann Bernhard xiii, 64

Berger, Peter L. xxxiii, 104

Blütenstaub (Novalis) xxix, 34, 55

Brinckmann, Gustav von xvi

Brunner, Emil xxxii

Buber, Martin xxx, xxxvii, xxxviii

Caryatides 71

Celebration of Christmas: A Conversation, The (Schleiermacher) xix, 37

Christ, *see* Jesus Christ

Christian Faith, The [*Glaubenslehre*] (Schleiermacher) xi, xxiii, 52

Christianity 115–23; characterized by holy sadness 119; original intuition of, and finite striving against infinite 115–17; as polemical religion 117–19

church, and clergy and laity as distinguished by function 75–6; and critique of parish system 89; and family as a preparatory society for religion 92–3; indifference toward 80; inspired role of leaders in 75; as mediating institution 88; not to be destroyed but to be related to true church

81–2; and rejection of religious exclusivism 77; rich luxuriant life of 75; and sectarian spirit rooted in religious opinions 82; and symbolic actions essential to fellowship 81; true, corrupted by state 82–91; union of, and state 90; unity of, contrasted with plurality of religion 96–7

Cicero 18, 46

Confessions from the Heart of an Art-loving Friar (Wachenroder) 69

Confidential Letters Concerning Friedrich Schlegel's Lucinde (Schleiermacher) xix, xxvii–xxviii

Critique of Judgment, The (Kant) xix

Critique of Practical Reason, The (Kant) xx, 23

Critique of Pure Reason, The (Kant) xix, xx, 23, 25, 26, 62

cultured despisers, argument based on contempt of 11; differ from practical people, who annihilate religion 63; do not despise society of religious people 79; ignorance of religion among 45; lack feeling for religion 3; more opposed to church and priests than to religion 72; preference of, for natural religion 98; rejection by, of positive religions misguided 107–11; and sensibility as help to rebirth of religion 67

David Hume on Belief; or, Idealism and Realism (Jacobi) xv, xxiv

determinate religion, *see* positive religion

Dierkes, Hans xxv, xxvi, xxvii

Dilthey, Wilhelm xix, xxiv, xxv, 64

Dohna, Alexander von xvi

Eberhard, J. A. xix

education, and *Bildung* 55; childhood 60; creative drive (*Bildungstrieb*) 40, 47; J. H. Pestalozzi 60; 67; and Philanthropin movement 64; and place of novices in religion 81–2; and self-formation

Cambridge texts in the history of philosophy

Titles published in the series thus far